ADVANCE PRA!

QUESTIONING TECHNOLOGY

"One of the greatest problems facing education in the contemporary world is the humanization and democratization of technology, firmly linked to questions of social justice and equity. Karen Ferneding's *Questioning Technology: Electronic Technologies and Educational Reform* provides us with an account that questions not only the technocentric rationale that pervades recent education reform but also lays out an emerging alternative social vision of education. It is both a humane and hopeful book directed toward a cultural approach to technology that views practices of educational innovation as contextual and situated processes.... Ferneding's book is an excellent contribution to the literature that ought to be required reading for teachers, administrators, and education policy-makers."

Michael A. Peters, University of Glasgow

"*Questioning Technology: Electronic Technologies and Educational Reform* provides a critical look at the use of computers in education that is grounded in both theory and actual observation in the field. It represents an important contribution to the literature on educational computing."

Eugene F. Provenzo, Jr., Author of Beyond the Gutenberg Galaxy,
Video Kids and Computers, *and* Curriculum and Cultural Change

QUESTIONING TECHNOLOGY

Studies in the
Postmodern Theory of Education

Joe L. Kincheloe and Shirley R. Steinberg
General Editors

Vol. 159

PETER LANG
New York • Washington, D.C./Baltimore • Bern
Frankfurt am Main • Berlin • Brussels • Vienna • Oxford

Karen A. Ferneding

QUESTIONING TECHNOLOGY

Electronic Technologies and Educational Reform

PETER LANG
New York • Washington, D.C./Baltimore • Bern
Frankfurt am Main • Berlin • Brussels • Vienna • Oxford

Library of Congress Cataloging-in-Publication Data

Ferneding, Karen A.
Questioning technology: electronic technologies
and educational reform / Karen A. Ferneding.
p. cm. — (Counterpoints; vol. 159)
Includes bibliographical references (p.   ) and index.
1. Education—Effect of technological innovations on—United States. 2. Critical
pedagogy—United States. 3. Educational change—United States.
I. Title. II. Counterpoints (New York, N.Y.); v. 159.
√ LB1028.3 .F47 371.33—dc21   2002152134
ISBN 0-8204-5047-2
ISSN 1058-1634

Die Deutsche Bibliothek-CIP-Einheitsaufnahme

Ferneding, Karen A.:
Questioning technology: electronic technologies
and educational reform / Karen A. Ferneding.
–New York; Washington, D.C./Baltimore; Bern;
Frankfurt am Main; Berlin; Brussels; Vienna; Oxford: Lang.
(Counterpoints; Vol. 159)
ISBN 0-8204-5047-2

Cover design by Joni Holst
Cover drawing by Karen A. Ferneding

The paper in this book meets the guidelines for permanence and durability
of the Committee on Production Guidelines for Book Longevity
of the Council of Library Resources.

© 2003 Peter Lang Publishing, Inc., New York
275 Seventh Avenue, 28th Floor, New York, NY 10001
www.peterlangusa.com

Printed in the United States of America

This book is dedicated in loving memory to my parents.

TABLE OF CONTENTS

TABLES

INTRODUCTION

The Politics of Educational Reform in a Technological Society

Reform proposals are like scripts, frames or 'cultural models' (Gee, Hull & Lankshear, 1996). They encode values intended to change people and social practices. . . . The key questions here are What kinds of 'visions' for life, people and practices more generally, are encoded in these scripts? What do we think about them? How do we respond to them?

de Alba et al., 2000

When the National Commission on Excellence in Education wrote its recommendations for educational reform in 1983, the report, *A Nation at Risk*, created a generative framework for educational reform policy and public opinion.[1] The particular discourse of this and other subsequent reform documents (e.g. *Goals 2000*) based the rationale for educational reform and restructuring on the emerging Information Age and a globalized market economy. The alignment of educational reform policy with economic imperatives is typical in American educational history. However, the sustained length of the current reform initiative, its overt functionalist aims that emphasize efficiency, are unprecedented, as is its focus on the infusion of electronic technologies (computers, networked systems, and telecommunications infrastructures) (Tyack & Cuban, 1995; Cuban, 1997). Also, the presence of "cultural wars" (Apple, 1995) illustrates the depth to which education has become politicized. Thus, although the development of educational policy has always been a forum for public discourse, the landscape of educational reform policy over approximately the past 20 years has been delimited by a narrow vision inspired not only by functionalist aims and politically conservative factions, but also a particular overarching technological utopianism. Although certain issues such as privatization of public schools and national standards are highly partisan, the official policy to reform education through the infusion of new electronic technologies is assumed both necessary and positive by many educators, the public, and all political factions (Zehr, 1997; Trotter, 1998; Turow, 1999). Why is this so?

The fact remains that there exists a growing omnipresence of electronic technologies in our lives. The application of electronic technologies within business and industry has enabled the development of a globalized market economy. The development of the Information Age indicates a shift from manufacturing to service-related industries and signifies that knowledge itself has become an informational commodity, a condition that raises issues related to power (Lyotard, 1984). Indeed, supporters of the new information-based economy describe information as a "new currency" for the 21st century. According to New Zealand educational theorist, Michael Peters (1996), this signals an alignment between education, science, and technology that is unprecedented in history. This alignment creates the basis for an "enterprise culture" whereby the aims and needs of a globalized market economy are actualized. This situation furthers education's repurposing toward functionalist ends, a direction that began at the turn of the 20th century with the adoption of scientific management techniques as a means to create a "one best system" (Tyack, 1974). The development of enterprise culture, because it is related to the globalization of market ideology and the technological production of information processing, "will generate a phenomenon, the ecological and cultural scope and impacts of which are still not clear" (de Alba et al., 2000, p. 54).

In addition, studies pertaining to the sociology of technology and society and the nature of technological innovation indicate that, as a culture, we construct technology as a neutral artifact (Winner, 1980). This is also the case in educational computing (Bowers, 1988, 1995; Streible, 1986). However, this apolitical stance seems to contradict the present situation where access to electronic technology is equated to nothing less than a civil right (Zehr, 1997). Although history shows that the use of technology to reform education is a story of hype and predictable failure (Cuban, 1986, 2001), these attempts nevertheless illustrate our culture's unwavering faith in a "technological fix" approach to social policy. Our culture historically demonstrates an uncritical approach to technology adoption, a phenomenon that political theorist Langdon Winner (1996) describes as "technological somnambulism," and places faith in technology's signification of progress and thus its ability to only positively affect the human condition. It is a paradox that our cultural bias is to depoliticalize the phenomenon of technological innovation as a mere tool when it is clear that through our social construction of technology-based policies, it constitutes sociopolitical processes, and in the case of telecommunications infrastructures, economic processes.

This paradox was clearly demonstrated in various projects in which I have been involved that aimed to assist teachers with adopting computer and telecommunications technologies. Unlike the simplistic approaches of typical reform efforts envisioned by policymakers, these experiences revealed how the process of technology adoption is highly contextual and situated. Significant influences arise from the socio-political sphere, a school's culture and local community, the level of individual teacher's perceptions, as well as the unique qualities of a technology. This composite of complex factors demands an "ecological model" of technology adoption that supports each component and which also recognizes the complex synergy of technology-based reform efforts, including negative or unintended outcomes (Christal, Ferneding, Kennedy-Puthoff & Resta, 1997). In addition, although new technologies, such as networked systems, offer the potential to deconstruct existing hierarchical structures, this aim needs to be highly specified and articulated within the adoption process itself. This is often not the case as it is assumed that the mere presence of such a technological infrastructure can generate such effects (Morrison & Gold-berg, 1996; Winner, 1986, 1996). Indeed, when adopting electronic technologies, educators often focus on simply acquiring the technology, leaving fundamental pedagogical issues to a mere afterthought (Smith, 1995a; Kerr, 1996). This could mean that despite their potential to engender positive reforms, these electronic technologies ironically could simply reinforce some of the worst aspects of the existing educational system.

Many factors led me to question the technocentric vision of current educational reform policymakers. For example, the sheer complexity of technology adoption within educational settings is overwhelming in terms of the challenges posed to the culture of schools, the changing roles of teachers, and the fiscal commitment necessary to build and sustain technological systems. In effect, a technocentric reform agenda acts to displace other values and aims by furthering a technicist means-ends. This situation is especially disturbing given the political drive to privatize the public sphere which includes public education. Also, the emphasis on standards and accountability reflects the worst aspects of competitive capitalism which has so much inspired current reform policy. In addition, there exists a growing marketization of education where teachers and schools are carefully constructed through advertising and marketing schemes as a viable "target audience" for computer-related products. With the increasing violence within schools and the number of children living in poverty, I grew suspicious about the "inevitable" technological utopian vision of education painted by what David Tyack and Larry Cuban (1995) call "policy elites" who largely envision schools being repurposed for the specific technical and functional needs of a globalized market economy. Given these factors, I wondered if teachers' visions of education's future in the 21st century reflected that which had been constructed by policy elites, entrepreneurs, and marketers. It is the findings of a study which aimed to address this question that is reported in this book.

The Creation of Political Dramaturgy

Educational historian, Herbert Kleibard (1992) has described educational reform discourse in terms of political theorist Murray Eldeman's (1985) idea of "dramaturgy in politics." Eldeman (1985) explains how the act of generating political discourse or "political dramaturgy" can be understood as the expression of a society's ideological narratives. In effect, the "dramaturgy in politics" exists as a manifestation of a culture's social construction—how it expresses its values and social vision. Thus, political-social discourse is inherently reflexive. According to Kleibard (1992), educational reform discourse has historically existed as a particular "social space" for sociopolitical discourse. Therefore, educational policy discourse may be understood as "the dramatization of ritualistic myths about America and its values played out on the proscenium of the public school" (p. 186).

Indeed, politics, according to Eldeman (1985), is concerned with who gets what or with the authoritative allocation of values through language. Policy talk "involves a competitive exchange of symbols, referential and evocative, through which values are shared, assigned and coexistence attained" (p. 114). Furthermore, Eldeman (1985) explains that a political act is always an incomplete symbol because the public does not experience it as a physical act, but rather as language, which is "the paramount form of action in creating political phenomena" (p. 196). He also points out that the social construction of politics is lived as a "ritualistic exchange of predictable gestures" among various interest groups and officials who justify their position to one another; a process which in effect creates a "political spectacle" of dramaturgy.

> The patterned nature of so much of the publicized political process provides a revealing clue to the function of the political spectacle. In effect, though not often in intent, it is dramaturgy rather than policymaking. Like drama, it is constructed to be presented to a public (p. 210).

Thus, the presentation of political spectacle is constituted on a symbolic level. However, political acts are both instrumental and expressive and therefore meanings are not in symbols per se but rather in society and also in individuals, which means they are reflective of one other (p. 92). Eldeman (1985) further explains that "condensation symbols" evoke emotions associated with a situation which then condenses into one symbolic event, sign, or act, such as patriotic pride or the promise of future greatness through technological progress. The development of a condensation symbol's power arises from the construction of a threat of crisis. Indeed, in the case of current educational reform policy, it is the supposed threat of economic failure due to the development of a global market and the demands of the information-based economy and the alleged failure of public education to adequately address such changes that have created an unprecedented "crisis" to which education must be made to respond. The social myth of progress through technological innovation coupled with the perceived threat of an impending economic crisis has thus led to a technocentric-based educational reform agenda imbued with the condensation symbolism of technological progress and its unquestionable "inevitability."

Also, as Eldeman (1985) suggests, political reform narratives act on a broad social level as well as an individual level. On an individual level, these stories are related to the construction of subjectivity and roles. As a consequence, in the campaign to infuse schools with information and computer technologies, we see a reconfiguration of many elements that impact teacher's roles, including curriculum development as standards and social interaction framed by elaborate accountability schemes. Reconfiguration of the model of the "good teacher" is highly exacted in advertisements for educational computing products that depict how a teacher's power is realized through pseudo control over the technology. On a broad, social level, educational reform discourse exists as a "narrative space" where the construction of social discourse reflects changes in the stories we tell ourselves about who we are. But what if the landscape of this narrative space is delimited; the possibilities diminished through constructed "inevitabilities" that secure legitimacy through official reform policies?

Moreover, educational researchers David Tyack and Larry Cuban (1995) describe how the discourse of current educational reform acts as a "dramatic exchange in a persistent theater of aspiration and anxiety," such that "conversation about schools is one way Americans make sense of their lives" (p. 42). As noted above, Kleibard (1992) would concur and also points out that educational reform discourse seems especially characterized by a struggle between interests related to equity and more pragmatic interests germane to serving national and economic needs, with the latter having secured and maintained dominance since the turn of the 20th century (p. 199). For example, although the current "dramaturgy" in educational politics ideally can be characterized as a struggle between various perspectives and interests to forge a "politics of meaning" (Shapiro, 1994/1996, p. 224), according to Kleibard (1992) and Labaree (1987), fundamentally, there is a tension between two broad perspectives. A traditional perspective on educational reform understands that the educational process needs to be anchored by a commitment to building a democratic society (Goodman, 1995; Purpel, 1996; Greene, 1986/1996; Dewey, 1916). A traditional perspective's focus on democratic principles emphasizes "equality and promotes participatory politics" (Labaree, 1987, p. 489). Another perspective, which reflects a functionalist orientation and the spirit of vocationalism at the turn of the last century, "elevates liberty and promotes free markets" (Labaree, 1987, p. 489). This dialectic between the values of a market economy and those of democratic politics generated two prescriptive approaches to educational policy—one that emphasizes competition and a meritocracy and another that envisions a more egalitarian purpose realized through open access and student-directed pedagogy (Labaree, 1987).

Similarly, in terms of the current policy to infuse schools with technology, Cuban (1997) understands the issue in the context of oppositional values between "techno-enthusiasts who seek efficiency and preparation for a computerized workplace vs those who are unconvinced that higher productivity is better for students or meets the social purpose of building literate and caring citizens." Cuban (1997) concludes that "value conflicts seldom succumb to technical fixes. These are honest-to-God dilemmas that need far more debate than they have gotten so far" (p. 41). Thus, it is not the messy political act of debate or the very dialectic between the dominate perspectives that has traditionally fueled conversations related to educational reform policy that characterizes the problem concerning current reform efforts. Rather, it is the lack of a pluralistic dialogue—a silence that arises from the assumption of certain "inevitabilities."

The functionalist discourse of current educational reform has rationalized changes in education by aligning the purpose of public education with that of economic interests and Information Age futurism, a purpose that includes rapid infusion of electronic technologies. Thus, the hegemony of current official reform policy, as expressed through its particular story or discourse of inevitability, acts to frame the dramaturgy in educational politics. Although the narrative space of educational reform continues to function as a "place" where social discourse is both constructed and constituted, it nevertheless is characterized as a procrustean bed, delineated by predetermined ends and means.

Educational philosopher Maxine Greene (1986/1996) perceives the position held by policy elites as an exercise in power in the manner expressed by Michel Foucault, where the naming of the problem and solution seems inescapable or inevitable. Greene (1986/1996) believes that technical rationalism, or an emphasis on efficiency, guides educational reform policy. A focus on technical rationalism, according to Jurgen Habermas (1989, p. 258) inadvertently "impedes making the foundations of society the object of thought and reflection." This is because the underlying tension between the values inherent in the social democratic vision of education versus a vision that emphasizes the values of a free market and liberty are in fact not addressed. The absence of such foundational elements from discourse effectively serves to depoliticalize the issues at hand, thus opening the way for a technical-rational perspective and "solution." The narrowing of the focus of reform discourse on economic issues at the expense of social democratic issues needs to be understood within the context of how economic changes spurred by computer and information technologies are putting pressure on the traditional institution of education (Hargraves, 1994; Peters, 1996).

The fundamental point is that the closure or narrowing of divergent voices may not necessarily indicate a consensus via debate as much as one forged through the power of the discourse of policy elites. If this situation exists, and several thoughtful educators hold this perception, then such a situation raises important and serious questions related to the democratic process and education's existence as a viable site for public debate. For example, several educational researchers (e.g., Shapiro,1994/1996; Hargraves, 1994; Apple, 1996; de Alba et al., 2000; and others) raise concern about the connection between the rise of an information-based economy and the alignment of education and technology toward serving corporate interests. Many supporters of technology-driven reforms assert that the marriage of technology and education is necessary to rebuild a new work force that can regain a competitive edge in a growing world economy and, in turn, would cure the "pervasive mediocrity" of schools. However, such a position is reductionary as all elements of the public sphere, including education, are positioned within technological means and ends even while the image of a crisis generates fear, and as a result, arrests the will to imagine things otherwise. In effect, the *de facto* vision painted by policy elites has been created without any citizen participation in its construction or ratification. Thus, even if the public becomes computer literate, citizen decision-making, in terms of educational policy, is essentially postpolitical.

In addition, the current reform movement involves an interaction of economic and social-based elements such that the relationship between schools and the economic base of society has intensified and shifted toward accommodating the values of the market economy, thus largely abandoning the social-democratic accord that has characterized education since World War II (Apple, 1995). Thus, according to critics of current reform policies, the dialectic between social democratic values and more functionalist interests is out of balance with the former eclipsed by the power of the latter's ability to name the crisis and its attendant solution in a manner that accommodates policy elite's interests. Therefore, the key issues that arise from the current dramaturgy in educational reform politics are as follows: (1) the process of the social construction of the crisis in education and the subsequent narrowing of reform discourse, which envisions the "inevitable" solution to education's crisis as serving corporate and national economic needs, (2) how policy talk acts as a framework for developing a social vision about the future of education in the 21st century, and (3) the influence of social and economic issues within the context of postmodernity, especially the "inevitable" infusion of electronic technologies into schools as a means to meet the needs of the Information Age. Also, another key element in educational reform, though often a forgotten one, is the role of teachers.

The Role of the Teacher and Educational Reform Policy

Despite teachers' relative powerless position in terms of their control over educational reform, teachers are not without their agency. The history of technology diffusion is characterized by teachers' resistance (Cuban, 1986; Tyack & Tobin, 1993). In fact, teachers are constructed as holding a privileged position by certain educators critical of the current reform movement (i.e., Apple, 1995; Greene, 1986/1996; Bowers, 1988; Nunan, 1983; Hargraves, 1994). The teacher as gatekeeper holds a key position as one who has the power to resist the current reform policies. A teacher's agency has been characterized as a form of trusteeship (Sergiovanni, 1994), as citizens serving the public interest (Reid, 1979), as well as initiators of social change (Freire, 1970; Greene, 1986/1996; Bowers, 1988; Hargraves, 1994; Fullen, 1993; Nunan, 1983). For example, Andy Hargraves (1994), who understands that the traditions of education are being challenged by postmodernity, believes that teachers are demanded to "engage effectively with the images and technologies of the postmodern world" while also maintaining "the cultural analysis, moral judgment and studied reflection they threaten to supersede." Within this paradox, Hargraves (1994) believes that teachers "must be both competent users and innovators with technology and moral guardians against its most trivializing effects" (p. 76). However, the position which Hargraves has outlined for teachers demands a highly critical awareness in relation to power, media, and technology. It also assumes that our commonsense understanding about technology reflects its true complexity within society, when in reality the bias is to construct technology in a singular, uncontested fashion as a neutral artifact (Winner, 1980, 1986; Bowers, 1988; Ellul, 1964). The perspective of Hargraves and other educators who understand a teacher's role as that of a social change agent, envisions teachers breaking out of the gravity of socio-economic biases and commonsense assumptions. This is not such an easy thing to do.

The issue of teachers' agency within the context of current reforms—the intensification and rationalization of their work to achieve greater professionalization and efficiency—needs to be considered within the historical context of teachers and the process of change. On the one hand, teachers have been historically constructed in an instrumental sense as mere "delivery systems"; a position which easily accommodates a functionalist approach to education's purpose. On the other hand, as mentioned above, teachers have also been privileged as gatekeepers who, through their resistance, defend the lifeworld of schools and the underlying democratic ideals of the educational institution. As public trustees and caregivers, it is the civic duty of teachers to defend the social sphere and the public good. However, the two forces, which characterize the fundamental roles of teachers, are inherently oppositional and, in fact, mirror the underlying dialectic between democratic versus market-based values, which characterize the dynamics of the dramaturgy in educational reform. Clandinin and Connelly's (1995) research indicates that teachers find the struggle to negotiate official knowledge (such as the latest instructional strategy), and administrative policy (often arising from state or federal mandates) with their personal moral reasoning and tacit, experiential knowledge, to be challenging and sometimes debilitating. Even if teachers do not see themselves specifically as gatekeepers, teachers become political agents by virtue of the fact that they are positioned to struggle against the power of official knowledge and top-down administrative policies in defense of their professional practice. Indeed, the role of teachers within the context of current reform policy is not only related to traditional areas of curriculum and instruction and its associated expressions of control as accountability measures and standards, there is also the issue of utilizing electronic technologies to reform education.

Questioning Technology

Many critics of current reform policy do not understand the rapid infusion of electronic technology as a specific issue, although there are some exceptions. For example, some critics are concerned that electronic technologies have become and end in themselves (Smith, 1995a; Bowers, 1988). Others perceive that technology's growing presence in schools acts as a form of "hidden curriculum" inculcating a technocentric way of knowing and values (Streible, 1986; Postman, 1995). Others are puzzled by the fact that so much energy and resources support a technology-driven reform effort when there is little evidence that technology-based learning environments improve achievement (Kerr, 1996; Oppenheimer, 1997; Healy, 1998).

The issue of restructuring schools through the infusion of electronic technology can also be questioned by examining our cultural bias toward the nature of technology. Our cultural bias is to view technology as a mere tool or artifact. This position is inherently apolitical and therefore leads to technology adoption without much reflection on how technology may change the social environment or inadvertently enable negative unexpected

outcomes (Winner, 1986). There is much more to understanding the
process of technology adoption if one understands technology not only as a
tool but as a "social process" (Schwarz & Thompson, 1990) whereby it is
recognized that "the study of technology cannot be separated from the
surrounding political structure" (Street, 1992, p. 181).

For example, in the context of educational policy development, one
needs to consider the intersection of what characterizes enterprise culture—
the privatization of the public sector, the development of globalized market
economy dependent upon information technologies, the valuing of
efficiency, individual liberty, and a minimalist state which in turn affects a
social process of a particular cultural engineering in the creation of a
sovereign, entrepreneuring self (de Alba et al., 2000). This reconstruction of
the ideal identity of a citizen (and student) into an "enterprise individual"
has immense bearing on the purpose of public education, as evidenced in
functionalist-based reform ends, although this point is seldom
acknowledged. As de Alba et al. (2000) observe, "Most curricula in Western
schools are being restructured by what can be called the informational
economy. But the *form* that this 'new' education should take in this new age
of electronic communication is seldom discussed or even problematized" (p.
139, authors' italics).

In addition, there exists a fundamental shift from an emphasis on
knowledge to information and from content to process, which is related to
the proliferation of information, a postmodern fetish, whose production
process depends upon electronic technologies. Specifically, the redefinition
of knowledge has shifted from an emphasis on knowing *that* to knowing
how, explicitly regarding the acquisition of a skill or reskilling ("lifelong
learning"), especially a skill in using computers or some other technical
know-how. Thus, it is not surprising that questions related to the nature of
knowledge and pedagogy within the context of enterprise culture and
society are seldom raised. This is nothing less than "a philosophical silence"
(de Alba et al., 2000, p. 139). Another related point is how the shift in
emphasis from content to process reflects how the values of enterprise
culture have deeply colonized the educational sphere. This shift also reflects
the subsequent unacknowledged influence of related issues, such as the
reconfiguration of the ideal self; the redefinition of the nature of knowledge
via the essentializing of information; the relationship of information
technologies to changes in human communication processes (i.e., from face-
to-face to mediated); and the disabling of the legitimacy held by traditional
authority structures associated with oral and written communication (de
Alba et al., 2000).[2]

Langdon Winner (1986) has also examined how electronic technologies
have become central to economic, business, and scientific processes. He
believes that "mythinformation" guides many of our political, economic,

and social decisions. He describes mythinformation as "the almost religious conviction that a widespread adoption of computers and communication systems along with easy access to electronic information will automatically produce a better world for human beings' (p. 105). Similarly, Theodore Rozak (1986) warns about the "cult of information," characterized by a mindless allegiance and acquiescence to the essentializing of information.

Winner (1986) points out that mythinformation is peculiar to the latter decades of the 20th century, as it has arisen with the invention of new information technologies, and seems particularly popular with those who are cynical or have become discouraged by other aspects of modern social life (p. 106). Mythinformation's projected vision of the future equates the sheer momentum of the computer revolution to "eliminate many of the ills that have vexed political society since the beginning of time" while information itself becomes "the dominate form of wealth" (Winner, 1986, p. 104). The proliferation of information and information infrastructures (networked systems) are envisioned to deconstruct entrenched systems of hierarchy while regenerating prospects for participatory democracy. However, according to Winner (1986) one can predict how the advantages of the computer revolution will further the interests of those of wealth and power, thus certain to make the "revolution" one of a conservative character. Although this trend can be assuaged through deliberate action, such an approach is seldom advised by computer revolution enthusiasts. To this end, a libertarian perspective characterized by an unquestionable faith in the computer revolution realized through market forces means that "technological determinism ceases to be a mere theory and becomes an ideal: A desire to embrace conditions brought on by technological change without judging them in advance. There is nothing new in this disposition" (Winner, 1986, p. 108).

In addition, the technological society is characterized by the fact that today "our *techne* has at last become *politeia*—our instruments are institutions in the making" (Winner, 1986, p. 54). Winner adds that "because technological innovation is inextricably linked to processes of social reconstruction," a society that endeavors to control "its own structural evolution" must necessarily "confront each significant set of technological possibilities with scrupulous care" (p. 54). Winner suggests that in contrast to an apolitical understanding about technology, a cultural approach to technology adoption embodies a reflective and contextual understanding and signifies that our relationship to technology is essentially socially constructed. Thus, for example, policy elites' technological fix approach "treats technology as an instrument when in fact it involves a complex set of interests" (Street, 1992, p. 172). However, an apolitical technology fix approach has the political advantage of neatly fitting into the context of a commonsense cultural bias about technology. Hence, the "inevitability" of a technology-based policy goes unquestioned. Winner believes that with a cultural approach to understanding technology adoption, "we should try to imagine and seek to build technical regimes compatible with freedom, social justice and other key political ends. . . . to accord with a deliberately articulated, widely shared notion of a society worthy of care and loyalty" (p. 55). Winner refers to his cultural approach to technology adoption as one which is "disciplined by the political wisdom of democracy" (p. 55).

Winner underscores the idea of imagining our future via the construction of a democratically inspired social vision within the context of technology adoption. Another important point he raises is that a choice truly exists in terms of constructing a social vision via the process of deliberation. This means that the "inevitabilities" offered by policy elites not only discount the political nature of technology adoption but also disengage people as citizens. The closure of public space, created by the political and technical elites' "inevitable" solution, brings into relief the contrived nature of the current social imagination and the restricted "dramaturgy" of educational reform policy with regard to education's relationship to society.

The Creation of Social Vision and the Politics of Crisis

Maxine Greene (1995) describes social imagination as "the capacity to invent visions of what should be and what might be in our deficit society— in our schools" (p. 5). The power to "invent visions" arises from the power of imagination. Envisioning involves the study of existing circumstances toward the goal of imagining other possibilities, and therefore is inherently a critical process. Greene (1995) explains that if the act of imaging, of envisioning, is closed down, a feeling of the inability to conceive an alternative order of things can "give rise to a resignation that paralyzes people . . . [and that] an accompanying effacing of the sense of personal and communal efficacy may submerge people into the given, in what appears impervious to protest and discontent" (p. 19).

Several critics of the current reform movement make reference to the importance of expressing a vision, specifically a democratically inspired "social-utopian" vision (Goodman, 1995), "utopian ideals" (Tyack & Cuban, 1995) or utopianism as a "vision of possibility" (McLaren, 1995). Shapiro (1994/1996) describes the dramaturgy in educational politics as a search for a "politics of meaning" where "questions of human purpose and social vision" enable a society to engage in a "cultural act" whereby it may secure "a sense of what our lives are about and what it means to live with others in community" (p. 224). This discourse counters that of a functionalist-based social vision, which has associated the concepts of privatization and business to education's ends, such that "the language of possibility and hope, one that is tied to social empowerment and active citizenship, has given way to the language of the instrumental" (Aronowitz & Giroux, 1985, p. 196).

Indeed, within a typical school environment a vision is a construct defined by values arising from a business administration framework rather than the act of negotiating a shared vision toward realizing social justice. In a business administration context only administrators and educational experts truly can have visions, as the practice of creating visions is solely an outcome of leadership (Bennis & Nanus, 1985; Seng, 1990). This perspective accommodates a top-down functionalist approach to the management of schools and further disengages and alienates teachers from decision-making. Although it is acknowledged that teachers may possess "personal visions," the existing power structure in most schools does not encourage teacher's sharing or acting on their personal visions (Barth, 1990). Given the current political context, characterized by the closure of deliberative space by the "inevitabilities" of policy elites and teacher's depoliticized position, how do educators construct a personal and social vision about the future of education specifically within a "technopoly," a state of a culture that seeks its authorization in technology (Postman, 1993) and which requires a particular kind of social order dominated by the values of efficiency and control? How might educators understand the meaning and function of education within the context of the postmodern condition?

One means is to critically examine the association between education and society in terms of the current crisis, as this is an essential aspect of political dramaturgy. However, the actual crisis is not that which is constructed by neoliberal technocentric discourse. Rather, there exists a systemic crisis within all levels of society—a generalized weakening of the relational systems within sociopolitical and economic realms, a condition described by Antonio Gramsci as an organic crisis (cited in Laclau & Mouffe, 1985). In fact, even neoliberalism exists in a crisis state in that "we currently lack new utopian horizons from which socio-political projects could emerge and enable a new hegemonic rearticulation of societies" (de Alba et al., 2000, p. 149). Elements of the current crisis are related to poverty, environmental problems and sustainability, the speed of change characterized by temporality (dislocation) over spatiality (structurality) and the consequent ambivalence of possibility, responsibility and morality. The crisis is also related to the rise of globalization and its effects on economics in terms of capital, scientific and technological developments, trade and transportation as well as the realm of politics, specifically democracy, participation, human rights and sustainable development (de Alba et al, 2000, pp. 161–186).

Social critic Andre Gorz explains that the crisis is more fundamental than any economic or social crisis, in that the utopia that has directed industrial society for the past two centuries is collapsing. He describes a utopia in a philosophical sense as a social vision of the future upon which a civilization builds its hopes and ideals. Thus, when a utopian framework collapses, it creates a systemic crisis such that the values regulating the social dynamic and which constitute a shared meaning, implode, in a postmodern sensibility, and effect a systemic loss of meaning. Therefore, industrialism's utopian promise, via the unfettered expansion of the economic sphere, to liberate humanity from scarcity, and emancipate all from injustice through the domination of Nature, has failed. Indeed, Gorz (1989, p. 8) concludes, "nothing remains of this utopia." This means, of course, that society must seek new utopias. However, the discursive process by which new social visions are constructed are essentially controlled by those in power who have a vested interest in maintaining the status quo (Eldeman, 1985).

Also, the current crisis in meaning and the vacuum that it creates has been filled not only by a mediated spectacle (DuBord, 1994), but also a benign system of control which Lyotard (1984) characterized as expressing a "performity principle." The performity principle operationalizes the criterion of efficiency as a cost-benefit (input/output) model within the context of all facets of lived experience including the lifeworld or the everyday experiences of social interaction. Those elements which guide and define the realm of economics and business have now been applied to other social realms such as education. Within the context of current technicist educational reform policy the nature of the discourse has fundamentally shifted. de Alba et al. (2000) explain that the "locus of operation is no longer based on questions of educational aims and ideals in the old sense which drew on language games involving values, aspirations, conceptions and beliefs about humanity, potential, personal worth and attaining emancipation and dignity" (p. 213). Rather, it has moved into the realm of means toward the ends of optimal efficiency. The legitimacy of policy elite's proclamation regarding educational reform policy is concretized and rationalized via the logic of efficiency, which has colonized all realms of the sociopolitical sphere. For example, an obvious expression of performance culture within the context of educational policy is the development of standardized testing and accountability schemes. Indeed, the "text" of performity is a complex intersection of "a technology, a culture and a mode of regulation" (Ball, 2001). It operates as a "system of terror" in Lyotard's words, which utilizes various means of control that serve to measure productivity and thus the value of an individual or organization. As an elaborate system of judgment, it raises questions in relation to the issue of power: Who establishes the legitimacy of control systems via procedures of competition, accountability, and standards? As Foucault's vision of a society of discipline eclipses into a society of control via feedback processes such as the database, the appraisal meeting, and other accountability procedures, it is not only the threat of surveillance but also the uncertainty and instability of being judged in various ways that creates a "flow of changing demands" that act as a "recipe for ontological insecurity" (Ball, 2000, p. 212). As individuals internalize these procedures of control, they become engaged by the logic of their own virtual representations and thus become "enterprising subjects" (Ball, 2000, p. 223). Thus, in terms of educational settings, the performity principle, embodied through accountability procedures and standardized testing, expresses the technical rationality of control technologies that act to configure the roles and social interactions of teachers, students, and administrators.

Therefore, it is important that educators question the basis of current reform policies and how it relates to the larger socioeconomic condition of enterprise culture because, as expressed in the quotation featured at the beginning of this chapter, reform policies function as scripts or frameworks and thus "encode values intended to change people and social practices" (de Alba et al., 2000, p. 216). Moreover, those who create educational reforms,

> . . . intend them to mesh with scripts for doing life as a whole. The key questions here are What kinds of 'visions' for life, people and practices more generally, are encoded in these scripts? What do we think about them? And how do we intend to respond to them? (de Alba et al., 2000, p. 216).

The creation of theories about the current crisis as well as our social visions are not only interpretations but rather possess constituting power to objectify the world. Indeed, technology, as an expressive media of communication, engenders what it pretends only to display (Carey, 1990). This effort to direct our world via narrative or language and communication media is essentially an instantiation of power, especially the need to control and dominate the world—more specifically, Nature. It is in effect a process of domesticating the world as an expression of a "will to power, a will to know, a will to establish a system, to configure an order, to objectify the world; a will to dominate that strives to give form to the world and impose that form upon it" (de Alba et al., 2000, p. 54). Thus, one may conclude that much is at stake and that great power exists within our social visions and political narratives that arise from the political dramaturgy of educational reform.

Focus and Structure of the Study

The study presented in this book suggests that the current incarnation of a "technological fix" approach to educational reform both reflects and exploits a constructed and unquestioning cultural belief in the power of information technologies. This factor is considered with regard to how educational reform discourse expresses a broader social discourse or social vision and how the landscape of this social vision has been narrowed by policy elites' "discourse of inevitability" expressed as technological determinism.

Traditionally, within the historical context of educational reform policy, a dialectic exists between a functionalist "discourse of inevitability" offered by policy elites and that of an alternative discourse reflecting an emergent social vision constructed by the critics of official educational reform policy, which emphasizes democratic values related to social justice and equity. Chapters One and Two delineate these two philosophical frameworks. In Chapter One we review current educational reform policies by specifically examining the discourse of key reform documents (e.g., *A Nation at Risk*, 1983; *Goals 2000*, 1989; *Goals 2000: Educate America Act*, 1994). In this chapter we examine the politics of the general technocentric vision of education in the 21st century embedded within these official policies.

In the second level of analysis (Chapter Two) we will investigate current reform discourse from the vantage point of its critics who represent a liberal/critical perspective and question how current technocentric reform policy essentially ties education to the needs of industry. Specific aspects of current policy such as its definition of the crisis in education and the assumption of the "inevitable" infusion of electronic technologies into educational settings are discussed. This section offers alternative perspectives on the dominant discourse through examination of how electronic technologies have affected changes in the economic and social spheres. A review of the literature of the sociology of technology serves as the basis for the examination of the commonsense understanding about the nature of technology and how this apolitical perspective may influence current functionalist educational reform policies and the maintenance of a technocentric social vision.

In the third level of analysis (Chapter Three) we shall locate the role of teachers in relation to educational reform in general, and more specifically, within the context of the infusion of technological innovations into schools as a means of reform. Teachers' roles within this context are discussed regarding their agency and practices of resistance. In addition, the work of Maxine Greene and other critical scholars are discussed in terms of how educators' social visions may influence the development of educational reform policy.

The first three chapters provide an analytical framework with which one may contextualize the experiences and perceptions of the individual informants as well as understand the context of two case study sites and their particular reform programs. The two sites are located in central Texas. The elementary school, in terms of its reform endeavors, represents traditional social democratic aims of educational reform as the school's major focus was to build community solidarity. In contrast, the middle school's reform efforts centered around information technologies and thus reflect the aims of current technocentric educational policy. Chapters Four and Five feature the individual case studies of these schools. Chapter Four presents the story of Shelton Valley Middle School whereas Chapter Five recounts the story of Zepeda Elementary. Chapter Six is a cross-case analysis of the two sites and also provides a discussion of the meaning of the study's findings.

The fundamental assumptions embodied in current educational reform discourse are examined through in-depth interviews with teacher participants and administrators. The aim of the study is to understand how the dialectic between a technocentric, and that which expresses an alternative social vision based on social justice, is experienced by educational practitioners. While certain educational theorists see a need for educators and citizens to counter and disrupt the closure of dominant educational reform discourse, is this tension, this resistance, evidenced in the lived experiences of teachers? How do educators who face the reality of the classroom perceive official educational reform discourse? Do they believe that education is in a state of crisis? If so, what characterizes this crisis? How do teachers define the Information Age and what meaning, if any, does it have for education? Do they hold any misgivings about the infusion of electronic technologies into education? Do they characterize the relationship between society and technology in a typical apolitical manner? Finally, how do they envision the future of education as we find ourselves within a new millennium of an absolute technologically dependent information society? What is their ideal vision of education's future in such a society and what do they think, given the current trajectory of educational reform, is likely to unfold? The participants' reflections on these questions are considered within the context of their own school's reform efforts.

I also examine the contextuality of the adoption and change process by considering each site in terms of its particular story of reform. The actual reporting of the data on each site is presented in a narrative or storied format. The two individual stories are thus set within a broader context of the socio-political narrative of educational reform policy. This contextual positioning enables the incongruencies and parallels between the concerns of policy elites and educational practitioners to emerge. However, this study is not a traditional technology adoption report that only focuses on the usage and nonusage of a technological innovation within a particular context. Rather, the case studies of two distinct schools reflect a cultural approach to understanding technology adoption. A cultural approach to adoption integrates two elements: (1) the understanding of the political context, and (2) technology assessment (Street, 1992). This study addresses the political context at the micro or school level through interviewing teachers and their principals about their school's reform program. A macro level political context was addressed by acknowledging the power of technocentric official reform policies and asking participants to reflect on the assumptions embodied in these policies. The technology assessment aspect of a cultural approach to technology adoption was addressed by observing the school's general facilities, including computer labs, libraries and classrooms. In addition, each school's academic plan was examined to ascertain the role of technology toward realizing the school's goals. A cultural approach therefore underscores what has been found by Cuban (1986, 2001) and Tyack and Tobin (1993) in their research on teacher adoption of technological innovation—that it is a contextual and situated process.

This research effort also offers an understanding of how a particular group of educators perceive the nature of technology, specifically how they describe its relationship to society. Although much research has been conducted to understand teachers' perceptions about technology in terms of computer phobia or computer anxiety, none of these studies have attempted to analyze how teachers perceive the construct of technology in terms of a philosophical understanding. As electronic technologies become more ubiquitous within education and other social, institutional, and economic realms, it may be beneficial for educators (and students) to become more aware of their own assumptions about the nature of technology. Winner (1986) reminds us that our apolitical understanding about technology ultimately enables technological determinism. The main question is whether or not individual teachers reflect a culturally biased perspective or is their construction of technology more complex? Do their perceptions about technology influence their attitudes toward technology-driven reform policy? Would teachers, for example, who assume an unquestioning artifactual view of technology, be more likely to accept the policy elites' rationale for restructuring schools with technology at face value than those teachers who possess a more complex and political understanding about technology? Perhaps those teachers who have a complex understanding about technology and society are nevertheless unable to connect their perspective to current reform policy. Also, do those teachers who possess a more critical, social process view of technology adoption, voice their perspective to help inform decisions related to technology adoption at their schools?

In addition, each informant-teacher and their school's principal were asked to reflect on their social vision in terms of the future of education and what is likely to unfold given the current reform trajectory, as well as what they would like to see happen—their utopian-based vision of education's future. The informants were invited to reflect on discrepancies or similarities between their two imagined outcomes.

Although this study offers a general critical perspective, it does not stand to elucidate an antitechnology position, for such a stance is futile. The reality is that electronic technologies are ubiquitous and integral to many social, military, and governmental institutions as well as the general economic system. Also, millions of dollars are being invested into a technology-driven vision of education. Rather, this research effort attempts to understand how, in the words of Maxine Greene (1988), educators may "reawaken concern for a belief in a humane framework for the kinds of education required in a technological society" (p. vii). Indeed, how may educational policymakers balance the present functionalist and technology-driven reform policy with alternative approaches to educational reform that focus on caring (Noddings, 1992) and building community (Sergiovanni, 1994)? Educators would be wise to ask themselves if these new technologies are simply to be used to further reforms and policies designed to control the work of teachers and their students. If teachers and administrators understand networked systems simply as conduits for sending information, then they may unquestionably accept technology's usage to further accountability and standards-based instruction, especially if such systems create greater efficiency in the delivery of curriculum and other information. Indeed, have the values that the technological system expresses become the measure of all things, including pedagogy?

In conclusion, this study, through the voice of educators, seeks to question the technocentric and functionalist-based assumptions that drive current reform policies. Through this research effort, I attempt to shed light on the serious issue of the narrowing or the collapse of educational reform discourse by examining the voices of individual educators as citizens, and cast in relief their social visions against the background of the absence of public discourse within the dramaturgy of educational reform policy.

Notes

¹ The concept of a frame refers to the definition offered by psychologist Jerome Bruner (1990) who explains that a framework acts on the level of common sense as a "means of constructing the world, characterizing its flow." The process of framing is rooted in language and thus is constructed in a narrative form. It works on both the individual and social level through "folk psychology" as well as through "historically rooted institutions" (p. 56).

² For example, historian Mark Poster (1993) emphasizes the *mode* of symbolic exchange processes and compares how societies over time have experienced face-to-face orally based exchange to written exchange via a print mode of expression and finally to electronically mediated exchanges. Poster claims that these various modes are not mere extensions of previous symbolic exchange processes. Rather, a particular mode of symbolic exchange has the capacity to restructure social relations, influence the manner of meaning making, constitute subjectivity and change the relationship between a subject and the world. These factors are especially important to education in terms of the nature of the linguistic dimension of electronic communication, which is also related to the epistemological shift from knowledge to information and content to process.

CHAPTER ONE

The Social Vision of Technological Determinism

Technology has an essential, but not independent, role to play in meeting the demand for a vastly more productive education system. Technology must be viewed broadly, embracing all the components of an education system, not just as an 'add-on' to an established educational infrastructure. Meaningful technological change of schools will depend on a comprehensive sociotechnical systems design process, *integrating technical systems, human resources, management and organization.*

Lewis J. Perelman, 1987, author's italics

This chapter reviews the major reform benchmarks of official educational policy established since the early 1980s. Beginning with *A Nation at Risk: The Imperatives for Educational Reform* (The National Commission on Excellence in Education, 1983) under the Reagan administration, the subsequent major reform measures are: *America 2000: An Educational Strategy* (U.S. Department of Education, The President's Educational Summit with Governors, 1991) under the Bush administration, and *Goals 2000: Educate America Act* (National Educational Goals Panel, 1994) developed under the Clinton administration and largely adopted by the George W. Bush administration. This section highlights the discourse of educational reform as expressed in these reform documents as well as examining the cultural politics and various interest groups that fueled the "dramaturgy" in educational reform since the publication of *A Nation at Risk*.

As explained in the Introduction, the repositioning of education to meet the demands of a competitive global market-based economy accommodated both technocentric and functionalist perspectives. In addition, because education holds a social and cultural function characterized as a highly contested site, various interest groups and political factions sought to configure the curriculum and general pedagogical values within their particular socio-political frameworks. For example, in the past few decades, educational reform policy was influenced by the political right represented by Neoconservatives, the Christian Coalition and the 1996 Republican's platform (i.e., Contract with America), and the "left" represented by Neoliberals and the more centrist-based New Democrats (i.e., the Clinton administration). Each of these political factions vied for the public's commitment to their particular vision of education's future in the next millennium (Spring, 1997; Apple, 1996). Thus, this review of official reform documents attempts to illustrate how the discourse of policy elites and particular interest groups acted to shape the vision of education's purpose within the 21st century.

A Nation at Risk

In hindsight, *A Nation at Risk* (1983) is described by some educational scholars as the most significant of recent reform documents in terms of how it set a trajectory for educational reform policy's direction into the 21st century (Tyack & Cuban, 1995; Shapiro, 1990; Spring, 1997). It is important to understand that the publication of *A Nation at Risk* opened the way toward questioning the legitimacy of public education itself. As we shall see later, this issue of choice became central to the evolving dramaturgical debate over educational reform.

Published in President Ronald Reagan's first term of office, *A Nation at Risk* was used as a political tool during a time of rising conservatism and economic downturn. The publicity surrounding this report and its particular language, likening the "rising tide of mediocrity" within education to an "act of war" against the American people, placed education at the forefront of political debate. *A Nation at Risk* spurred subsequent reports by several task forces and commissions on the status of education. In fact, a few months after its publication, several states submitted their reform proposals to the Commission, listing specific policy objectives designed to meet the recommendations made by the Commission (U.S. Department of Education, 1984). These responses were characterized by a strong focus on accountability, a feature that state policymakers defended in order to meet the Commission's standards of excellence (Snauwaert, 1993).

The Commission, noting that the American economy was faltering due to the poor state of schools and the ineptitude of educators, painted a vision of the future where education, within the present context of a waning industrial-based economy, was becoming central to an emerging new world order based on international markets and information technologies. The Commission defined, as follows, the risk the American public was facing at that time.

> Knowledge, learning, information and skilled intelligence are the new raw materials of international commerce and are today spreading throughout the world . . . learning is the indispensable investment required for success in the 'information age' we are entering (p. 11).

The reform of education was thus closely tied not only to economic welfare but to the emergence of an era uniquely defined by the dominance of information technologies. The Commission noted how the lowering of United States students' performance on standardized tests scores, in comparison to other industrialized nations, had occurred during a time when "computers and computer-controlled equipment are penetrating every aspect of our lives—homes, factories, and offices" (p. 11).

At the time in which *A Nation at Risk* (1983) was published, the writings of futurists such as Alvin Toffler's (1980) *The Third Wave* and John Naisbitt's (1982) *MegaTrends: Ten New Directions Transforming Our Lives* were very popular, especially with the business community to whom the authors addressed their writings. Generally, these writers projected a picture of a future where electronic technology is a central force engaging wide economic, political, and social change, although the major emphasis is given to the economic sphere. Their utopian views of the new information technologies as a generative force for a new global economy is perhaps a vision in a becoming or actualized state, as evidenced by various multinational corporation's growing worldwide power. However, the vision that such technologies will automatically create an "anticipatory democracy" seems dangerously naive. Segal (1994) explains how these particular authors' ahistorical perspectives ignore the fact that technological progress has been a mixed blessing. He also perceives that it is the very success of such books that in fact betray a deep social unease.

> It is precisely when American business and professional people, among
> others, are so unsure of the country's or the world's future, so desperate
> to be handed sugar-coated soma pills in book form, that [such books]
> can be so successfully packaged, purchased and consumed (p. 188).

Although the works of Toffler and Naisbitt are not specifically referred to by the Commission, the particular impacts of new technologies as envisioned in these writings were not lost on the policy elites and business executives who were, more so than educators and citizens, most instrumental in formulating official educational reform policy.

The Infusion of Electronic Technologies

As with the *National Defense Act* of 1958, a reform proposal inspired by Cold War politics and America's response to the Russian launching of Sputnik, *A Nation at Risk* also emphasized the importance of science and mathematics, citing that "we are raising a new generation of Americans that is scientifically and technologically illiterate" (p. 11). It was predicted that if this problem was not addressed by altering school curriculum, a growing chasm would arise between a "small scientific and technologically elite" and most other "ill-informed citizens" (p. 11).

In the report's "Indicators of Risk" section, it was noted how low levels of academic achievement exist at a time when computer and high technology are rapidly transforming several occupations. In response, not only did the Commission recommend emphasis on the teaching of science and math, but also the teaching of computer science in high school. The Commission's rationale is as follows:

> The teaching of computer science in high school should equip graduates to: (1) understand the computer as an information, computation and communication device (2) use the computer in the study of the other Basics and for personal and work-related purposes; and (3) understand the world of computers, electronics and related technologies (pp. 71–72).

In the "Standards and Expectations" section of the report, the Commission instructed educators that "new instructional materials should reflect the most current application of technology in appropriate areas" (p. 75). In response to *A Nation at Risk* (1983), the National School Boards Association (NSBA) established in 1985 the Institute for the Transfer of Technology to Education (ITTE), a federation of state school board associations "to help advance the wise uses of technology in public schools" (Perelman, 1987, p. 1). The ITTE developed the organization, Technology Leadership Network (TLN), as a means to facilitate a dialogue about technology in education among school districts. Since that time, several professional organizations and journals dedicated to the infusion of electronic technology into schools have been established.[1]

The recommendations made by the Commission and subsequent reports had a definite impact on the curriculum in schools as the teaching of keyboarding in primary schools and computer literacy and computer programming languages in the upper grades became a part of the general curriculum. In addition, schools invested revenue into building computer labs. Today many schools utilize computer-based networked systems to organize their library inventories whereas many state technology expenditures are devoted to the building of local and wide-area networked system infrastructures. These infrastructures provide electronic communication within and between schools and their statewide educational system for distance education programming, a shift augmented by current federal funding such as the Federal Communication Commission's Education Rate or "E-Rate." Also, the diffusion of computers and access to the Internet into schools and homes since the mid-1980s, shortly after the personal computer was developed, reflects a steady and rapid increase.[2]

Establishing National Standards

The Commission's recommendations directly addressed meeting the needs of the Information Age and reconfiguring schools to meet its perceived demands largely through the diffusion of electronic technology. Yet there was also a related concern—the viability of U.S. economy in the face of growing competition in a global economic sphere. This concern was met by setting "standards of excellence" through developing national standards and testing. The Commission also recommended that while equity remains a challenge, educators should turn their energies toward realizing "excellence in education" with adopting higher standards and accountability—the ultimate goal being the creation of a "learning society" which reflected "standards of excellence." Not only did the Commission's recommendations point educators in the direction of national and state standards, they clearly aligned the goals of public education with those of the national economy and business enterprise. Indeed, schools were cited as being the major reason why American businesses were falling behind their international competitors in an emerging global market. Subsequent reports directly linked economic productivity to education.[3] The relationship between school reform and the strengthening of U.S. corporation's presence within an global economy also demanded new roles for teachers. In *A Nation Prepared: Teachers for the 21st Century* (1986), the Carnegie Forum on Education and the Economy attributed the low quality of education (and, in turn, the poor state of the U.S. economy) to inept and/or poorly trained teachers (Spring, 1997). In addition, the assumptions outlined in this document were later used by the Bush administration to justify research and development of alternative charter schools and fueled justification for the restructuring of schools to meet the demands of an information-based economy (Spring, 1997, p. 52).

The Entrepreneurial Factor

In addition, the Education Commission of the States' Task Force on Education and Economic Growth published *Action for Excellence* (1983), which sought to restructure education through the entrepreneurial power of U.S. corporations. The Education Commission, composed of governors and executives from major U.S. corporations, was funded by IBM and Xerox, two major high-tech multinational U.S. corporations. The Education Commission concluded the following: "If the business community gets more involved in both the design and delivery of education, we are going to become more competitive as an economy" (p. 18). Also, despite the fact that neoconservative support of direct involvement of business enterprise with educational reform counters traditional libertarian, market-based ideology, the relation between business and educational policymakers continued to strengthen (Spring, 1997). [3] In addition, some conservative congressional members, under the leadership of Newt Gingrich, organized the Conservative Opportunity Society (COS) in the early 1980s, which defined itself as being high tech, futurist, populist, and conservative. The purpose of COS was to counter the "epidemic of techno abhorrence" inspired by welfare state bureaucrats by promoting a high tech optimistic future based on growth through technological progress.

America 2000: An Education Strategy

Whereas the publication of *A Nation at Risk* (1983) marks the beginning of the "first wave" of reform characterized by an emphasis on standards, accountability and achievement, the "second wave" aimed to restructure education. Tyack and Cuban (1995) explain that the meaning of "restructuring" is indeed quite varied, but has one common thread—raising academic achievement.

> People regard restructuring as a synonym for the market mechanism of choice, or teacher professionalization and empowerment or decentralization and school site management or increased involvement of parents in their children's education, or national standards in curriculum with tests to match or deregulation, or new forms of accountability, or basic changes in curriculum and instruction, or some or all of these in combination. But underlying most conceptions of restructuring is the goal of raising academic achievement (p. 80).

The second reform phase was the result of a meeting held in 1989 at Charlottesville, North Carolina, where President Bush and 50 state governors discussed the state of public education since the publication of *A Nation at Risk*. The governors emphasized the traditional functionalist perspective—human capital, standards, and the reform of schools to suit demands of the economy. Their plan offered six goals that were to be achieved by the year 2000 and underscored a need for national performance goals and offered detailed strategies for meeting such goals—in effect, a national curriculum. The president and governors also recommended decentralization of decision-making by instituting site-based management, especially regarding accomplishing reform goals and systems of accountability. Thus, the term "restructuring" developed to signify not only national standards and curriculum, but also the adoption of market-based administrative goals, teacher professionalization via the adoption of technology skills, and increased parental involvement through site-based management.

According to Tyack and Cuban (1995), policy elites became frustrated with educators' "lack of compliance" to state-mandated reforms and the sustaining of low academic performance and also realized that top-down mandates could not create increases in achievement. As a result, policy elites turned their attention toward reworking the structure of the education system or "systemic reform" (p. 81). Ironically, the "noncompliance" arose from confusion around the increase in contradictory bureaucratic mandates. For example, in their effort to respond to the call for reform demanded by *A Nation at Risk,* many states "promulgated more educational laws and regulations than they had generated in the previous 20 years" such that "exhortations for change and mandated practices often worked at cross purposes" (p. 78). Tyack and Cuban (1995) refer to one educator, frustrated by the compounding and often contradictory mandates, having commented that "we are asked to reinvent schools, to break the mold . . . and they put a moat of mandates around us. Its like putting on handcuffs and leg irons and saying climb Mt. Everest" (p. 78).

The suggestions offered by President Bush and the governors were implemented through a specific plan, *America 2000: An Education Strategy* (1991). This document illustrated a direct association between national standards and "human capital," as indicated in the following quote: "We believe that the time has come for the first time in U.S. history, to establish clear national performance goals, goals that will make us internationally competitive (U.S. Department of Education, 1991, p. 73)." [4] Also, the justification for a "back to basis" approach to curriculum and instruction was often couched in the rhetoric of "cultural literacy," where a conservative vision of curriculum focused on fundamental knowledge that eschewed the perspective of a more multicultural inspired understanding of curriculum content. Publications by E. D. Hirsh, Jr. (1987), Alan Bloom (1987), and William J. Bennett (1984) reflect this conservative vision.

The Establishment of NASDC

In terms of the privatization or choice issue, both the Neoliberals and Neoconservatives made reference to a 1990 study conducted by the Brookings Institute, which proposed that the effective management of schools was being prevented by political factions and that management problems could be assuaged if schools adopted a market-based structure of administration and fiscal support (i.e., Chubb & Moe, 1990). In fact, phase two of *America 2000: An Educational Strategy* (i.e., "For Tomorrow's Students: A New Generation of American Schools," 1991) invited business leaders to utilize the initial $1 million offered by the Federal government to garner private resources for underwriting a private corporation referred to as the New American Schools Development Corporation (NASDC). NASDC, devoted to creating alternative "break the mold" schools, was supported by Chris Whittle's Channel One and Edison Project, a business venture designed to exploit voucher revenue by developing and franchising for-profit, conservative-based, and technologically advanced schools. [5]

The basic reform tenents of *Goals 2000*, which were later adopted by President Clinton as *Goals 2000: Educate America Act* (1994) and generally guide the present George W. Bush administration, were national achievement tests, academic standards, and corporate involvement with the restructuring of schools. The institutionalization of these tenents was rationalized as a means to increase the quality of "human capital" and give U.S. corporations a competitive advantage within an information-based global economy. In 1991, Aronowitz and Giroux observed, for example, that in some cases "school curriculum has been fashioned in the interests of an industrial psychology that attempts to reduce schools and learning to strictly economic and corporate concerns (p. 89)."

Goals 2000: Educate America Act

The subsequent national reform policy, *Goals 2000: Educate America Act*, proposed by the National Educational Goals Panel (1994) specified eight goals that were to be achieved by the year 2000. [6] Generally these goals mirror those outlined in Bush's 1991 proposal—national standards, accountability, and choice. Sounding much like the Neoconservatives, the Neoliberal Clinton administration expressed a political centrist position and grounded their rationale for educational reform within Information Age and "human capital" rhetoric (Spring, 1997). For example, in February 1996, the Technology Literacy Challenge Fund, a Department of Education program offering grants to states, allocated over $2 billion over a five-year period to mobilize "the private sector, schools, teachers, students, parents, community groups, state and local government" to meet the goal of making all U.S. children "technically literate" by the "dawn of the 21st century." The strategy aimed to ensure that all teachers would have the necessary training and support to teach students to use the Internet. President Clinton's technology plan for schools included "four pillars": connectivity, modern computer hardware, high-quality software, and on-line resources and teacher preparation. It is significant that teacher preparation was the only nontechnical item on the list.

In 1998, President Clinton asked Congress to double its funding for the Technology Literacy Challenge Fund to $425 million. The contributions of business to educational technologies were also impressive. Pacific Bell, for example, paid an estimated $100 million between 1994 and 2000 to a technology program, "Education First," which provided ISDN lines (digital based internet service) to California schools and libraries. Although schools acquire only twenty-five percent of their technology funding from federal sources (the remainder is acquired from local districts, states and private businesses), by 1997, projections indicated that educators would spend $5.2 billion annually on technology alone (Trotter, 1997). Indeed, education clearly became a viable market for high-technology products. Consequently, one of the major challenges added to the burden of managing a school is sifting through the hype of marketing and negotiating the complexity of planning, financing, developing, and sustaining an electronic-based instructional environment with very limited funds and technical support. One means by which educators secure the additional funding for technology is to cut back on traditional instructional services, especially those in the arts, and teacher's aids (Trotter, 1997).

The leadership power that the Clinton administration held to shape the vision of educators and policymakers was significant, as was its fiscal influence. As one observer put it, "dollars follow vision" (White, 1997, p. 40). Thus, by 1999 a consensus grew regarding the fact that "an increase in educational technology is not only inevitable but could also serve as a powerful tool in the quest to improve the nations schools" (*Education Week*, 1997, p. 3). The politics of technology-based reform was also reflected in the fact that the "inevitable" infusion of electronic technologies had become the "education initiative du jour for lawmakers across the nation and of every political stripe" (White, 1997, p. 40). Indeed, Representative Newt Gingrich in his "Contract with America" proposal placed his arguments for educational reform within the context of the "Third Wave Information Age" rhetoric. His proposal, much like that of the New Democrats and President Clinton, required a restructuring of the Industrial Age bureaucratic model of school through information technologies, especially distance education. Students are envisioned to comprehend world problems through the use of computer databases or general access to information. This technocentric vision of learning and instruction, however, was understood to be stymied by "the aversion of professional educators to the use of technology" (Gingrich, 1995, p. 147). Thus, although policymakers may argue vehemently about standards and school choice, "they're in almost total agreement when it comes to the need for computers and other kinds of technology in the classroom (White, 1997, p. 40). The American public is also convinced: Eight of every ten Americans believe that understanding computers and technology is critical for students' success in the future (see footnote number two).

In addition, although the availability of computers in schools has risen over the years, access to computers remains a divisive issue, with schools in poor urban areas having the least access to new technologies (U.S. Deptartment of Education, 1994; Martinez & Mead, 1988; Sutton, 1991; Executive Office of the President of the United States, President's Committee of Advisors on Science and Technology, 1997) whereas the form of the instructional application is often limited to remedial drill and practice (Campbell, 1984; Loop, 1986; Chann, 1989; Sutton, 1991; Executive Office of the President of the United States, President's Committee of Advisors on Science and Technology, 1997). Given that low socio-economic status and minority students are overrepresented in these categories of students, this may inadvertently lead the "appropriate" uses of computers in schools to become a form of tracking. This situation may be exacerbated by the fact that computer-based Integrated Learning Systems (computer-based instructional systems utilizing behaviorist learning models to improve remedial skills), often purchased with federal Chapter One aide for minority and poor students, are being tied into schools' wide and local area network systems and used to disseminate emerging state and national standards (Morrison & Goldberg, 1996).

Despite these details, having access to computer and information technologies is a highly politicized issue as it is perceived as a great equalizer or even a civil right. If equity in the quality of education cannot be legislated (such as fairer distribution of tax-based public funding), then, at minimum, each child, whether their school resides in a crime-ridden inner city or a sedate suburban setting, will have access to information on the Internet. Although this perspective essentializes access or the delivery of information over other economic and social challenges, which directly affect the quality of education for poor children, it is nevertheless a rather common perception of policy elites. If nothing else, the idea that access to information exists as a civil right, in the sense that it can manifest equality, expresses the depth in which technology has been vested with so much hope and vision within the context of the current educational reform movement.

Other issues, besides the policy to infuse schools with electronic technologies as a means of reform, brought consensus between various political factions. The issue of school "choice," for example, a policy which encompasses the privatization of public schools through a voucher-based system of school financing, was favored by most political factions to some degree. The religious right (e.g., the fundamentalist Christian Coalition), for example, favors "choice" as it enables parents to utilize public funding toward offsetting the costs of private, religious-based schools. The Neoconservatives, inspired by libertarian free-market–based ideology, believe that choice can lead to more effective and efficient schools.[7] The Neoliberals also embrace choice, albeit in the form of charter schools within the existing educational system, a political decision reflecting the interests of the teachers' unions constituents. Charter schools, an alternative to a choice plan based on vouchers, envisions the creation of a "new public school system" formed by educators, parents, and social service agencies or private groups in "learning industries" (Kolderie, 1990).

The "Reinvention" of Education and Equity in School Funding

Specifically, the Clinton administration embraced choice in the form of charter schools as a means toward "reinventing" schools to meet the demands of the Information Age. This goal was also assumed by Neoconservatives, although the neoliberal New Democrats emphasized improving the skills of individuals while the Neoconservatives were more concerned about increasing the competitive advantage of American businesses (Spring, 1997). Inspired by the work of Daniel Osborne and Ted Gaebles' *Reinventing Government: How the Entrepreneurial Spirit is Transforming the Public Sector* (1993), the Clinton administration followed the author's principles for "reinventing" schools which expressed the goals of competition, accountability, and choice. Thus, where the policy of restructuring education rationalized government intervention to ultimately improve academic achievement, "reinventing" education signals a turn specifically toward the power of the marketplace to "reinvent" schools (Spring, 1997).[8]

The adoption of Osborne and Gaebles' "reinvention" framework reflects a fundamental shift in policymaking that emerged in the early 1980s. This shift is generally referred to as "New Public Management" (NPM) (Hood, 1990). NPM is characterized by a shift from policy development to management (e.g., planning and public service welfarism to cost-cutting) and from process to accountability/performance measurements. NPM also combines "new institutional economics" such as public choice theory or transaction cost theory with "corporate culture" doctrine. Peters (1996) describes the general impact of NPM as representing "a development of the scientific management of Taylor and has become a vehicle for new-right ideology, emphasizing an avoidance of direct state management and a corresponding favoring of marketlike arrangements for the allocation of scarce public resources" (p. 142).

The NPM model, for example, can be realized through network system technologies, which cut the costs of labor and also act as efficient systems of information control. In fact, one particular usage of technology applied to the management of schools advocated by the Technology Leadership Network, as featured in their publication, *Technology and the Transformation of Schools* by Lewis J. Perelman (1987), was Socio-Technical Systems (STS), an approach utilizing corporate-based models of networked system technologies, which configures the activity of educators around networked computer systems with the aim to reduce costs and maintain control of information. The quotation by Perelman (1987), featured at the opening of this chapter, describes how the technicist framework of STS would effectively corporatize the institution of public education. As mentioned in the previous chapter, within the past decade an approach to the management of educational environments, which utilizes information systems, has developed in the U.S. and abroad, and because this approach is related to the privatization of education, it emphasizes values related to efficiency and control expressed via performance standards and accountability schemes. This approach has become so normalized within the context of reform policy that its operationalization has effectively constituted what some critics call a "performance culture" within schools (de Alba et al., 2000).

The emphasis on "reinventing" schools, therefore, reflects concern about the needs of the Information Age and the plight of the modern worker in a global economy that demands changing job skills centered around computer technology. This perspective has resulted in a general economic plan that emphasizes educational policies (Spring, 1997; Peters, 1996; de Alba et al., 2000; Kenway, 1998). Thus, current educational reform policy is configured to meet the challenges of unemployment, workers stymied by low-income service industry jobs, restructured and downsized employees, and increased inequality in the distribution of wealth and income by expanding educational opportunities, especially the skills of knowledge workers (i.e., symbolic analysts). However, those who possess economic advantage have traditionally secured their position through the exclusion of the disadvantaged from education and economic opportunities (Reich, 1991). This results in "educational inheritance," a condition that will likely counter policies designed to meet the needs of modern workers, especially within the current political vacuum (Spring, 1997; Shapiro, 1994/1996). In addition, the current "dramaturgy" of educational reform policy can be distinguished by an absence of attention to the inequity in the quality of education (Spring, 1997; Kahne, 1996).[9] This is further evidenced in the rise and fall of "Opportunity to Learn" standards.

The Rise and Fall of "Opportunity to Learn" Standards

The two major assumptions underlying the 1994 *Goals 2000: Educate America Act* educational reform policy are: (1) increasing educational standards will improve the educational quality of the potential work force and in turn decrease economic inequities through increased wages as all Americans become trained as symbolic analysts, and (2) all students will have equal access to the necessary elements (e.g., trained teachers, technology, support, and adequate facilities) that will enable their meeting national or state academic standards. In addition, the rationale behind state and federal standards arises from "effective schools" research. This body of research, supported by both Neoconservatives and neoliberal Democrats, focuses on how the attitudes and beliefs of teachers and administrators affect the academic achievement of students. However, as Spring (1997) points out, the "effective schools" research has been used erroneously and to further a particular conservative political agenda.[10]

In terms of the second assumption, the creators of *Goals 2000: Educate America Act* had departed from their predecessors in their attempt to directly address the issue of equity in the quality of education. Specifically, the Opportunities to Learn (OTL) standards in the *Educate America* legislation focused on "enhanced opportunities" for poor and "disadvantaged" students to learn "the same challenging standards as other, more advanced students" (Smith, 1995b, p. 9). According to Andrew Porter, a member of the Wisconsin Center for Education Research, the OTL standards stem from "an equity concern that high-stakes assessments of student achievement are fair only if students have had an adequate opportunity to learn the content assessed in those high-stakes tests" (cited in Spring, 1997, p. 80). Thus the OTL standards were an attempt to address the fundamental reality of "savage inequalities" (Kozal, 1991), which unfortunately characterize our school system. In effect, the OTL standards set a criteria for assessing the ability of a school system to provide their students with an Opportunity to Learn curriculum content featured in voluntary national standards or state standards.

However, the 104th Congress eliminated the U.S. Department of Education's authority to establish OTL standards and the requirement that states provide all schools with the necessary resources that allow all children to achieve the required standards. This retracting of OTL in 1996 occurred as Neoconservatives realized that the national standards and *Goals 2000: Educate America Act* could be used as a tool to further entrench the political power of educators and "liberal elites" rather than subdue or undermine it. The Christian Right, the Contract with America Republicans, and libertarians began a campaign to disable the role of state and federal government in education, indeed calling for the elimination of *Goals 2000: Educate America Act* and the U.S. Department of Education. This coalition of interests began to emphasize choice by focusing on site-based management and parental control over schools, especially the control over curriculum, versus the role of the federal government to reinvent or restructure schools (Arons, 1997, p. 141). However, essentializing the power of parental involvement can act to divert the gaze away from structural elements that exacerbate inequity. In fact, federal and state governments have shifted responsibility and blame for education's problems on the backs of low income parents (Fine, 1993). Also, attempts to democratize educational decision-making are simultaneous to the contraction of the public sector. Thus, in many school districts there is little support for public schools and parents to take on the responsibilities of management (Apple, 1996). In addition, through her research, Michelle Fine (1993) acknowledges that although "deep parental involvement" can improve academic achievement and a sense of trust between schools and the community, without a broad-based political commitment to serving *all* students and to restructuring schools in low income neighborhoods, parental involvement itself "will do little to positively affect—or sustain— low income students or their schools and outcomes" (p. 69).

The issue of choice and that of equity drives to the heart of the symbolic power that public education holds regarding its meaning as a *public* institution, which expresses social democratic principles. Although the political "dramaturgy" generated by the choice issue elicits various perspectives on the purpose of schooling, in reality the framework of choice-based reform does not offer great latitude when it comes to defining the ends of education. In effect, a system of educational reform offered by the 1994 *Goals 2000: Educate America Act* provides flexibility in exchange for accountability and focuses on standards, tests, curriculum frameworks, and accountability with regard to ensuring that students learn "what they need to know to compete and win in the global economy" (Clinton, 1994). Also, privatization/marketization is not, as the libertarians would have it, a value-free perspective. The focus on efficiency and other utilitarian values does not necessarily obviate the political struggle, but rather absorbs it into a civic silence characterized by a false apolitical reality of "inevitabilities." Finally, there is evidence that a privatized system of education furthers the inequities in public education for poor and minority families while simultaneously increasing bureaucratic management (Whitty, 1994; de Alba et al., 2000).

Although the United States has not officially adopted a privatized system of education, the blatant refusal to address issues related to equity could foster similar results. For example, the removal of the OTL standards from *Goals 2000: Educate America Act,* while maintaining national and state standards of achievement and "excellence," could possibly lead to increasing "savage inequalities" among schools and ultimately "result in education actually causing greater economic inequalities" (Spring, 1997, p. 81). While high income U.S. families fight to protect their "educational inheritance" and policy elites ignore the inequities within the educational system, Spring (1997) envisions that "U.S. routine production workers and in-person servers will experience declining wages as they compete with workers in other countries. If educational inequalities are not eliminated, national and state standards and high stakes tests will doom children of the poor to a world of the underclass" (p. 82).

Spring (1997) is not alone in his dire predictions. Although national standards can be used by parents as a form of "quality control" to evaluate schools in the context of a market-based system, it can also set into motion "a mechanism for differentiating children more rigidly against fixed norms, *the social meanings and derivation of which are not available for scrutiny*"; thus further entrenching the underlying common sense of the current meritocratic school system (Johnson, 1991, p. 79, author's italics). In addition, Michael Apple (1996) believes that policies based on "choice" and national standards, "a mechanism for the political control of knowledge," will unlikely manifest social cohesion, but rather further differences between "we" and the "others" and in turn exacerbate "the attendant social antagonisms and cultural and economic destruction" (p. 33).

Moreover, the process of privatization and marketization of education removes educational polices from the arena of public debate. Choice shifts the landscape of policy discourse from public space to the privatized sphere of the individual. Thus, as pointed out by Michael Appel (1996, p. 30) "the very idea of education being a part of a public political sphere in which its means and ends are publicly debated antropies." Indeed, while political dramaturgy acts to extend politics through discussion and deliberation, thus expressing a "vision of democracy that is seen as an educative practice," the process of market privatization seeks to contain politics by reducing it to an economic framework that expresses an ethic of consumption and choice. In other words, "the world, in essence, becomes a vast supermarket" (Apple, 1996, p. 30). Despite education's position as a contested political site, the neoliberal and neoconservative hegemonic bloc has moved so deeply into the zeitgeist that it has "transformed our very ideas of what education is for," where "democracy becomes an economic rather than a political concept and where the idea of the public good withers at its very roots" (Apple, 1996, p. 38). Thus, the underlying values of efficiency and competition and a view of human nature as solely motivated by maximizing self-interest are paramount.

Perhaps the most disturbing aspect of policy elite's refusal to recognize equity as a key issue to be addressed within educational policy is the truth of the reality with which many children live. Changes in school populations and societal changes demand that schools face challenges without precedents. Schools are now expected to meet students' needs that arise from systemic social problems within the context of a postmodern society epitomized by the breakdown of the family unit; high crime and violence; increasing drugs, alcohol and child abuse rates; increased poverty for women and children; and a perceived lack of morals and values among citizenry. However, it is these issues that form the basis of a socioeconomic crisis that current educational reform policy does not address. Thus, in the next chapter we shall examine how it is that issues related to social justice and equity, within the context of current educational reform policy at the turn of the 21st century, have been eclipsed by a technocentric discourse that reduces the purpose of public education to the needs of a globalized market economy.

Notes

[1]   Just to name a few: International Society for Technology in Education (ISTE), Technology Education Research Centers, National Educational Computing Association, Inc. (NECA), The Association for Educational Communication and Technology (AECT), as well as an array of local or regional associations (e.g., Texas Center for Educational Technology). There is also an array of international education technology organizations such as the National Council for Educational Technology (UK) and the Ibero-American Network of Informatics and Education (Chile) to name a few. The annual conferences are typically underwritten by hightech organizations (e.g., Sun Microsystems, Inc. or Microsoft) and national professional organizations (e.g. American Association of School Administrators) and local universities and businesses. There are also various journals dedicated to the applications of electronic technologies into schools (e.g., *Journal of Research on Computing in Education, Journal of Computing in Teacher Education, T.I.E. Telecommunications in Education News*) as well as those aimed specifically toward teachers, such as the journal *Technological Horizons in Education*.

[2]   For example, in 1983–1984 the ratio of students to computers was 92:1. In the 1996/1997 school year that ratio dropped to 7:1. These figures, however, do not indicate the quality or datedness of schools' computer technology, an important factor given that constant upgrading is the nature of computer technology. Even with the increase in availability of hardware/software, only one of every five teachers uses a computer regularly for teaching (National Center for Educational Statistics, 1997). However, by 1998, 59% of teachers had Internet access at home and 90% reported that having access in the classroom is essential for teaching (Becker, 2000). Also, the federal government policies between 1994–1999 have resulted in an increase from 35% to 95% of schools having Internet access (National Center for Educational Statistics, 2000). Moreover, national polls show widespread support for children having access to computers in schools (Trotter, 1997, 1998). Most parents believe that access to the Internet can have a positive effect on academic achievement and those without access are at a disadvantage (Turow, 1999). Thus, many parents are providing Internet and computer access to their children at home. Households with children ages two through seventeen had an increase in home computer ownership from 48% in 1996 to 70% in 2000 and Internet access increased from 15% to 52% during the same time period (Woodward & Gridina, 2000). The rate of diffusion of Internet access is higher than all other previous electronic technologies including computers (Chaney, 2000).

[3]   For example: *Action for Excellence: A Comprehensive Plan to Improve Our Nation's Schools* (1983), Task Force on Education for Economic Growth; *Education and Economic Progress: Towards a National Educational Policy*, 1983, Carnegie Corporation of America, and later, *What Work Requires of Schools: A SCANS Report for American 2000*, Secretary's Commission on Achieving Necessary Skills, 1991.

[4]   The title of a section in *American 2000* that discusses the development of systemic accountability and achievement tests—*For Today's Students: Better and More Accountable Schools* —is interesting to contemplate (p. 21). The title indicates how the creation of standardized tests and accountability measures are justified in order to serve the "customer"—students. However, this particular manner of serving the

needs and demands of students arose from the agenda of policy elites, not the discourse of students, parents, or teachers.

[5] Time revealed that the Edison Project faced feasibility problems when the likelihood of a government-financed, public-private-based school voucher system diminished with the election of Clinton in 1992. Still, in the state of Massachusetts one-fifth of its 25 charter schools are for-profit based, two of which are operated by the Edison Project (Spring, 1997, p. 63). Also, Whittle's Channel One, which involves the selling of American students as a specific "target audience" to advertisers who underwrite the Channel One "news" programming in exchange for giving schools leases on television equipment, has been relatively successful. The success of profit-based programs such as Channel One, the growing presence of corporate-sponsored curriculum materials, and the selling of school property as advertising space, illustrate a shift in perception or a "boundary crossing," which accepts as commonsense commercialization of public spaces such as schools.

[6] President Clinton (former governor of Arkansas and present at the 1989 Governor's meeting) generally adopted Bush's *America 2000* as the framework for his administration's education initiative: *Goals 2000: Educate America Act*. This initiative, authorized by the National Educational Goals Panel (1994, pp. 13–14), offers the following general educational goals:

1. All children in American will start school ready to learn.
2. The high school graduation rate will increase to at least 90%.
3. All students will leave grades 4, 8 and 12 having demonstrated competency for challenging subject matter including English, mathematics, science, foreign languages, civics and government, economics, arts, history and geography, and every school in America will ensure that all students learn to use their minds well, so they may be prepared for responsible citizenship, further learning, and productive employment in our Nation's modern economy.
4. The Nation's teaching force will have access to programs for the continued improvement of their professional skills and opportunity to acquire the knowledge and skills needed to instruct and prepare all American students for the next century.
5. United States students will be first in the world in mathematics and science achievement.
6. Every adult American will be literate and will possess knowledge and skills necessary to compete in a global economy and exercise the rights and responsibilities of citizenship.
7. Every school in the United States will be free of drugs, violence, and the unauthorized presence of firearms and alcohol and will offer a disciplined environment conducive to learning.
8. Every school will promote partnerships that will increase parental involvement and participation in promoting the social, emotional, and academic growth of children.

[7] Joel Spring's (1997) analysis of the various political interest groups, which influenced educational reform policy since the publication of *A Nation at Risk*, underscores how the Neoconservatives and New Democrats fell under the sway of libertarian ideology. Libertarians have grave distrust for government intervention and place great faith in the power of the market to govern the allocation of resources. The libertarian perspective, inspired by the conservative economists at the University of

Chicago (e.g., Friedrich Hayek and Milton Friedman), asserts that prices or social values are determined by individual choice and that the use of vouchers would essentially overcome the class stratification that is reflected in the inequity of the quality of schools. Unlike the libertarians, however, the Neoconservatives, whom Spring describes as a blend of Christian right and conservative economics, believes in the moral and social authority of government over education "while letting the marketplace determine the best methods for inculcating government supported ideologies" (Spring, 1997, p. 32). Nevertheless, the Christian Right's affiliation with the neoconservative/libertarian coalition parts ways in terms of the federal government's right to create national standards and testing, as they seek curriculum guided by religious beliefs. However, the libertarians, Christian coalition, and the Neoconservatives, believe that both governmental and educational institutions are controlled by a "liberal elite." Spring explains how a coalition of conservative and libertarian ideologues, via several think tanks (e.g., John Olin Foundation, the Cato Institute, the John Birch Society, the Center for Independent Education, the Institute for Humane Studies, the Heritage Foundation which highly influenced the Reagan Administration, the American Enterprise Institute which focuses on producing neoconservative scholarship such as Richard Hernstein and Charles Murray's *The Bell Curve* (1994), the Hudson Institute's Educational Excellence Network and the Manhattan Institute's Center for Educational Innovation which promotes school choice programs, to name a few), sought to undermine the legitimacy of public education and push for choice and national standards. Spring (1997) concludes that, "it is important to emphasize that a conscious effort is being made to disseminate ideas and influence public opinion by conservative think tanks" (p. 44).

[8] Osborne and Gaebles' five principles are as follows: (1) competition between service providers, (2) citizen control through site-based management, (3) focus on outputs versus inputs thus rewarding students and teachers with merit pay for high achievers, (4) since mission statements, not rules, guide government agencies, schools are to be governed by the mission of *Goals 2000*, and (5) the government considers citizens as "customers" thus "choice" is necessary for customer-citizens to exercise their right of choice.

[9] Spring (1997) proposes that the New Democrats centrist shift on education and other issues was a political move to recapture those former democrats who perceive that the democratic party only represented the interests of poor and minority citizens. Thus they shifted emphasis from attaining equity in educational quality for the poor to equity in opportunity to aid middle class families with rising costs in college education through a series of tax cuts and other educational aid programs.

[10] "Effective schools" research focuses on the attitudes and beliefs of teachers and administrators. Both Neoconservatives and the New Democrats find the political implications of this research attractive—that high expectations result in greater academic achievement. However, Spring (1997) points out that policy elites conflate the idea of national standards and teachers' expectations. There is no evidence that national or state standards heighten a teacher's or administrator's expectation that students will learn. Thus Spring concludes that "effective schools" research has been used "to justify a particular political agenda. Effective schools research has justified educational policies that embrace the contention that the problem is not money but a lack of high expectations" (p. 85). One may also add that focusing on "effective schools" research as a justification for a standards-based reform agenda also passes the responsibility and blame on the individual student/teacher/parent rather than

acknowledging the systemic inequity in the distribution of support for education. Also, the basic indicators of effective schools are: clear goals, strong leadership, parental involvement and site-based management. Yet the effective school model adopts a neutral stance with regard to these indicators. Kahne (1996) explains that describing a school as having "clear goals" or "strong leadership" says little about "the values that guide students and teachers." He asks rhetorically, "Are these 'clear goals' narrow and utilitarian or do they reflect a commitment to what humanist education might call the 'whole child'" ? (Kahne, 1996, p. 113)

CHAPTER TWO

Alternative Visions: Questioning Technocentrism

Current technology is no mere affair of curriculum scholars. The school is now the tail, the whole world the computerized dog.

Israel Scheffler, 1990

In the previous chapter we examined official educational reform policy and the technocentric discourse of policy elites. But as we shall see, although it is the dominant discourse it is not the only perspective on educational reform. Thus, in this chapter we shall examine an alternative position, which essentially offers a critical perspective on the dominant discourse of educational reform policy and reflects the stance of those educators concerned with issues related to social justice. This chapter is divided into three main sections. In the first section we revisit policy elites' assumptions about the crisis in education and their construction of the Information Age by investigating the economic realities of an information-based global market economy. In the second section we examine the politics of using technology to reform education, specifically how our culture constructs technology as a neutral artifact and how this factor may impact current technology-driven reform policy. This section also features a review of concerns that some educators have about the instructional uses of electronic technologies. Given all of these factors, in the third section we examine the significance of the dialectic between the two spheres of educational reform discourse with regards to the construction of social visions within a technological society.

Revisiting the "Crisis" in Education

The creators of official educational reform policy base their functionalist position on two assumptions: (1) in comparison to other nations, U.S. children's academic achievement is below acceptable standards, especially within the areas of mathematics and science, and therefore more effective academic standards and accountability measures are necessary, and (2) the rise of the Information Age demands job skills for high technology and therefore schools need to change to address these skills. Much of the criticism written about the current reform movement questions the validity of these two assumptions especially in terms of the way they have been used to rationalize specific reform measures. For example, David Berliner and Bruce Biddle (1995) believe that the conservative right's political faction has a mission to delegitimize public schools, and that this political faction used the publication *A Nation at Risk* (1983) as a springboard for their campaign. The Commission on Excellence in Education based their justification for reform on the assertion that education's poor performance directly caused the U.S. economic downturn. Although Berliner and Biddle (1995) admit that U.S. schools need some improvement, such needs arise from inadequate funding and fundamental inequity in the distribution of funding. They argue that international comparison studies, although flawed due to the vast differences between populations, also do not account for the comprehensiveness of the U.S. student body that tends to lower overall scores in U.S. schools. In fact, the academic performance of U.S. students equals and, in some cases, exceeds that of European and Japanese students when comparisons are based on similar curriculums. But such reasoning has not seemed to quell the anger toward public education and the political vision to restructure the system.

Perhaps it is not surprising that scapegoating seems to lie at the heart of the matter. Educational historian Lawrence A. Cremin (1988), for example, believes that to assume that problems related to international competition can be solved by educational reform "is not merely utopian and millennialist, it is at best foolish and at worst a crass effort to direct attention away from those truly responsible for doing something about competitiveness and to lay the burden instead on schools" (p. 103). From Tyack and Cuban's (1995) perspective, this situation creates an "ideological smokescreen," and as a consequence much of the recent "policy talk" about schools "has restructured discussion of educational purposes and obscured rather than clarified the most pressing problems, especially those of the schools that educate the quarter of American students who live in poverty" (p. 34). Also, they explain that blaming schools for the nations economic decline not only scapegoats educators but also distorts the reality of a labor market in which the majority of new jobs are relatively unskilled and millions of skilled workers are either underemployed or jobless (p. 38). Indeed, other politically conservative-based assertions, such as the poor productivity of American workers and the projected shortage in technically trained individuals in math and science, are debunked by Berliner and Biddle (1995). In fact, the United States leads the world in worker productivity in the service sector, the fastest growing labor category. Also, although supposed low productivity is blamed on the poor education of typical U.S. workers, a workers' education level is not as strong of a predictor of worker productivity as is the policies and behavior of management (Berliner & Biddle, 1995; Berliner, 1993).

In addition, Berliner and Biddle (1995) refer to two fundamental economic factors that discount the rationale to reform schools based on the Information Age rationale. (1) "Educational inflation" describes an indirect relationship between an increase in highly educated individuals and a decrease in the inherent value of higher education. In fact, in 1994, the Economic Policy Institute announced for the first time in history that the economic value of a college degree had fallen (Uchitelle, 1994). In an economic framework aligned with education, educational advantage becomes a form of "educational inheritance," where current knowledge workers protect the educational advantages of their children, leaving little concern for the educational quality of poor and minority children (Spring, 1997, p. 77; Reich, 1991, pp. 268—300). (2) The slow growth (only 6% by year 2000) of the highly skilled and technically trained occupational groups weakens the rationale for aligning educational curriculum with the needs of high-tech businesses (Uchitelle, 1994).[1]

Without exception, those who discount these two (and other) underlying assumptions, which form the foundation of current official reform policy, situate the overt functionalism of such reforms against socio-democratic concerns of equity, poverty, violence, and racism. For example, Berliner's (1993) examination of policy elites' and conservative right's rhetoric of educational reform, in comparison to these data, has led him to the following conclusion.

> The agenda America should tackle if we want to improve schooling has nothing to do with national tests, higher standards, increased accountability, or better math and science achievement. Instead, we should focus our attention and our energies on jobs, health care, reduction of violence in families and in neighborhoods and increased funding for day care, bilingual education, summer programs for young people and so forth. It is estimated that 100,000 handguns enter the schools each day. It seems to me that this is a greater problem than the nation's performance in international mathematics competitions (p. 638).

Educational theorist Siv Shapiro (1990) believes that education, "whatever its practical and ideological autonomy, is not closed off from disruptions and dislocations found elsewhere in the society" (p. 9). Therefore, the material conditions that result from policy related to urban decay, discrimination, and economic disenfranchisement can no longer stand outside the reality of classrooms. Indeed, it is possible that the challenges arising from these conditions can open up school reform.

> We are looking at the displacement into the areas of schools and education of a wider series of crises that confront the lumpen class in America—crises are experienced as economic deprivation, political disempowerment and cultural disintegration. . . . The ideological wall that up until now seemed entirely impervious to the possibilities of an alternative agenda for education reveals some cracks (p. 9).

Shapiro (1990), therefore, perceives that the *real* crisis in education relates to broader, systemic social and economic crises and that today schools are inescapably a part of these challenges. Shapiro also explains that the discourse of school reform during the 1980s was "ideologically encircled before there was ever the possibility of breaking out of the dominant form of educational discourse." He describes the discourse as being generally "saturated with values that affirmed the dominant positivist outlook" and how there exists a "strongly shared desire to assimilate the process of schooling to the forms and methods of technology." This positivist perspective has worked to "shape teaching and knowledge to a technical discourse in which these would become amenable to the manipulation of improved and expanded inputs" (p. 13).

In addition, educational researcher David Purpel (1996) argues that *a Nation at Risk*, "the single most important document of what is called our current educational reform movement . . . ostensibly directed at making basic educational changes, offers a revealing picture of the essentially unchallenged assumptions about the purpose and nature of American education." The report, he contends, "arrogantly and blithely posits the role of education as servant to the state: incredibly enough it blames the schools for the nations' crisis" (p. 208). Purple (1996) believes that the narrowing of the definition of the crisis which necessitates educational reform—international economic competition—thinly veils systemic crises that are to a great extent consequences of the very economic competition educators are asked to intensify.

> I share the belief that our most serious crises involve the staggering degree of poverty, hunger, and homelessness; that our very existence is threatened by economic greed and moral callousness; and that our security is endangered by the arms race, the proliferation of chemical and nuclear weapons, the intensification of nationalism and chauvinism, and the ravaging of the planet (p. 208).

The issues that Purpel raises are also well taken within the context of a discourse which seeks to reform schools so that it generates success for *all* students and specifically meets the needs of so many who live in poverty, have diverse cultural and linguistic backgrounds, and for the forgotten ones with histories of failures in schools. The realities of many children have forced educators to revisit what and how they teach. However, even though educators are driven by the needs of all students and not just those of white middle class privilege, and struggle to make schools more caring places and communities, the campaign to change schools has become co-opted by the technical, functional, and individualistic language of reform, which in turn emphasizes the professionalization of teachers through technical training and standards of competence toward professional advancement. In effect, this approach to educational reform has reconfigured schools as "corporate, rational businesses concerning their missions analogous to shopping malls, restaurants, clinics or private clubs, when the main purpose of the organization is to serve individual private needs and wants" (Newmann, 1993, p. 7). Within this context, the will to create and serve a caring community has lost its foundation.

Also, it is important to consider how the development of any reform policy is often rationalized by the rhetoric of crisis (Eldeman, 1971, 1985). For example, Israel Scheffler explained that the educational reform policy of the United States in 1964 had shifted from a child-centered perspective toward a new formalism, which emphasized basics, excellence, and standards as well as educational technologies. In fact, the rise of the influence of educational technology was expressed as both the development of devices for the delivery of programmed instructional materials and as the control of the distribution of knowledge to guarantee its efficient delivery to students. This occurred at a time when youths were also encircled by the emerging mediated environment of the televisual and the world's technological dream projected via the cold war and the space race (i.e., Sputnik), which in fact was used to construct a rationale for a crisis in education and the necessity of reform. The publication of *A Nation at Risk* in 1983 signaled a return to formalism after the brief interlude of the 1960s more child-centered policies and instructional strategies. Although parallels exist between the two periods of crisis and reactionary formalism, essential differences are important to examine. The formalism against which the first progressivism reacted against was not as intense as that required to arrest the broad social and economic forces of the antiestablishment of the 1960s and 1970s (Scheffler, 1990). Also, the intensity and scale of the first reactionary formalism was more contained because the focus was primarily on schools and school-based technologies. However, the current trend of formalism is much more broad in its social impact in that computer and information technologies are transforming the foundation of society and economic reality. As Scheffler (1990) notes in the quotation at the beginning of this chapter: "Current technology is no mere affair of curriculum scholars. The school is now the tail, the whole world the computerized dog" (Scheffler, 1990, p. 94). Indeed, the pressure to add the computer to educational curriculum arises from the generalized influence of computerization. But what does this really mean to education? Scheffler (1990) indicates in the following quotation how the momentum of a generalized computerization has become not only the means but also the ends of education's purpose and thus creates a totalizing framework.

> The general point is this: as the computer's presence grows, the whole array of our educational ends tends to shrink to what is achievable or supposed achievable by the computer. Instead of understanding the computer as a means to goals independently sought, we tend to redefine our goals so as to match what computers may do. From its initial status as a technology for promoting independently specified educational values the computer thus becomes transformed into a general criterion of value. And the whole process is facilitated by language transfer.

> Even without hard evidence for the educational efficacy of the computer, the mere promise of such efficacy promotes the transfer of computer language to education. Such transfer tends to filter out ends and values that do not fit the metaphor—for example, ethical sensitivity, social perceptiveness, artistic expressiveness—so the efficiency of the computer is expanded by definition. For it is the merest tautology that ends achievable by the computer are achievable by the computer. It is, however, far from tautologous that all educational ends are indeed achievable by the computer. Indeed, it is false, and impoverishes education in fundamental ways (p. 101).

It is ironic also that although computer language promotes a reductive realm of teleological and mental processes, "it is teleological language which has enriched the view of computer processes" (Scheffler, 1990, p. 102). This reductionary process is also evidenced in how the computer has been used as a metaphor for the mind and how information is often conflated with knowledge.

> To speak of information and memory, not to mention knowledge, in reference to the computer, is itself a metaphorical transfer from the human case. To transfer such terms back from the computer to the mind, now emptied of the connotations of human activity, interpretation, need, and purpose, is an example of the irony I mentioned earlier. This double transfer in the context of practice leads us unwittingly to shrink our initial ideals of education and our conceptions of mind and schooling (Scheffler, 1990, p. 104).

Scheffler (1990) and other educators who resist the received technocentric discourse of educational reform are attempting to articulate a process by which the lifeworld, the realm of human lived practices and traditions, norms and relational knowing, is being reconfigured by instrumental rationality as it breaks out from its original place of economic production and seduces the realm of the social and cultural. Jurgen Habermas (1989) believes that an interpenetration of instrumental rationality into the lifeworld lies at the center of our struggle to negotiate the complex challenges of postmodern reality. In fact, Neil Postman (1993) has described our present age of technoscience as that of a "technopoly," which is characterized by a culture's complete surrender to technology. Indeed, one of the profound characteristics of postmodernity is the technologization of our everyday lives, which includes the experience of teaching and learning. Thus, Scheffler's (1990) examination of how, through language, we have come to essentialize the computer addresses the social construction of computer technology in that it exists as an apolitical tool/artifact even as it simultaneously embodies our deepest desires to control and secure power. Thus, reconfiguring schools to address the manufactured crisis arising from the needs and demands of the Information Age can only further the colonization of education, and the realm of the lifeworld in general, by the logic of instrumental rationalism. Thus, the real crisis in education may in fact be the technocentric reform policy with which it now struggles to negotiate.

Revisiting the Global and Economic Dynamics of the Information Age

Scheffler's (1990) point that the current formalism expressed in educational reform policy reflects a broader functionalist shift in the economic landscape is essential to understanding the sociopolitical dynamic surrounding current educational reform and its emphasis on computerization not only in the United States, but in many westernized nations. For example, the current U.S. reform movement, from its inception, emphasized the centrality of infusing electronic technology into schools as a means to reform public education and to accommodate the assumed needs of an Information Age economy. In *A Nation at Risk* the Commission rationalized their recommendation for change based on the understanding that "knowledge, learning, information and skilled intelligence are the new raw materials" for a global economy. Further, learning itself became an "indispensable investment" required for success in the Information Age (National Commission on Excellence in Education, 1983). Indeed, the reconfiguration of the purpose of education within a postindustrial Information Age is related to the "inevitable" infusion of electronic technologies into education. Also, one must consider how the development of a specific era bearing the nomenclature of Information Age signals a fundamental change in the purpose and meaning of knowledge itself. In Lyotard's (1984) analysis of the postmodern condition in the late 1970s, he examined the changing status of science and technology specifically regarding the control of knowledge and information. He argued that the emerging technology and sciences based on information systems (cybernetics, telematics, etc.) are language-based and have thus transformed two principle functions of knowledge—research and the process or transmission of knowledge (e.g., education). Thus, Lyotard (1984) asserts that as knowledge is reduced to a commodity, the focus becomes the process of exchange and not the intrinsic value of knowledge itself. He explains that "knowledge is and will be produced in order to be sold and it will be consumed in order to be valorized in a new production: In both cases, the goal is exchange. Knowledge ceases to be an end in itself, it loses its 'use value' " (p. 45).

In addition, educational researcher, Michael Peters (1996) explains that as knowledge loses its "use value," the technical transformation "wrought by a continued miniaturization and commercialization of knowledge machines will further change the way in which learning is acquired and classified" (p.139). Knowledge, therefore, is a product exteriorized outside of the learner and the role of the teacher and student is reconfigured into a "commodity relationship of supplier and user" (Peters, 1996, p.139). Within this reconfiguration of knowledge, education has been reconstructed through the discourse of policy elites and the prevailing Neoliberal economic rationale. Peters (1996) believes that education has been "discursively restructured" within a marketized framework, where science, technology, and education have been given a special place in the economic order. Restructured and fully rationalized as "a public good, science and state education have been commercialized and commodified in the name of increasing national competitive advantage" (Peters, 1996, p. 16). Peters explains that "within the information society, science and education are hypothesized as the principal forces of production." He adds that because of the growing influence of information technology within corporations and industry, "knowledge becomes an informational commodity indispensable to the economy and future basis of international competitive advantage." Peters concludes, therefore, that science and education had become the main "knowledge industries" within an "information state" (p. 16). But, one might ask, how might we understand the nature of this "information state"?

Peters' (1996) examination of the information state's genesis indicates the dominance of a particular neoliberal discourse which, in poststructural terms, exists as a powerful metanarrative. This metanarrative, which he has labeled "enterprise culture," portrays a "totalizing and unifying story legitimating the prospect of economic growth and development based on the triumvirate of science, technology and education" (p. 88). This "ideological vision" is not based on sociodemocratic ideals, which reflect the language of equality or multiculturalism. Rather, Peters (1996) asserts that neoliberalism has reworked its version of classical economic liberalism "as a totalizing vision of the future." This project, as an ideology, "construes the future in terms of a post industrial utopian vision based on a faith in science, technology and education" as key sectors that create a national competitive advantage in a global economy (p. 80). Peters (1996) believes that enterprise culture as a "national ideological vision," differs from past "stories." It is not based on any attempt to rewrite the past, to redress power imbalances or socioeconomic inequities. Rather, within the context of enterprise culture, "questions of equity and social justice have receded under the economic imperative" (p. 88). Also, concerns about national economic survival and competition within a global marketplace "have come to be seen under neoliberalism as one of cultural reconstruction" (p. 89).

Enterprise culture has several ideological interpretations and is constrained within its own rationalized framework. For example, with emphasis on collaborative decision-making and the potential for network systems technologies to undo hierarchical systems and redistribute decision-making, enterprise culture could invite a postindustrial democracy. However, according to Peters, enterprise culture has been "construed in its narrowest sense—postindustrialism of reaction rather than exploring social-democratic possibilities" (p. 89). Thus, even as the scope of influences on education arising from sociopolitical and economic discourses such as enterprise culture widens, the social vision or landscape of possibilities seems to have narrowed considerably. Indeed, education has been "discursively restructured" under the sign of "homo economicus," a main tenet of neoconservative politics, which asserts that people act on cue as "rational utility maximizers," to the extent that this principle has become "a paradigm for understanding politics itself " (Peters, 1996, p. 80). In the following quotation Peters (1996) explains how this framework has secured the power to silence the "dramaturgy" in the politics of educational reform, as "the solution" is offered in the form of an inevitability.

> The metanarrative of "enterprise culture" projects a unity on the future. It is future-oriented although anchored in the past. In a violent act of closure it represents the future in totalizing terms, excluding in the process other possible stories we might inscribe on the future by arguing there is no alternative. There is perhaps no better example of the extension of the market to new areas of social life than the field of education. In particular, it is clear that under the principles of neoliberalism education has been discursively restructured according to the logic of the market. Education, on this model, is treated no differently from any other service or commodity (p. 81).

In addition, Peters (1996) asserts that an evaluation of the "information society thesis" must necessarily "acknowledge the technological deter-minism" underlying this thesis, where technology is presented in unproblematic terms "as somehow being autonomous, having a life of its own and driving the modernization process." This apolitical perspective, tied to a linear notion of progress, has "greatly restructured imagination in the policy process" and thus restricts social vision and obscures the need for public deliberation (p. 143).

> [N]ot only does it obscure questions of power in selecting the form and direction of technology and its relations to issues of national growth but it also prevents reflection on the need for making choices. It also serves to discourage public participation in debate over the criteria that ought to be used in making public choices. Technological deterministic postindustrial theories postulating the existence of the new economy proceed from simplifying assumptions about the role of new information technology in driving economic development and the demand for new skills. They generally interpret these developments as neutral, natural and inevitable outcomes of market logic (p. 143).

Peters' (1996) observation that "technological deterministic post-industrial theories" arise from a simplistic understanding of the role of information technologies and the economy reveals how the particular myths that our culture holds about technology quietly directs our public policies, including educational reform policy. The use of the term "myth," however, may be misleading as its connotations may be contradictory. On the one hand, a myth is understood as something that has no standing and is an idea to be dismissed. However, this is not the meaning or interpretation that is being referenced in this particular case. For example, Murray Eldeman (1971) defines myth as "an unquestioned belief held in common by a large group of people that gives events and actions a particular meaning" (p. 53). The myths of progress and economic rationality are associated with technology. In addition, technology itself is constructed in a mythic sense as being an apolitical or neutral artifact. More specific aspects about the nature of technology are discussed later in this chapter.

Other educational researchers have couched educational reform within the context of a globalized market economy. For example, Colin Lankshear (1997) refers to the work of Manuel Castells (1993) and outlines some of the specific qualities of what Castells describes as "new capitalism," which delineates the Information Age. The sources of "new capitalism" are applied science, technology, information and knowledge, organization based on flexible specialization and horizontal networks of management structures, and "real time globalism"—all of which depends on information technologies including microelectronics, telecommunications, and biotechnology. Lankshear (1997) explains Castells' (1993) conclusion, that the central means for generating wealth is "the ability to create knowledge and apply it to every realm of human activity by means of enhanced technology and organizational procedures of information processing" (p. 20). Lankshear (1997) adds that another distinguishing factor of "new capitalism" is how it is "enfolding in the context of a powerful, intrusive, highly regulatory, techno-rationalist business world-view, which—as manifested in educational reform as well as in wider changes at the level of the state—has impacted powerfully on language processes and practices" (p. 4).

Lankshear (1997) explains how the "techno-rationalist business world-view" has been embraced by many governments as the framework for governing public sector institutions including public education. The specific elements of this worldview are as follows: (1) the "techno" refers to "privileging technicist approaches to realizing social purposes," essentially expressing a technocratic instrumental rationality in the conduct of human affairs. The utilization of systematic procedures to reduce human goals into discrete tasks, processes or categories, so as to operationalize outcomes into measurable forms (e.g., observable behavioral objectives and defining values in terms of commodities) is one example. (2) The "rationalist" refers to the "currently pervasive tendency to analyze and measure institutional processes and provisions in cost-benefit terms, with a view to 'rationalizing' them accordingly" (p. 4). In addition, the ubiquity of computer technology has in turn prompted official policy aimed to increase within the context of education "technology literacy" (p. 9). Lankshear (1997) understands that technology-driven reform policies generate the creation and maintenance of "enlarged markets for products of the information economy—extending beyond curricular exhortations to advocate also the extensive use of new technologies within administrative tasks of restructured schools (Kearns & Doyle, 1991)" (p. 10). For Lankshear (1997), a techno-rationalist approach raises fundamental moral issues for educators committed to equity-based reform policy.

> Apologists for the new capitalism, like apologists for the magical educational powers of new technologies, are currently surfing the tide of history with seemingly unbounded confidence. They have assumed the right to define the role and purposes of education in terms of service to the unfolding new work order. Their confidence is backed with the power of educational policies decreed, enforced, and policed by administrators high on the waft of the techno-rationalist business world view. The choice facing educators who are committed to alternative visions is clear cut. We either 'put up and shut up,' or we struggle to live out the faith that education is not the servant of any single end or purpose. . . . But if educators like ourselves, who are committed to understanding language and social processes, do not participate actively in public debate about this issue, it will rapidly become much more closed than the interests of a healthy, moral, educative society can afford (p. 10).

However, there are those who insist that education's restructuring can most effectively be achieved through meeting current economic needs. Schlechty (1990), for example, envisions that the structure and aim of schools should closely align with that of business, such that schools should be engaged in the act of "knowledge work."

> It is reasonable to expect that, as the American economy becomes more information based, and as the mode of labor shifts from manual work to knowledge work, concern with the continuous growth and learning of citizens and employees will increase. Moreover, the conditions of work will require one to learn to function well in groups, exercise considerable self-discipline, exhibit loyalty while maintaining critical faculties, respect the rights of others and in turn expect to be respected. . . . This list of characteristics could as well be a list of the virtues of a citizen in a democracy (p. 39).

Schlechty (1990) also explains that the current structure of schools, based on the self-contained classroom and discrete subjects and single-teacher formats, is not conducive to inculcating the above-mentioned skills.

However, Canadian educational researcher Andy Hargraves (1994), who has conducted extensive research on the effects of current reforms on teachers' work, argues that assessing the reforms outlined by Schlechty (1990) and other "writers and policy makers in tune with corporate agendas begin to seem selective and seductive" (p. 51). The above-mentioned skills may be necessary for a small percentage of "technical elites," but for many citizens who could be faced with chronic unemployment or under-employment, "education for leisure and constructive recreation" and education for "citizenship, political participation and social responsibility," which enable citizens to engage in discussion and "deliberations about constructive socially valuable uses of technology, along with associated patterns of employment," will be most essential (p. 51). In addition, Hargraves (1994) points out that a closer examination of Schlechty's (1990) vision portrayed in his book *Schools for the Twenty-First Century*, "talks of respect, but not of care—either for persons or the environment. Justice and equity are also absent. Productivity is paramount. This doesn't distort, but it does restrict what is seen as appropriate for schools and teachers to do" (p. 51).

In addition, Australian educational theorist Jane Kenway (1998) explains how the current reform movement within her country as well as in countries such as the United States are characterized by positioning education within the context of the high-tech global economy. The current impetus to reform education has moved from the initial phase characterized by a plan to economize and marketize education to that of technologizing both the general economy and education. Kenway explains that the technocentric reform policy is a socially constructed story, a yarn spun around the Information Super Highway (ISH), which is "as much fantasy and fiction as it is fact, and as much a social construction as a technological construction" (p. 63). In effect, she notes, "at the same time the information super highway is being constructed technologically, it is being constructed discursively, with a range of very different values implied and interests at stake" (p. 64). As a metaphor, the ISH stands as the promise for the future, a future without oppressive hierarchies and bureaucracies as new virtual communities create a new, albeit virtual, geography of networks free from the concerns of terrestrial-based social relations anchored in racial, gender, age, and cultural barriers, while each citizen immersed within this marketized neoliberal "reality" has ultimate individual freedom expressed as consumer control. In effect, ISH signifies a libertarian techno-utopia.

The metaphor of the ISH also underscores the feature of media as spectacle, but with a peculiar twist—"the media is no longer just a vehicle for the spectacle; rather, the media becomes the spectacle" (p. 67), thus making new technologies expressions of status politics, image, and style, while barriers that offered a semblance of meaning within the simulacra's flux of images has dissolved, hence infotianment and edutainment. Indeed, children are described as "techno-tots" and "vidkids." The hype surrounding the infusion of new technologies (i.e., ISH) into the realm of education is almost unbearable. As Kenway summarizes the situation: "Technology is where the money is in education" (p. 76). The creation and maintenance of both the schools and home markets have generated billions of dollars in revenue. In addition, producers of home-based computer products create and exploit parental anxieties about their children's education. Children are saved from the fallout of incompetent teachers by the apparent salvation of the computer.[2]

In any case, Kenway explains that as parents are goaded into taking charge of their children's education because schools have allegedly no credibility, "children are strongly positioned as both the objects and subjects of the technological utopia" (p. 77). Within this context, the ISH reflects anxiety about social justice, specifically regarding the notion of "information rich and information poor." However, essentializing the notion of access to information as signifying the plight of poor children in public schools, when inverted, "points to the problem of being 'rich in poor information' and encompasses enduring social justice questions about access to what?" (Kenway, 1998, p. 70). Kenway asks about the quality of such information and "the nature of the content we will have dramatically increased access to" as well as how the increase in mediated communication will change the nature of identity formation and social relatedness (p. 70). These are important issues not addressed by educators. Neither is the assumption that information access assuages the systemic social and economic inequities which are at the basis of social injustices. Moreover, global markets and the technologies that sustain them express capitalist ideology as they are the forces that fuel sociocultural and economic change. These changes, in particular, challenge the power of nation-states, which must, in turn, accommodate the economic processes of globalization. And this means a retrenchment from welfare and social services toward greater privatization of state, and public-funded provisions, which create the "rise in market forms in remaining state-provided services and the development of new government and market technologies of ideological manipulation and control" (Kenway, 1998, p. 73). Thus, concludes Kenway (1998), "markets and information technology and the relationship between them are the primary forces driving educational change today" (p. 77). Under the sign of economizing, governments sponsor commercialization, marketization, and the privatization of public education, which, according to Kenway (1998), has led education into the "zone of the unknown" (p. 78).

> In exposing education to various technologies market forces, global, national and local policy makers have placed themselves in a paradoxical position. Not only have they put at risk the vulnerable steering capacity of the state with regard to education, economics and social justice, they have encouraged onto the center stage of education a range of relatively new 'players.' In effect, it is these new players who/that are currently developing new educational forms which will take education into the zone of the unknown. The likely long-term consequences of these new directions are not at all clear, although we can make some informed guesses. They suggest that now that the technologised market genie is out of the bottle, policy makers' hopes for rational, goal-directed change 'in the national interest' are likely to be unfulfilled (p. 78).

It is clear that electronic technologies and the signification of their centrality within the socioeconomic realm, the Information Age, exist as generative metaphors that guide educational reform policy. As Kenway (1998) suggests, the politics surrounding technocentric reform are complex because electronic technologies exist as a cultural code whereby they denote actual technological artifacts and simultaneously connotate discursive-based social constructions or social visions. Thus, our relationship with such artifacts is hardly apolitical although this assumption is common sense. Thus, some questions arise: Why do we choose to construct technology in an apolitical fashion? What is the relationship between how, as a culture, we define technology and issues of power and control? What does it mean to say we live within a technological society and what relationship does this have to the growing presence of instrumental rationalism within the social and public sphere? And, what do possible answers to these questions mean to education within a postmodern technological society? Thus, it is to the subject of how we, as a culture, construct our relationship to our inventions that we turn next.

Questioning the Politics of Technology as Reform Policy

In this section we examine how technology is understood in an apolitical fashion and review the policy to use electronic technologies to reform education. We begin by examining alternative conceptualizations of the politics of technology and then consider technology's symbolic value and how, as a society, we define our relationship to technology. Following this review, we discuss educators' concerns about the infusion of electronic technologies into educational settings.

Presently, educational reform policy clearly indicates that electronic technologies are central to the overall vision of education in the 21st century. This intersection of technology and policy ironically illustrates how technology is not apolitical (Winner, 1986). John Street (1992), for example, believes that technology and politics are related through a process of social construction whereby our economic sphere and cultural beliefs act as a framework for policy discourse. Change, therefore, is about both the creation of *techne* and its introduction into society. Thus, politics shape technology inasmuch as technology shapes politics (Street, 1992, p. 179). How do we make this hidden process become more apparent? Street (1992) proposes an eclectic approach, which attempts to tie the "technological imperative" with the "cultural context—the internal force of *techne's* development with external forces of society's needs and aspirations"(p. 41). However, technology is frequently employed to reinforce existing dominant interests (Street, 1992; Winner, 1986, 1996). A cultural approach to technology recognizes this factor and in fact seeks to place technology as a "crucial aspect of the way political aspirations and actions are organized. This does not mean technology cannot be judged, but it does mean that analysis of both the technology and the politics cannot proceed along conventional, separatist lines" (p. 182). Street (1992) adds that political principles are not only derived from introspection or reflection. They are also derived in part "from our relationship with our technology." Thus, he reasons, "we are forced to ask not what we mean by 'democracy,' but what does it mean to be a democrat, given our technology?"

Richard Sclove (1995) understands technology as "a species of social structure." He defines social structure as "the background features that help define or regulate patterns of human interaction." Examples are laws, dominant political and economic institutions, and systems of cultural belief. Sclove (1995) explains that technologies qualify as social structures "because they function politically and culturally in a manner comparable to these other, more commonly recognized kinds of social structures." Sclove (1995) raises the issue that laws and political and economic institutions are "contingent social products" and thus it is commonly understood that alternative choices are possible. However, "people are prone to misperceive a society's technologies as inevitable, as naturally determined rather than socially shaped and chosen" (p. 23). Also, because laws and other social structures are indeed understood to function explicitly as social structures they can be implicated as generating various social consequences and thus also act to shape social interaction and history. However, people generally expect most technologies "to prove structurally inconsequential, and because on the surface of things they do, their expectations appear confirmed" (p. 23). Still, it is technologies' nonfocal aspects (additional and recessive effects such as pollution) "that conspire to manifest profound structural consequences." Thus, even though technologies are as consequential as other social structures, "people tend to be more blind to both the social origins of technologies and to their social effects." This is partly due to the myth that technologies are "autonomous self-contained phenomena and the myth that they are morally neutral (p. 24)." In fact, the symbolic position that technology holds within our culture has evolved into an unquestioned "technological utopianism" (Segal, 1994) or a "technocratic spirit" (Marx, 1994). Such perspectives were criticized by Lewis Mumford in 1934 because they discount moral and political goals by assigning technological means as ends in themselves.

In addition, communication scholar James Carey (1990) points out that our cultural bias to understand technology simply as a tool naturally influences how we conceive of information technologies. Carey (1990) describes how a transmission model of communication generally guides our understanding and thus leads us to construct telecommunications infrastructures as mere conduits for the transportation of data. In contrast, he proposes a ritual or community model of communication, which configures such technologies operating not only as conduits for information transport but also signifies a means of cultural transformation. For example, Carey conceives a ritual view of understanding communication as "a process through which a shared culture is created, modified and transformed." (p. 43). Thus, the focus is not so much on the transport or transmission of messages/goods through space but rather the maintenance of society in time through the creation of shared beliefs. Carey (1990) proposes that "if a transmission view of communication centers on the extension of messages across geography for purposes of control, a ritual view centers on the sacred ceremony that draws persons together in fellowship and commonality" (p. 43). Carey poses questions about the nature of technology-based systems of communication, such as how changes in *forms* of communication technologies affect how we construct our experiences and how such technologies change the experience of community. He also asks the following: "What, under the force of history, technology and society, is thought about, thought with and to whom is it expressed? That is, advances in our understanding of culture cannot be secured unless they are tied to a vivid sense of technology and social structure" (p. 64).

Carey's ritual or cultural-based understanding about electronic communication technologies and the questions that he raises regarding how such technological systems are intricately embedded in cultural practices may in turn raise serious questions about the nature of technological communication systems within educational settings. Indeed, from the perspective of certain educational theorists, the infusion of electronic technologies, especially networked systems, is unprecedented in terms of its potential to change the foundational elements associated with educational institutions and the process of learning and the nature of knowledge itself. Fox (1991), for example, explains that distance learning, which utilizes telecommunications for the distribution of televised instruction to mass audiences of students, exists as a "new form of market mechanism for the distribution of knowledge which is increasingly presented as a commodity like any other" (p. 217). Fox (1991) theorizes that the proliferation of electronic technology is "replacing the agency of human speculation with a kind of impersonal, disembodied, free-floating, public dissemination of information," while the purpose of knowledge is quietly moving away from the role of social, spiritual, and moral critique and deliberation to that of "performity" (p. 218). He describes performity as "the capacity to efficiently augment power by producing 'competitive edges' for decision-makers" (p. 217). Fox (1991) believes that the "large ethical and social issues are being effectively lost in the technological race" and unless they are addressed, he predicts that "a thousand years of humanism will end in collapse" (p. 219).

Also, Frank Smith (1995a) asserts that developments in computer and telecommunication technology are creating profound changes in our lives as "the developments are not merely technological—they are social, political and existential" (p. 76). He perceives that "social, economic and technical developments bring new attitudes toward education, many of them not propitious for teachers. Their extinction is a distinct possibility" (p. 65). Smith (1995a) believes that the logic behind replacing the classroom teacher with "virtual on-line instructors" or artificial intelligence-based instructional programs arises from our conventional understanding of how we view the teacher as a mere "delivery system" of information. The Internet, understood as a vast resource of information, could possibly replace the teacher, and Smith adds, be more efficient. However, he cautions that "our social institutions are of a different and deeper order than the social organization of the Information Highway . . . people should be able to meet face-to-face or side-by-side, demonstrating the essential humanity of humankind" (p. 75).

Indeed, although access to information via the Internet has been essentialized, thus becoming the center of educational reform, some educators worry that despite the potential gains such technology offers, focusing on a technocentric solution to the problems in education inadvertently acts to diminish larger social issues such as racism and economic and social inequity which directly influence education (Bredo,

1989; Kozma & Croninger, 1992). Thus, the Information Age rationale for technology-driven educational reform offered by policy elites can act as a smoke screen, directing our gaze away from broad socioeconomic issues. Moreover, the development and infusion of electronic technologies, because of their political nature, are related to issues of power. Carey (1990), in fact, believes that technology's symbolic power within our culture operates as a "master trope," where "visual literacy, computer literacy, and the information society," create a world in which "the computer is the master trope" (p. 19). His analysis is based on the ideas of Canadian economist, Harold Innis, who proposed that the power of communication technologies "is exercised through the production and reproduction of real social life," elements which are expressed in the fundamental coordinates of space and time (Carey, 1990, p. 30). Carey (1990) proposes that power is the term that holds economics, politics, and culture together and is "realized in control over time and space. The very framework within which action is exercised or over which control is asserted are themselves imaginative or cultural constructs. Power to act and control time and space are exercised through technology." Thus, Carey concludes, "technology engenders what it perversely pretends only to display" (p. 30).

Carey is arguing Sclove's (1995) thesis, that technology embodies "social structures" and thus engenders power. Carey (1990) further argues how the configuration of basic structural forces (i.e., time and space), which act to inscribe and maintain power, are themselves socially constructed. Thus, it is erroneous to assume technology as being apolitical. If technology is inherently political and the political operates on both a collective socio-logical level and individual level (Eldeman, 1985), then technology affects human reality on both levels. Indeed, Winner (1996) asks what type of person are we manifesting with our new information technologies. He reasons that "to invest in a new technology requires that (in some way or another) society also invents the kinds of people who will use it" (p. 64). In terms of today's development of a "cyber culture," Winner (1996) believes that questions related to conditions that sustain selfhood and civic culture are most important, as there exists a "digital transformation" of vast arrays of material artifacts interwoven within social practices. Thus, he asserts, people are readily converting existing practices into digital formats, such as the classroom teacher where "blackboard, books and verbal exchange [are replaced with] materials presented in computer hardware and software and call it 'interactive learning'" (p. 64). Therefore, to move to the computer-ized and digitized means that several "preexisting cultural forms have suddenly gone liquid, losing their former shape as they are retailored for computerized expression" (p. 64). Winner (1996) suggests that as new patterns solidify, "both useful artifacts and the texture of human relations that surround them are often much different from what existed previously.

This process amounts to a vast, ongoing experiment whose long-term ramifications no one fully comprehends" (p. 64).

Indeed, Winner (1996) describes some of the social and personal characteristics peculiar to the current Information Age as that of no longer belonging to and being crucial to any enduring framework of social relations. "To an increasing extent our organizations assume perpetual expendability. How people will respond to that, how they will recreate selfhood in an era in which everyone is expendable, could well become a far more serious issue in coming decades than even the often lamented decline in real wages" (p. 69). Winner (1996) adds that the values of the Information Age culture are "protean flexibility, restless entrepreneurism and the willingness to abandon social bonds for material gain," and wryly adds that "many of those enthralled with globalization as the wellspring of economic vitality also bemoan 'the weakened family,' 'collapse of community' and 'chaos of the inner cities,' failing to notice any connection" (p. 69).

In addition, Sclove (1995) explains that technologies "do not merely affect society or states, they also constitute a substantial portion of society and states." Sclove (1995) concludes that because technology acts as "social structures," one is forced to recognize how technologies contribute to "defining who people are, what they can and cannot do and how they understand themselves and their world should dispel the common myth that technologies are morally or politically neutral" (p. 17). Sclove (1995) also believes that in the ostensible interest of efficiency, convenience, and safety, many contemporary technologies experientially separate ends and means that were formally integrated within holistic local practices or forms of life. Sclove (1995) asks if this experiential separation might "contribute to the observed modern eclipse of moral reasoning by instrumental rationality" and how the growing dependence on personal computers for our communication "may contribute to a morally problematic deepening of the experiential split between emotion and reason" (p. 97).

Sclove (1995) also points out that technologies possess a "focal function" (its ostensibly intended purpose) as well as "nonfocal functions" (additional and often recessive functions, effects, and meanings). Thus, "all technologies are associated with manifold latent social effects and meanings and it is largely in virtue of these that technologies come to function as social structures" (Sclove, 1995, p. 21). For example, prepackaged computer-based instructional materials are designed to facilitate instruction but they contribute nonfocally to the deskilling of teachers (Apple, 1986).

The work of Winner, Sclove, Street, and Carey indicate that a simplistic artifactual view of technology is problematic and in fact reflects a bias that complements a positivistic framework and also what Lyotard (1984) has described as the "grand narrative of progress," a point which is discussed

later in this chapter. But it is the work of French social theorist Jacques
Ellul (1964) that delineates how, in the tradition of Max Weber's criticism
of bureaucracy, technology serves not only as a tool/artifact but also
embodies a specific process through which technical rationality is actualized.
Ellul (1964) describes this process as *technique*, which he defines as follows:

> The term technique, as I use it, does not mean machines, technology, or
> this or that procedure for attaining an end. In our technological society,
> *technique is the totality of methods rationally arrived at and having absolute*
> *efficiency (for a given stage of development) in every field of human activity.*
> Its characteristics are new; the technique of the present has not common
> measure with that of the past (p. xxv, author's italics).

To Ellul (1964), *technique* expresses the "consciousness of the
mechanized world" and of a collective sociological reality (p. 6). The only
means by which modern society can overcome the determinism of *technique*
is to "seek ways of resisting and transcending technological determinants"
through overcoming our complacency and trivial existence characterized by
a greater adaptation to the rationalized system we've created. In effect,
society needs to awaken from the techno-utopian dream. But in doing so, it
will necessarily be called to take responsibility for its inventions.

Within the context of education, Ellul indicates that utilitarian aims have
driven education to the degree that "instruction must above all else be
technical" to accommodate specialization and the production of
technicians. Thus, education will no longer be "an unpredictable and
exciting adventure in human enlightenment, but an exercise in conformity
and apprenticeship to whatever gadgetry is useful in a technical world" (p.
349). Indeed, the billion dollar investment toward infusing schools with
computer-based technology illustrates the power behind the technocentric
dream of the current reform movement as well as Ellul's insightful
prediction. In fact, the instantiation of *technique* in education was also
noted by Foucault who suggested that British utilitarian Jeremy Bentham's
principle of panopticon control was first adopted by teachers and social
workers who required the use of data to monitor a student's progress.
Within the panopticon system of discipline and control, individuals being
monitored, as in the case of electronic surveillance technologies and
computer-based feedback systems, act to change their behavior such that
they become collaborators with the monitoring system. Changes in behavior
to accommodate the system of control and surveillance become internalized
as commonsense practices enabling participants to exact their own
oppression within a hegemonic system. The underlying logic of panopticon-
based control is efficiency; thus it epitomizes *technique*. The predominance
of systems of control over teachers' work and students' learning experiences
via accountability schemes and standardized testing illustrates the degree to

which technique has come to articulate "sound decision-making" even while its reification process acts to normalize a dehumanized and commodified learning experience. Thus, within the context of a technocentric reform framework, it is not only the actual infusion of electronic technologies that needs to be considered, but also the practices that constitute *technique*. How *technique* actualizes the control of teachers' work within a performance-based culture is more fully examined in the following chapter.

The Characteristics of Technology Adoption in Education

Our unquestioning, commonsense perspective on technology has been described as "technological somnambulism" (Winner, 1996) or "techno-logical anesthesia" (Ellul, 1964). This stance is reflected in traditional top-down models of technology diffusion guiding the process of institutional and organizational change. These models reflect a commonsense cultural bias and therefore support top-down management approaches to institutional or organizational change. In addition, because this approach to technology diffusion does not recognize how the process of change and adoption is both contextual and situated, its usage has been most unfortunate for teachers (Tyack & Cuban, 1995; Cuban, 1986, 2001).

Moreover, educators are not immune to the bias of technological utopianism, for such a perspective is bolstered by the very forces that frame education—a bureaucratic structure based on Taylorism, the pragmatics of learning theory/psychology and models of management and administration borrowed from business, and instructional technology, an applied field of training founded within the military. Thus, according to Douglas Noble (1991) educators have unwittingly adopted a larger military/scientific enterprise to be the agenda for public education because the specific language of this enterprise (i.e., intelligence, learning, thinking, and problem solving) is very similar to that of education.

Educational psychologist Frank Smith (1995a) believes that electronic technologies have been thoughtlessly ushered into education because the possible negative side effects have not been addressed, nor has consideration for what has been lost in the perceived instrumental gains achieved in their adoption. This view is shared by other critics (see, for example, Kerr [1996], Goodman [1995], Sarason [1995], Bowers [2000], and Cuban [2001]). This situation could lead to "change without difference," where new technologies can unwittingly be used simply to further entrench the least desirable elements of the existing educational system. It may also be argued that the potential for computers and networked system technologies to facilitate positive changes in educational practices may not be exploited or fully understood if technology adoption is simply driven by a transmission or delivery system framework. Also, Seymore Sarason (1995), who has conducted extensive research on school reform, acknowledges that computer technology offers some positive possibilities for education but asks, "for what purposes? Are all purposes coequally important? On what basis do we decide where on a priority list a purpose should be, which is not to suggest you downplay, let alone ignore, purposes not at the top of your list" (p. 144).

Despite these concerns, securing access to the technology with little consideration given to its actual instructional purpose or possible nonfocal effects seems the norm. For example, Kerr (1996) relates this experience with educators when discussing their approach to the diffusion of technology.

> In virtually all of these cases, however, the discussion has gone forward without an examination of one central underlying assumption: that we should think of education, and schools as sites for the application of computers, software, networks and associated technologies. Technology itself, rather than particular goals and ends we wish to have students achieve by using it, often seems to have the priority. . . . The issues of what technology is 'good for' are often either ignored or postponed until their consideration has become a moot point. . . . this approach to technology is fundamentally flawed, and that we ignore these concerns at our future peril. An approach to technology in education that puts hardware (or even software) in first place will ultimately lead to impoverished schools (in the moral, not the financial sense) where students learn things that are unimportant—but possible—to learn (p. 4).

Kerr (1996) also believes that the wider uses of computers and other technologies in schools "may have unanticipated results" as the ways in which technologies are typically used "may define and limit, as well as extend, student (and teacher) perceptions" (p. 4). However, the issues raised by Kerr (1996) are generally not discussed by educators, even if their threat remains tacitly present. The fact remains that most educators embrace the blind enthusiasm of a "technological fix" approach to educational reform in their quest to meet the reform demands made by business and government. However, not all educators are so enthusiastic about the use of electronic technology in educational settings. For example, educators Pepi and Scheurman (1996) use the story *The Emperor's New Clothes* (Hans Christian Anderson, 1949) to illustrate the blind willfulness of fellow educators who engage the vision offered by policy elites. So profound is the power of policy elites' technocentric vision, argue Pepi and Scheurman (1996), that even if the overt power and manipulation that drives certain aspects of current educational reforms are revealed to educators, having invested so much time, money, and energy, they will nevertheless continue to have faith in the charade. Indeed, in a 1996 poll, teachers expressed that acquiring computer skills was more essential than studying traditional subjects or schools dealing with social problems such as drugs and family breakdown (Oppenheimer, 1997, p. 2).

Also, supporters of technology-driven reforms assume that the sheer accumulation and generation of information disseminated via computers will automatically create a power shift from centralized decision-making of a few to a decentralized process negotiated by many. This is one of the central tenants of "mythinformation" (Winner, 1986), a perspective which assumes that increased information necessarily equates to increased knowledge and power when the evidence does not support this assumption (Segal, 1994, p. 184; Winner, 1986, 1996). Consider how it is in the interest of existing corporate and state organizations to control the generation and flow (production and consumption) of the "new currency," information, a point that popular futurists carefully ignore (Segal, 1994, p. 184). In addition, as mentioned above, it is the conflation of information and knowledge that signifies the interpenetration of the computer as a totalizing metaphor into the realm of the lifeworld.

Research conducted by Morrison and Goldberg (1996), members of Co-NECT a national school design team funded by the New American Schools Development Corporation, on the effects that local information infrastructures may have on school reform, raises some important points regarding the application of telecommunications systems within educational settings. Morrison and Goldberg (1996) believe that such infrastructures can open schools to the outside world, offer teachers greater professionalization through flattening hierarchical structures, and support collaborative learning-based instructional practices. However, they also point out that "the same technology, put to different uses, may have exactly the opposite effect—tightening central controls, narrowing the scope of teaching and learning and concentrating management of resources among a small number of designated experts" (p. 127).

This possible outcome arises from the fact that schools, when perceived as highly decentralized organizations that offer teachers too much autonomy, need to use networked systems to administer systems of account-ability and standards. Under such conditions "it is not hard to integrate the two systems—instructional delivery with assessment" (Morrison and Goldberg, 1996, p. 133). On the other hand, schools can also be viewed as rigid bureaucracies offering teachers little freedom and control over their work. In this scenario, networked systems are applied to foster teacher professionalism and community involvement. The main difference between the two scenarios is the primary purpose of the network—as accommodating interactive communication versus mere transmission of information (p. 139). Thus, when assessing the adoption of networked systems, Morrision and Goldberg (1996) recommend that both the information infrastructure (e.g., computer network connections, telephones, file servers, human resources devoted to maintenance, etc.) and the "environment of the system" (e.g., the school community including businesses, universities, textbook and software publishers, national professional organization, etc.) or "all the different networks in which schools are embedded" be considered.

Morrision and Goldberg (1996) predicted that most schools' adoption of information infrastructures would resemble a hybrid of the two scenarios because reforms would largely be driven by state and national standards. Indeed, given the current standards-based reform effort, it is naive to believe that simply diffusing information infrastructures into schools will manifest a restructuring of their management framework that results in a more democratic structure of decision-making.[3]

Considering the Nature of a Technological Medium
Within Educational Settings

The questioning of technology's legitimacy within the context of educational settings has a long albeit somewhat forgotten history. For example, in 1969 Hutchins expressed skepticism in terms of technology-based instruction, stating that "the means of education does more than affect the ends of education; they become the ends" (p. 95). Hutchins (1969) noted that technology acts as a two-edged sword, for although it may increase effectiveness and reduce costs, technology can also promote efficiency and standardization and therefore may also "reduce discussion . . . promote centralization . . . [and] drive out teachers." In effect, noting technologies' nonfocal effects, it could very well "dehumanize a process the aim of which is humanization" (Hutchins, 1969, p. 105).

In 1988 educational researcher C. A. Bowers examined the particular qualities of computer technology and how these may affect the nature of learning. For example, he characterized computers as expressing a particular "language of computing," whose expressive traits are linear, logical, and rational and thus accommodates positivistic thinking. An emphasis on the "language of computing" displaces the presence of relational, intuitive, and tacit aspects of knowing. The question arises as to whether or not the "language of computing" and the positivistic framework it engenders are congruent with a learning experience characterized by social relations and intersubjectivity (Bowers, 1988). In fact, Bowers (1988) proposes that an "overemphasis on facts and data in the educational process" and electronic delivery systems (telecommunications and networked systems) has de-emphasized the teacher's responsibility in the intellectual realm for "guiding the process of primary socialization" and has left many teachers to feel uncertain about their role (p. 115). Bowers (1988) foresees that until teachers "reclaim their moral and intellectual responsibilities to students, and educational computing experts recognize that the nontechnical educational issues are the primary ones yet to be addressed," the use of electronic technologies in schools "will be driven by the forces of the marketplace and by the cultural myths that put out of focus what we are doing to ourselves and our environment" (p. 115). Thus, Bowers (1988, 1995, 2000) associates the policy to infuse schools with electronic technologies as furthering market-based values and associates technocentric policy as challenging broader sociocultural issues including environmentalism.

In the area of instructional technology, Michael Streibel (1986/1996) applied critical analysis in order to disclose the socio-cultural dimensions embedded within typical computer-aided instruction (CAI) (i.e., tutorial, drill and practice, and simulation). Streibel (1986/1986) explained how such CAI utilizes a behavioral approach to instruction and constructs the learner as a generic information-processor and that the goals of such instructional systems essentially create a narrow set of learner performance outcomes and thus impedes the development of the learner's personal intellectual agency. His critique of CAI is situated by his understanding about the nature of learning, which, giving reference to the writing of Maxine Greene, he describes as a socially constructive process that entails human collaboration and dialogic engagement with "interpretive communities" (p. 285). Such interpretive communities create a public space within the minds of the participants, whereby shared meaning via symbol systems of language and cultural codes is generated. Indeed, these interpretive communities define the very basis of our humanity. Education, therefore, is an essential part of the process of creating and sustaining interpretive communities and shared public spaces. In this sense they are inherently a meaning-making forum that generates a shared moral reality for children and the larger sociocultural community. Hence, formal education is far from simply being a "rationally managed process" and teachers are more than mere "instructional managers" even though such reductionary conceptions are common language in instructional technology (Streibel, 1986/1984, p. 288). Rather, teachers play a critical role in the dialectical community of creating a shared relationship between themselves, their students, and the subject matter (Greene, 1978).

Given these factors, one major concern that Streibel (1986/1994) has about the use of CAI is its power to inculcate conformity and uniformity. He explains how the work culture, which has to exist in a classroom for a technological instructional system to operate, can only result from "intentional human engagement, negotiation and interaction." However, ironically, those processes required to create such a work culture "then have to be *denied* because they contradict the technological framework." This is so because the technological framework necessarily shapes human culture to its own ends (author's italics, p. 302). A shift occurs from emphasizing the needs demanded by interpersonal interactions to that of procedural skills and information processing functions, systems efficiency, reliability, and economy. As these needs become the focal point of the learning environment versus those of the actual learner, it creates a highly controlled and diminished experience for both the role of students and teachers.

Thus, Scheffler's (1990) point about the introduction of computer technology in general can also be applied in the case of CAI. The danger is that the technology delivery system becomes a deterministic and central organizing factor in the classroom while it weakens individuality via conformity and uniformity and mitigates personal empowerment and critical thinking (Streibel, 1986/1994, p. 303). Streibel (1986/1994) further explains that within such a technology-based system humans are constructed as "data-based, rule-following, symbol-manipulating, infor-mation processors" as opposed to individuals with unique intentionalities (p. 309). And because computers only engage data and not the actual person, "the computer can never semantically or affectively engage human beings. Human beings therefore have to adapt to the *nature* of the computational environment" (author's italics, p. 309). Although machine processes can never replace interpersonal interaction, they can, according to Streible, act to shape them in a reductionary fashion.[4]

Both Streibel (1986/1994) and Bowers (1988) underscore the bias inherent within CAI and computer-based systems and how this bias acts as a totalizing means-ends rationalized paradigm, which shapes the learning experience, indeed the nature of thought and social interaction. Streibel (1986/1994) summarizes this effect in the following quotation.

> Knowledge acquisition and skill building (the terms themselves are revealing) become subject to efficiency and performance criteria, and learning becomes a systematically designed and rationally managed process. Furthermore, knowledge and skills become commodified because they are conceptualized in utilitarian terms and because the design and the conception of instruction are separated from the execution of instruction. This commodification, in turn, permits a fine-grained control of the learner's, the teacher's and even the system's performance. The computer formalizes this whole process and makes it capital intensive (p. 315).

In addition, sociologist Sherry Turkle (1984) studied children's perceptions of computer technology and found that they play a significant role in the transformation of children's psychological development, specifically their understanding of self and moral reasoning. In a more recent study on children's usage of computer technology, specifically simulation software, Turkle (1997) discovered that such software programs as "SimCity" often, instead of opening up questions, "close them down." She adds that "simulations enable us to abdicate authority to the simulation; they give us permission to accept the opacity of the model that plays itself out on our screens" (p. 14).[5] Turkle (1997) explained how the typical rationales for the diffusion of simulation software in schools—simulations are less expensive than science teachers, of which there is a dearth—beg another question: "Are we using computer technology not because it teaches best but because we have lost the political will to fund education adequately?" (p. 11).

Other studies on the nonfocal effects of electronic technology, specifically within the context of computer-based communication (i.e., the Internet) characterized by computer-mediated communication (CMC), indicate that the particular qualities of the medium filters out nuance, nonverbal communication and contextuality, which are fundamental to morally engaged human interaction (Ihde, 1979; Borgmann, 1984). Also, some researchers have found that screen-based technology such as computer and television monitors induce escapism, withdrawal from social engagement, psychological distancing from moral consequences (Mander, 1978) and obsessive and compulsive behaviors (Turkle, 1984). In addition, computer-based instruction for young children, especially those of the "edutainment" sort, do not facilitate learning as deeply as hands-on learning (Healy, 1998). In another study, "Reading Rabbit," a computer-based reading program used in thousands of schools, caused some students a loss of fifty percent in creativity (Oppenheimer, 1997, p. 10).

Similar concerns have been raised by instructors of architecture and physics at the Massachusetts Institute of Technology. The use of computer-aided design (CAD), while compensating for poor drawing skills, can also induce lower aesthetic value, thus reducing the role of an architect from that of an artist to an engineer. Some instructors observed that the computer-generated drawings seem dispossessed of human creative agency, which results in a distancing or loss of attachment to their work (Turkle, 1997, p. 12).

Tom Snyder, president of Tom Snyder Productions, which produces instructional software, believes that educators really do not need computers, "rather what they need is time communicating with students" (Snyder, 1997). He believes that computer technology "is not an educational machine. It's a cultural moment." Snyder also perceives that computer-based instruction is not interactive, but rather responsive. Interactive, he insisted, refers to conversational intercourse. Because much of the instructional software is "configured as games and games have no rules or conversation, only limits, with the goal to win rather than negotiate the meaning of the game" and because browsing the Internet basically has no depth, neither are optimal instructional sources.

Given these limitations of new technologies, Snyder believes that the role of the teacher, in the context of technology diffusion as official policy, is to "slow the whole thing down [the diffusion of electronic technology into schools] and make sure that you bring back the conversation." Snyder offered an example from his own research, which sought to discover how children use computer-based instructional programs. He explained that oftentimes when students were using a CD-ROM on civil rights, for example, and observed an intense moment in Martin Luther King's "I Have a Dream" speech, the students would click and jump to another place and then another and another. He pondered the meaning of this particular reaction, wondering if the nature of the medium fostered what he interpreted to be nonengagement, detachment, lack of depth, and unreflective thinking.[6] Indeed the act of "surfing" Internet "space" may inculcate a detached orientation of consumerism toward a virtual parade of endless readily available text-image commodities. In effect, it is not so much a focus on learning as much as the pleasure of consumption that directs engagement.

Burniske and Monke (2001), in their research on the use of information technology within the classroom, found that the nature of the technology raised profound challenges for them as educators. Although some educators who develop and use online courses note that the medium offers a virtual forum characterized by race, age, status, and gender neutrality, Monke problemitizes this assumption by questioning how such social egalitarianism is achieved in human terms, given the fact that the actual human contact is removed from the communication process.

> Thus, the lack of bigotry displayed in some online communication is accomplished not through the elevation of human sensibilities but by the amputation of human senses. Are blindness and deafness the means by which we wish to teach our children to suppress (rather than overcome) bigotry? Is it a great benefit of the 'Net that we cripple our children in order to spare them the trauma of colliding with social injustices? To what extent does this sight-out-of-mind approach to teaching tolerance actually foster tolerance in face-to-face relationships, where the issues of race, age, status, gender, etc. can not be hidden behind an electronic wall? And finally, what does this say about the evolution of our concept of education, when in order to reveal the world to students intellectually we willingly conceal the full humanity of those with whom they learn (p. 143)?

Furthermore, there exists a paradox: On the one hand the Internet enables students from diverse backgrounds to engage in some form of com-munication and possibly understanding, while on the other hand, it enables an isolating and fragmenting effect which inculcates the false sensibility that communicating with another via a virtual process equates to knowing them.

Monke concludes that this paradox is epitomized by the fact that as we construct "psychological walls that keep us apart from those physically close, . . . we commiserate at a distance through the 'Net with only those who share our narrow interests" (p. 144).

Shenk (1997, p. 127) explains how one can mistake tribalism for real, shared understanding. Monke (Burniske & Monke, 2001), as an educator, reflects on the meaning of this paradox to educators, describing it as an "internal contradiction in the technology's relationship with the educational community" in the sense that the two forces work against one another— "one profoundly human, attempting to bring diverse peoples together; the other, a product primarily of a communication technology that overwhelms us with information and an accompanying bureaucracy that gives us little room to maneuver, lures us into circles of special interests and like minds" (p. 145). This paradox is further complicated by the fact that as globalization promotes the rapid diffusion of electronic technologies all over the world, nontechnical cultures are being destroyed in the actual process of adoption, which in turn leads to diminution of cultural differences, languages, and a geographic-based sense of community.

Monke's experiences with using the Internet with students also revealed another factor—the reflective nature of computer technology. He found that students wanted to use the computer, not to research ideas or issues, but rather to write "fun stuff " about themselves and share it with others. Both Monke and his colleague (Buddy Burniske) understood that the computer, a tool that reflects human consciousness, signifies for students an extension of themselves, a notion first proposed by Marshall McLuhan. Thus, they refer to the myth of Narcissus as a metaphor to explain the phenomenon that both of them witnessed in the classroom. For youth, the computer not only feeds adolescent narcissistic tendencies but also provides a false sense of security within the context of its distancing, detached but enticing and thus safe environment—a situation highly distinctive from the complexities and uncertainties of their personal lives (Burniske & Monke, 2001, p. 147). The challenge facing educators is how to pull their students out from the whirlpool of their own narcissism as it is enabled by the seduction of computer's inherent reflective capability.[7]

The insights of Burniske and Monke (2001) are furthered by considering the nature of the electronic-based communication process itself. The mode of information exchange restructures social relationships and the process of identity formation, meaning formation, and the relation between subject and the world (Poster, 1990). Thus, an educator could ask, how might the mode of computer-mediated communication affect a way of knowing? de Alba et al. (2000) offer one possibility:

> By distancing emitter and emittee, electronic communication disturbs our normal conceptions of relations between speaker and hearer, or between writer

and reader, thereby reconstructing both subjects and their relations to symbols. Indeed, for a subject in electronic communications, there seems no longer to be a material world as normally represented by language, but just a flow of electronic language. Instead of a real world behind the language we have, instead, a simulated world, with simulacra and no real objects (p. 142).

de Alba et al. (2000) are referring to Jean Baudrillard's (1983) thesis that a specific characteristic of postmodernity is the overwhelming influence of hypermedia, a condition that creates a simulation of reality, a totalizing effect described as simulacra. The essence of this condition resides in how the simulacrum masques the absence of a basic reality and consequently the loss of meaning regarding the real or the original as a referent.

In addition, recent publications question the efficacy of computing technology within educational settings for elementary age children. Armstrong and Casement (2000) explain that although there exists no conclusive evidence that computer technology improves the quality of instruction, "children have become unwilling participants in what can only be described as a huge social experiment" characterized by radical restructuring of the educational system, the infusion of electronic technologies, and incredible changes in the way children learn and experience the world (p. 2). The social experiment is based on two beliefs: (1) that computer technology will make education more productive and (2) technology literacy is essential in order to be productive in an information-based economy. Moreover, Armstrong and Casement (2000), utilizing medium theory as their analytical framework, explain that for children, time spent sitting in front of the computer screen is rivaling time spent before televisions. They note how the medium of the computer is qualitatively different from television in that it does present some measure of interactivity. Although, as noted above, Tom Snyder argues that computer-based instruction is *responsive* not interactive. Indeed, Armstrong and Casement (2000) argue that, especially with video games, the nature of interaction largely emphasizes speed and control at the expense of thoughtfulness, reflection, and understanding (p. 12). Such obsession with speed and control, they assert, "reflects the ethos of our frantic times" (p. 13). Indeed, educational psychologist Jane Healy (1990, 1998) explains how the mediated experiences of television and computers interfere with children's development of inner speech, which in turn leads to problems with abstract reasoning, writing, and problem-solving. Thus, ironically, the technology, which is thought to enhance student thinking, may in fact act to diminish it. Indeed, stimulation from media, including computers, may contribute to a higher incidence of learning disabilities, attention deficit disorder (ADD), and auditory-processing problems (Armstrong & Casement, 2000; Healy, 1998).

Armstrong and Casement (2000) draw upon antidotal evidence, which indicates that using computers often deskills in ways that one may not expect. For example, caring for animals and taking field trips offer students direct experience with the natural environment and teaches them to understand and appreciate nature. They explain how children's direct experiences are being replaced by computer and video-generated images and thus their understanding of the natural environment is shaped largely by a mediated reality. Although some of the computer-based software can bring the world of nature to children, it also creates a relationship with nature that is essentially commodity based in that nature is easily accessible by the click of a mouse and can be manipulated and processed to entertain and thus consumed like any other commodity. It is ironic how such programs intended to induce appreciation for nature might have an opposite effect. For, as Armstrong and Casement (2000) point out, after the glitz of video and computer-mediated images, "when confronted with the real thing, children may either be bored or feel threatened and may well prefer to settle for the screen version" (p. 181). Especially, I would add, if the screen version offers the illusion of control and power.

Also, given the critical situation that the world faces regarding environmental degradation, is it wise that direct experiences with nature are being replaced by mediated ones? Indeed, a vital question for educators is: What is the basis for learning to appreciate and respect nature? Thus, another point to consider regarding the use of simulated versus field-based experiences or hands-on science experiments is the value and practical experience of direct observation. Indeed, research indicates that greater frequency in conducting hands-on science experiments resulted in higher achievement scores on standardized science tests (Stohr-Hunt, 1997; Jacobson, 1997). In conclusion, Armstrong and Casement (2000) propose that those in favor of replacing real-world outings with digital "field trips" do not consider or value the emotional and intellectual association that necessarily must be created for children to care enough about the environment to preserve it.

Also, in her book *Failure to Connect* (1998), educational psychologist Jane Healy points out how for young children it is important that they engage in "whole-body three dimensional sensory experiences" to ensure proper cognitive and emotional development (p. 208). She explains that such activities, which includes "emotional and language interaction from human caregivers" especially for ages two through seven, are related to learning to use all senses within a social context that enables knowing how to think logically, focus attention, learn visual imagery, and develop memory capacity (pp. 207–219). Healy reports that early exposure to such media as television and computers can act to impede the development of these fundamental cognitive-emotional abilities.

Children and adolescents experience the use of media not only in the context of educational settings but also as forms of entertainment such as with television, computer games, and online communication via the Internet. These mediated experiences, perhaps because they are not situated in educational contexts, nevertheless exude a powerful socializing force within youth culture. Kenneth Gergen (1991) calls this process of "social saturation" an expression of the postmodern condition accommodated by electronic technologies and, in terms of the development of identity, is characterized by a loss of traditional values and a fragmented sense of self. Indeed, in a recent report on children and computer technology sponsored by the David and Lucile Packard Foundation, a review of current research on children, adolescents, and technology indicates that long-term exposure to computer games (30 plus hours per week) can hamper social and educational development, increase aggressive behavior, and desensitize one to violence (Provenzo, 1991; Irwin & Gross, 1995; Kirsh, 1998; Graybill et al., 1985). Other conditions related to increased media exposure are loneliness, depression, physical problems such as obesity and a higher risk of premature sexual activity. [8]

All of these factors need to be considered within the context of the ubiquity of media in children's lives. For example, within homes with children ages 2–17 computer ownership increased from 48% in 1996 to 70% in 2000 and Internet connectivity increased from 15% to 52% in the same time period. There is also evidence that children ages 2–17, with access to television, video games, and the Internet, spend an average of five hours a day in front of a CRT monitor (Woodward & Gridina, 2000). This increase in usage is paralleled by an increase in children's purchasing power which is overtly exploited by marketers. [9]

There is one other point related to the issue of media, children, and postmodernity. Educators such as Steinberg and Kincheloe (1997), Giroux (1997, 2000), and McLaren (1995) have criticized the manner in which producers of media exploit youth, especially in terms of their sexualization and commodification. In 1997, Giroux pointed out the inexplicable irony and complete failure in social responsibility exemplified by the fact that our youth, via conservative rhetoric, have in turn been demonized for becoming what they had been constructed to be via the process of commercialization. More recently, Giroux (2000) observed that childhood at the close of the 20th century "is not ending as a historical and social category; it has simply been transformed into a market strategy and a fashion aesthetic used to expand consumer-based needs of privileged adults who live within a market culture that has little concern for ethical considerations, noncommercial spaces, or public responsibilities" (p. 19).

Steinberg and Kincheloe (1997) explain that the very processes by which social reality is constructed via media's commercialized framework, or what they term "kinder-culture," is largely ignored by educators to the detriment of their student's ability to be critically engaged citizens and also to the detriment of the legitimacy and meaning of the traditional educational system within the postmodern condition. Indeed, Peter McLaren (1995) describes the current quest to colonize the hearts and minds of children via commodification as an expression of a "predatory culture." He invites educators to engage in a "pedagogy of critical media literacy" and thus in turn teach their students to make "critical judgments about what society might mean, and what is possible or desirable outside existing configurations of power and privilege" and also "to rethink the relationship of self to society, of self to other, and to deepen the moral vision of social order" (p. 22). He reminds educators that "pedagogy occurs not only in schools but in all cultural sites," and that the electronic media exists as perhaps the "greatest site of pedagogical production that exists—you could say that it is a form of perpetual pedagogy" (p. 21). Thus, it is important that educators give consideration not only to the artifacts of technology as tools but also to their power as media, as means of transforming the processes of communication and thus how we experience lived reality, including social relationships and identity formation. Also, educators need to give consideration to Ellul's notion of *technique*, in that technologies can be used to express values of efficiency and control and other sociocultural contextual factors such as the processes of commercialization and commodification. Thus, it is both the artifact and the content, the medium and the message, that needs to be addressed within the process of technology and/or media adoption.

In general, the concerns raised by educators wary of current technocentric reform efforts pertain to a means-ends issue, where technology is feared to have become an end in itself, and that consequently the learning environment will be restructured around the technology. They also express concern about the particular qualities of these new media, especially as they grow to be dominant forms of representation in schools. In total, these perceived outcomes raise the specter of dehumanization and the possible diminution of attention to the practical lived experiences of teachers' and students' daily lives. Thus, despite the history of resistance to change in education, the current reform effort seems to have created for some educators a gestalt characterized by wariness or questioning of technological and instrumental rationalism, which threatens the lifeworld of education and other social spheres.

It might be that the recognition of the symbolic value of technology may help to demystify the assumption that the diffusion of technological innovation into education arises solely from necessity (i.e., the demands of the Information Age). This commonsense rationalization disallows political deliberation and moral responsibility and raises serious questions regarding the functionalist aims, which guide current technology-driven educational reform. What is at issue here is the questioning of our underlying values, such as efficiency and instrumental rationalism, which guide policy elites, and how such efforts override social democratic concerns. Policy elites' rationales and our cultural myths about technology act to delegitmize a more cautious or critical perspective on the adoption of technology to the extent that such a position would not be understood as an alternative discourse but rather, the voice of the Other. In fact, C. A. Bowers (1995) explains that educators who are concerned about the positive *and* negative effects of computer technology, specifically regarding its usage for surveillance, thus posing a threat to democratic values and traditional civil liberties, will necessarily have to face the cultural bias that "all technological experiments with the culture are viewed as inherently progressive in nature and thus not requiring any sort of questioning attitude" (p. 88). Moreover, although official educational reform policy indicates that because of the central importance of new technologies in our information society, citizens need "technology literacy," experts and policy elites who are empowered to make political decisions about technology's diffusion typically know very little about the nature of technology, especially how it operates as a social structure (Sclove, 1995, p. 53).

Thus, the adoption of new technologies into education reflect common-sense assumptions while opposition to its infusion becomes polarized in a pro versus antitechnology configuration. Equating technology with the cultural myth of progress makes its adoption an "inevitability," thus public deliberation becomes a moot point. However, Winner (1986) argues that it is precisely at the point *before* adoption that deliberation must take place— for once a technology is adopted and integrated into norms, social practices, and economic structures, it is nearly impossible to reverse. This is why a deliberative-based framework for technology adoption, especially for technologies such as information infrastructures, is so important. However, Winner (1996) has found that, historically, a calculated narrowing of discourse and exclusion of other perspectives often characterizes the diffusion and adoption of an innovation. These factors, in terms of current technocentric educational reform policy, need to be considered in light of the fact that education itself has become marketized. Also, an examination of the alternative discourse that questions technocentric reform policy thus reveals two distinctive spheres of discourse which create a fundamental dialectic. And it is the specifics of this dialectic and its meaning to the general narrative of educational reform policy that we shall examine in the next and final section of this chapter.

The Dialectic of Educational Reform Policy

Many critics of current educational reforms refer to policy elites' power to create a particularly narrow vision of education's purpose and future. Their arguments against current reform policy portray an underlying and fundamental dialectic between what has been depicted as the dominant technocentric perspective and that of a social democratic view. Also, the power to construct a social theory or social vision about the purpose and nature of education within society is a subtle and profound process of constructing a sociocultural narrative. Michael Apple (1996, p. 98), for example, believes that behind every "story we tell about education—even if only tacitly—is a social theory about what this society 'really is.'" Apple explains that these theories or what he calls "social visions" are in conflict, "and education sits center stage." Thus, Apple's understanding of social vision is the narrative a society constructs about its purpose and identity. This political quest to "name our world" is inherently related to power—specifically who exercises voice to speak and represent a society to itself.

Political psychologist Murray Eldeman (1985) believes that, although their power remains hidden and tacit, it is those who hold power who largely construct a political framework. Eldeman (1985) explains that "valued beliefs are indeed allocated through politics (usually by maintaining established allocations), but the value outcomes that matter usually flow from unpublicized administrative implementations and the actions of corporations" which are often not expressed as political decisions (p. 201). Therefore, in terms of educational reform policy the political interests of the "New Right alliance" possess great power (Apple, 1995). However, it is the coalition of interests between the state and corporations that has positioned education to meet the needs of the Information Age and the globalized market economy. In addition, the alignment of education's purpose with the ends of enterprise culture is constructed as "inevitable" and thus politically exists as a rational *fait accompli*. Therefore, according to Michael Apple (1995), the narrowing of current educational reform discourse occurs on two levels—the scope of issues and solutions as well as who can speak. Within this broad context a fundamental paradox exists: simultaneous to the narrowing of scope and voice regarding educational reform discourse, the growing influence of social and economic forces act to broaden the context of educational reform and serve to reconfigure the purpose and meaning of education itself.

Siv Shapiro (1994/1996) believes that President Clinton's Educate America Act (1994) and the "School to Work" initiatives solely defined the value of education in vocationally related terms, "a direction which acts to place education in the service of promoting corporate expansion" (p. 220).

Shapiro (1994/1996), however, proposes that education's purpose is to serve much deeper and meaningful civic goals.

> It is easy to forget, in the constant reiteration of this discourse and its association to shimmering images of electronic super-highways, and new computer technologies, that there is another tradition and language concerning the purpose and meaning of education in this country. It is one that connects people, especially the young, to the making of a democratic culture. It is about creating and nurturing the individual's capabilities to live critically-aware, humanly sensitive and socially responsible lives. This, needless to add, has never been dominant in the public struggle to define goals of education—though it does persist in the ideals, and sometimes the practices, of educators in this country. Sadly there is little room in the ideological framework of expanding markets and corporate development for an education that might emphasize this democratic tradition (p. 220).

Shapiro adds that the essential technocentric framework that guides policy elites, stands in stark opposition to what truly lies at the heart of the matter with education and the society it serves—a struggle for a politics of meaning and a humanistic social vision.

> Education and educational change must be quite clearly linked to the struggle for a politics of meaning. This means to assert clearly that at the heart of the educational enterprise are questions of human purpose and social vision—what does it mean to be human, and how should we live together? Education, at its core, is *not* about the transmission of information and skills, but it is the quest for lives lived together in fuller and more meaningful ways (author's original italics, p. 224).

Thus, Shapiro (1994/1996) relates the dramaturgy of educational reform politics to the forging and expression of "human purpose and social vision," which he defines as expressing our humanity through building a meaningful community.

Also, Shapiro (1994/1996) believes that the publication of *A Nation at Risk* (1983) had wide and deep effects on the framing of educational policy. He found evidence for this claim through analyzing the discourse of the political debates about education in the 1984 and 1988 primary campaigns for the Democratic party. He discovered that the rhetoric of major candidates, with the exception of Jesse Jackson, was "unremittingly suffused by corporate priorities and capitalist values." The candidates' discourse generally did not relate education to "issues of empowerment, justice or human dignity" (p. 3). Rather, the reforms of education were tied to the modernization of industry, economic growth, and the education and training of workers for high technology. He noted how these goals "lead to a preoccupation with education as an economic investment, evidenced in a particular kind of educational discourse: 'the training for skilled minds,' 'new knowledge for improving productivity,' and 'modernizing schools for the information age'" (Shapiro, 1994/1996, p. 4). Mike Davis's (1986) analysis of the political discourse of the 1980s indicates that the traditional welfare concerns of the Democratic party were abandoned "for a high tech industrial policy." Moreover, the technocentric trajectory for educational reform policy set by the Clinton administration of the 1990s has been largely adopted by the George W. Bush administration for the 21st century.

In addition, Shapiro considers the omission of democratic values from educational reform discourse as creating "enormous ideological and political significance" because it represents "a selective response to the problems or crisis of the present era, a mobilization of bias around which issues or concerns ought to constitute the educational or political debate" (p. 15). Shapiro (1994/1996), therefore, believes that the silence about democratic issues within the context of educational reform discourse reflects a narrowing of political concerns on a broader scale.

> Failure to speak to democratic values in the context of schooling represents a larger failure to address a sense of critical issues in American public life—the pervasive and largely uncontrolled influence of television and the media, the alienation from the instruments of political democracy, and the absence of just about any form of economic democracy. Most important, there is an absence of any rhetoric that speaks to the erosion of those traditions concerned with community empowerment (p. 15).

Indeed, the masking of this process of social envisioning by the discourse of competition, accountability, and standards strikes some critics as a morally questionable act. David Purpel (1991/1996), for example, believes that the educational process "needs to be rooted in the commitment to build a democratic society" and that "one of the scandals of the present public and professional dialogue on education is the way we have successfully disguised our most fundamental crises by trivializing them, by converting the profound struggle for meaning into the vulgar pursuit of competitive advantage" (p. 207). In addition, Purpel (1991/1996) states that as a citizen he is "appalled by the arrogance reflected in *A Nation at Risk* which reeks of an obsession with power, control, domination and certainty." As an educator, he is "dismayed by the disingenuineness of the professional establishment in its zeal to do its master's bidding" (p. 209). However, Purpel (1991/1996) also understands how many educators become "unwittingly and naive accomplices" and support reforms and systems of education that run counter to the true spirit of teaching.

> Alas, the dominant streams of educational policy and practice run not in the currents of love, justice and joy but in the straits of inequity and competition. This situation is all the more tragic because it corrodes the true spirit of the impulse to teach. My view is that educators find themselves for the most part to be unwitting and naive accomplices to those who are bent on perpetuating a

society and culture that exists in sharp conflict with our deeply felt moral and
spiritual vision (pp. 209–210).

Moreover, Purpel (1991/1996) also raises the issue that educators'
awareness of a "moral and spiritual vision" of education may be obscured by
the drive to exact expertness and professionalism.

> Even worse, many educators and people in the public sphere are not even aware
> of the chasm between the dominant educational ideas and our highest
> aspirations as a people. Educators, in their haste and pride to be professional and
> knowledgeable—to be experts—actually deny the social, cultural, moral and
> religious implications of educational policy and practice. What we have is a
> powerful and awesome coalition between those committed to the political,
> social, and economic status quo and those who insist on sticking their collective
> heads into the blinding muck of neutrality and objectivity (p. 208).

Shapiro (1994/1996), who is also dismayed by educators' responses to
current reform discourse, was especially disheartened by the public's
response to *A Nation at Risk* rhetoric because it had seemed to resonate with
the public's frustration and fears about public education. This factor is
evidenced by the majority of citizens having accepted without question the
association between schools and international economic competition and
stricter controls on accountability and standards.

Maxine Greene (1986/1996) specifically explains how the narrowing of
reform discourse is characterized by "an instrumental rationality" or a
technocentric framework, which acts to close down the spaces for
alternative perspectives. Greene (1986/1996, p. 421) adds that "the lack of
dialogue in the public spaces today makes people forget that there are other
American traditions, other visions of what constitute the good life and the
humane society." Making reference to John Dewey's role of the public in
civic society, Greene states that educators have a special responsibility "to
choose themselves as an 'articulate public'" (p. 421). Greene's view is similar
to that expressed by educational historian William Reid (1979), who
believes that educators possess a "civic duty" to act in the public interest.

In addition, Tyack and Cuban (1995) explain that reform may be
understood in a manner of scale. "Tinkering" refers to short-range solutions
that express commonsense remedies for everyday problems. Whereas the
long-term goal of education, as expressed through "utopian discourse," is to
negotiate a pluralistic conception of education as serving the public good,
thus functioning as a forum of trusteeship (p. 142). However, although
school reform exists as a "prime arena for debating the shape of the future of
the society" and where such debate expresses "a broad civic and moral
enterprise in which all citizens are stakeholders," Tyack and Cuban (1995)
also reflect on the fact that since around the time of the publication of *A
Nation at Risk* (1983), discourse about the purpose of education has become

"radically narrowed" by focusing on "international economic competition, test scores and individual 'choice' of schools" (p. 140). Although not new, this underlying rationale is nevertheless unprecedented in its dominance (p. 36).

Indeed, writing just one year after the publication of *A Nation at Risk*, Barbara Finkelstein (1984) was dismayed by the reality that policy reformers endeavored to shape symbolic action through a functionalist discourse as they "seem to be recalling public education from its traditional utopian mission—to nurture a critical and committed citizenry." Rather, these policy elites "seem ready to do ideological surgery on their public schools—cutting them away from the fate of social justice and political democracy completely and grafting them instead onto elite corporate, industrial, military and cultural interests" (pp. 280–281). Finkelstein (1984), therefore, also referenced a closure or narrowing of discourse, especially in terms of abandoning a "utopian mission" toward realizing the ideals of political democracy and social justice.

Educational scholar Jesse Goodman (1995) understands the narrowing of educational reform discourse in terms of a dialectic, which casts functionalist or "socio-temporal" aims in relief against those that are situated within the tradition of "social-utopian" or democratic ideals. Functionalist-based reform discourse, for example, describes educational reform in terms of broad economic movements, which have occurred in three distinct "waves." For example, the first wave refers to an agrarian society and the one room schoolhouse and the second wave, at the turn of the century, met the demands of the Industrial Age. The current "third wave" of restructuring reflects the needs of a "highly technological, rapidly changing, information-oriented society" (Reigeluth, 1987). According to Goodman (1995), the second and third wave reform efforts are categorized as "socio-temporal," because their rationale reflects a functionalist ideology. Also, Goodman (1995) criticizes the current "third wave" reformers' discourse as having "an unsettling crisis mentality" (p. 25) while offering "the impression of inevitability woven into its socio-temporal vision. The future is presented as a *fait accompli* " (p. 6). Goodman (1995) believes that this closure of civic discourse especially silences the voices of teachers and their students.

> Rather than initiating a school transformation movement in which there is generative discourse about the kind of society we wish to create collectively, both the industrial and now the third wave restructuring movements place teachers and their students in the passive role of merely getting prepared for a destiny that someone else has determined for them (p. 7).

While not denying the changes brought about by technology and global market economics, which inspire a technocentric vision, Goodman (1995), however, questions the wisdom in how this element has been "mindlessly prioritized over other equally (or more) valuable social visions" (p. 7).

In contrast to a predetermined socio-temporal perspective on educational reform, Goodman suggests that educators understand school reform from a "social-utopian" perspective where teachers, students, principals and other interested individuals are "actively engaged in visualizing the type of society we wish to create. Once opened for inspection, any number of social visions might emerge that will move us substantially away from the functionalist tradition that has dominated schooling for most of this century" (p. 7). Goodman's (1995) notion of a "social-utopian" perspective therefore is very similar to Tyack and Cuban's (1995) proposal that schools as sites of policy debate work to enliven long-term social ideals which give expression to the "public good" via "utopian discourse" (p. 10). This perspective also parallels Maxine Greene's (1995) idea of "seeing schools big" through emphasis on the relational, tacit knowledge versus a functionalist-based framework that "sees schools as small." Tyack and Cuban (1995) point out that although the history of educational reform is characterized by a "pie-in-the-sky brand of utopianism," there is a different form of utopianism that educators and citizens need to address (p. 10).

> There is, however, a different kind of utopianism—a vision of a just democracy—that has marked the best discourse about educational purpose over the past century. We believe that debate over educational and social goals has become radically restricted in the past generation. An essential political task today is to renegotiate a pluralistic conception of the public good, a sense of trusteeship that preserves the best of the past while building a generous conception of a common future (p. 11).

Undoing the functionalist discourse of policy elites therefore depends upon democratization of the reform process, of opening up the spaces and allowing alternatives and oppositional voices the means—to borrow a concept from Paulo Freire (1970)—to "name their own world." It requires an awakening from our commonsense perceptions and cultural myths in order to forge a social vision that balances functionalist techno-utopian aims against social-utopian ideals. The development of a social vision is, therefore, an integral part of the "dramaturgy" of the educational reform process.

Educational Reform Policy and the Meaning of Social Vision

The first two chapters provided background information and a foundation for understanding current educational reform discourse. It was found that such discourse reflects a narrow scope—a functionalist framework with a focus on standards, accountability, and the rapid infusion of electronic technologies. These changes are rationalized by the demands of the Information Age and a globalized economy, an aim that directly accommodates corporate and state interests. The current reform movement is generally characterized by a technological utopian futurism. The proposed reforms are presented as "inevitable," thus the current policy exists as a *fait accompli*. Politically, this situation closes down the spaces for public discourse, which, in the context of education, includes the voices of teachers. In general, there is an emphasis on positivistic and functionalistic ends at the expense of the social democratic ideals of social justice.

Given the factors thus far discussed, it is proposed that educational reform discourse exists as *social* discourse. According to Murray Eldeman (1985), the political dramaturgy is a means through which a society articulates its ideological narratives—the stories we tell ourselves about who we are. These broad social narratives, on an individual level, are related to the construction of subjectivity and roles. For, as Eldeman (1985) explains, the symbolic process of political dramaturgy is not inherent in the symbol, but rather in the observer and their situations. Eldeman (1985) believes that the social construction approach to understanding the political process— because of the reflexive power of language—holds out the possibility that we can remake our social reality through the process of renaming it. Thus, one could describe educational reform as a "narrative space" where social discourse is constructed. It is argued that at present this narrative space is characterized by a dialectic between two social visions—that of official policy's "language of inevitability" versus the "language of possibility" which is negotiated and emergent. Therefore, the "language of inevitability" constitutes a closure on the landscape of possibility and seeks to fully realize functionalist ends within education and ultimately the creation of a globalized "enterprise culture" (Peters, 1996). In contrast, the realm of possibility, which signifies an opening-up and broadening of the "narrative space," engages praxis and the realization of our social democratic ideals through social institutions such as schools. The major features that distinguishes each of these particular discursive frameworks, as explained in this and the previous chapter, are detailed in the following table.

Table 2.1: The Dialectic of Educational Reform Policy

Dominant Framework	Emergent Framework
Technocentric discourse *(fait accompli/*closure)	discourse of possibility (deliberative/pluralism)

Continued

Table 2.1—Continued

technological fix/ technological determinism	questions technology/media infusion
technology as artifact/tool (apolitical)	technology as a sociopolitical process
information as commodity	"mythinformation" and *techne* as *politea*
discourse of progress	technological pessimism
functionalist/vocationalist	politics of meaning/social justice
techno-utopian social vision	emancipatory social vision
efficiency/*technique*	questions *technique*
enterprise culture	questions technical rationalism
libertarian/technocentric	"cultural wars"/multiculturalism
privatization/commodification	the public good/social democratic process
crisis exists and related to the rise of Information Age and global market economy	crisis exists and related to systemic socioeconomic problems and postmodern crisis in meaning
educators without agency/ performance culture	educators as citizens and social change agents
technopoly	lifeworld
solution: infuse technology and adopt standards/accountability measures/ control technologies	solution: address sociocultural issues and economic disparity

It is important to recognize how the acknowledgment of possibility is essential to avoiding "an apolitical postmodernism," which unwittingly articulates a certain form of "technological utopianism that is seemingly postpolitical and simultaneously worshipful of the infinite possibilities for learning and teaching inherent in new computer technologies" (Aronowitz and Giroux, 1991, p. 190). Aronowitz and Giroux (1991) also note a shift within educational policy from arguments that underscore "the instrumental value of computers . . . to the emergence of a fully elaborated cultural theory that wishes to subsume pedagogy—indeed, the entire educational enterprise, under a new will to totalization" (p. 190). These new "prophets of hyperreality" recognize the existence of politics, but only as an obstacle to the creation of an electronic-mediated community. "Thus the struggle for social power, having been rendered obsolete by the now realized dream of total individual autonomy, made possible by the machine, may be conceived as an illusion" (p. 191).

Therefore, the dialectic between a language of inevitability and possibility also expresses the politics of technology and how its envisioned usage is socially constructed. For example, the "language of inevitability" assumes an apolitical, artifactual/tool function of technology. As discussed above, this simplistic perspective rationalizes rapid top-down infusion, a conduit or transmission view of knowledge and learning, and an expression of a teacher's role as a mere "delivery system." In contrast, the realm of possibility problematizes technology. Perceiving its function as both tool and social structures, technology is understood to be intimately connected with culture and politics. A political framework for understanding the relationship between technology and society disengages the priority of pragmatic questions (e.g., How do we accomplish our goals?) and equally considers moral and socially based questions (e.g., What ought we accomplish?). Thus, a top-down infusion model is untenable, as is a transmission model of knowledge and learning. Also, the role of the teacher expands to encompass not only demonstrating technical skills, but equally, if not more important, is active in decision-making whereby their professional tacit knowledge and moral reality are honored and incorporated into the decision-making process.

In addition, as the above discussion indicates, several scholars made reference to the notion of social vision. Jessie Goodman (1985) wrote about the importance of democratic ideals expressed as "social-utopian vision." David Tyack and Larry Cuban (1995) made reference to "utopian ideals" and the democratic tradition. Siv Shaprio (1994/1996) believes that we can only create a "politics of meaning" by asking questions of "human purpose and vision," a process that enables a society to engage in a "cultural act," which he describes as follows.

> At the heart of the educational enterprise are questions of human purpose and social vision—what does it mean to be human and how should we live together? . . . It is clear that there is very great support for an educational vision that might speak to our children's moral and spiritual needs. . . . [and] educators role in shaping human consciousness and communal purpose must be affirmed and reaffirmed (p. 224).

Also, educational theorist and poststructuralist Peter McLaren (1995) has made reference to how educational reform discourse can inspire a "vision of possibility" and a "theology of hope." Indeed, a vision is paradigmatic and encompasses a holistic understanding of sociocultural themes. It generally expresses deeply held values, beliefs, and personal philosophies on the individual level. It is also a reflective act as it requires the comparison of the given to an idealized image. Thus, a social vision of possibility requires reflective and imaginative thinking. However, because the notion of visions or the process of envisioning within the context of education has been co-opted by business administration rhetoric, it is strictly associated with leadership. Only administrators or policymakers are imbued with the need or power to envision. Therefore, although teachers may hold "personal visions," which express the deeply moral and emotional basis of their personal and professional lives, these visions have been largely diffused or buried as they are generally not given voice or acknowledged to exist within the current administrative framework guiding educators (Barth, 1990). Moreover, it is not so much the establishment of a permanent vision that requires complete consensus that is important, as this is an artifact of the business model of establishing an institution's vision or mission (Hargraves, 1995). Rather, the process of envisioning within an educational context needs to be fully recognized as both a community and political act and therefore considered as a process—temporary and approximate—in order to serve the changing demands and needs of a school's community as it strives to realize social democratic ideals. This is to recognize that "people cannot be given a purpose: purposes come from within" (Hargraves, 1995, p. 16).

In conclusion, the technocentric framework constructed by policy elites acts as a particular social vision grounded in the functionalist tradition. In contrast, critics of the dominant perspective base their policy framework and social vision on the tradition of democratic ideals. Although this dialectic exits, the reality is that within the context of current educational reform policy, the technocentric discourse, due to the power of the rhetoric of inevitability, has significantly dominated and thus narrowed educational reform discourse. Chapters Four and Five report the stories of two case study sites, which in fact reflect this fundamental dialectic, in terms of each school's respective approach to reform. What we shall discover, however, is that despite these very different settings and reform agendas, the informants shared very common concerns. Also, despite the fact that teachers are generally not invited into the process of policy development nor acknowledged for their capacity to envision, their social visions, grounded in their personal practical knowledge (Clandinin & Connelly, 1995), were not only insightful but raise serious questions regarding the validity and morality of current educational reform policy. It is in fact the role of teachers within the context of a technocentric reform agenda to which we turn in the following chapter.

Notes

1 Also, certain economists hold that contrary to political elites' rhetoric, there is little evidence of an accelerating skills mismatch, especially if many jobs are being deskilled by computerization (Gordon, 1996, p. 187). In addition, the vision that all U.S. workers, through equal education opportunities—a factor that is unlikely to be realized in the present political climate—will become symbolic analysts rests on shaky ground, for the real growth in jobs is within the "in-person services" sector, which Robert Reich (1991) describes as dead-end jobs with low pay and no benefits, a job category into which many well-paid factory workers have fallen. The promise of new telecommunications technologies spawning an "electronic cottage industry" also needs to be reconsidered given the reality of access, and the fact that many of such jobs will likely fall into the service sector category (Peters, 1996).

2 Indeed the allure of the gilded computer has turned naysayer William Bennett, former U.S. Secretary of Education, from a skeptic about the efficacy of computer-based instruction to one of its staunchest supporters. As founder of a for-profit K–12 online school, a venture funded by Michael R. Milken and his brother who have contributed $10 million in start-up funds, Mr. Bennett has not ruled out utilizing corporate sponsors to develop materials for his online school. Indeed, Chester Finn, an advisor to Bennett and supporter of the privatization of public schools, explained that teachers and students do not need to be in the classroom together, as such things as classrooms and blackboards are antiquated 19th century technologies (*New York Times*, Dec. 29, 2000).

3 In addition, as the sale of ILS continues to grow, especially to schools receiving Chapter One and other state and federal funding, "it is predictable that developers of these systems will attempt to incorporate the emerging national and state standards into their courseware" (Morrison & Goldberg, 1996, p. 136). The authors also point out that publishers are already using wide area networks to download courseware to local ILS servers (Newman, 1992), "a practice that seems almost certain to grow as increasing numbers of schools purchase network connections" (p. 136).

4 For example, Streibel (1986/1994) compares the different qualities of a technological and community framework for learning. A community framework encompasses individual uniqueness, a dialectical rationality that synthesizes oppositional perspectives and emergent community goals. In contrast, a technological framework emphasizes "the generic characteristics of individuals, a means-ends rationality and a predetermined set of performance goals" (p. 311).

5 In fact, it is this very abdication of authority that reflects how simulations are used in real world economics, politics, and social planning when such modeling is used by the Congressional Budget Office, for example, to project various economic and social scenarios. Thus, according to Turkle (1997), simulation games are not only objects for thinking about the real world, but also illustrate "how the real world has itself become a simulation game" (p. 14). Therefore, Turkle (1997), noting that students and the general population lack critical awareness about the nature of simulations while dependency on their usage in decision-making processes, recommends that "understanding the assumptions that underlie simulation is a key element of political power," and that students be taught a "new class of skills: readership skill for the

culture of simulation" rather than simply being left to act as passive users of yet
another entertaining medium (p. 15).

[6] Snyder (1997) advises teachers to guide students to abandon such "surfing" and rather
     "surrender to debate, shared language and storytelling, and teach them to commit to
     emotional discussion and being an author of their own authentic ideas." These
     recommendations are remarkable given the fact that Snyder is in the business of
     producing instructional software, a business not generally known for advising teachers
     to be cautious about their attitudes toward using and purchasing instructional
     technologies.

[7] Students, lacking in self-knowledge, look into the computer and see their own self-image
     and fall in love with themselves (p. 146). Moreover, as the story goes, Narcissus
     became so enamored with his own image he became eternally fixated by it, thus
     becoming a servomechanism of his own extended, repeated image (p. 146). It is
     possible, therefore, that within the context of a socioeconomic reality that emphasizes
     possessive individualism (Bowers, 1988, 2000; Bellah et al., 1986; Putnam, 2000), the
     computer can act to further what Christopher Lasch has described as a *Culture of
     Narcissism* (1979).

[8] Indeed, violent video games are used to train U.S. and British soldiers to desensitize them
     to other's suffering (Platoni, 1999). Also, the use of computers for engagement in
     online computer-mediated communication (chat, MUDs, etc.) are related to changes
     in socialization resulting in increased loneliness and depression in adolescents (Kraut et
     al., 1998). There is also evidence of changes in the development of identity and loss of
     the ability to distinguish between fantasy and reality (Turkle, 1997). Additionally,
     increased usage of such media as television and computers can raise the risk of
     childhood obesity (American Academy of Pediatrics, 1999; U.S. Department of
     Health and Human Services, 1996), seizures (Glista et al., 1983; Graf et al., 1994) and
     repetitive stress syndrome injury to wrists and hands (Brasington, 1990). Some adults
     fear that exposure to pornography and sexually explicit materials on the Internet as
     well as engaging in online "cybersex" may encourage premature sexual activity,
     although it may also encourage better sexual decision-making (Subrahmanyam et al.,
     2000). Also, use of the Internet by children may pose a threat to the safety of children
     who could be targeted by pedophiles.

[9] A market survey has found that 8.6 million children and 8.4 million teenagers were online
     in 1998, a figure expected to increase to a combined 69% of children ages 5—18
     (Jupiter Communications, 1999). This same survey forecasts that by 2002 teens, who
     are directly targeted online by advertisers, will spend 1.2 billion and children 100
     million of e-commerce dollars. Indeed, marketing research indicates that children
     under age twelve have control or influence household spending to the degree of $500
     billion a year. This does not only include toys but also major purchases such as vehicles
     (Russakoff, 1999). Furthermore, it is not surprising that many of the Websites
     developed for children and teens are commodity based and are essentially
     advertisements for licensed products. Sites such as Mattel's Barbie.com also portray
     themselves as a "community for girls" and many other Websites "targeted" towards
     children integrate advertising with informational content to promote brand awareness
     and loyalty—a "cradle to grave" marketing strategy that exploits children's
     developmental needs of belonging (Montgomery, 2000, p. 156). In fact, some
     Websites went as far as to gather personal data about children, luring them into
     compliance thorough games and contests. Consequently, Congress passed the Child

On-Line Privacy Protection Act of 1998 to restrict personal data collection from children under age 13 on the Internet.

CHAPTER THREE

Technocentric Reform and the Rationalization of Teachers' Work

If teaching and learning are to remain vital, creative and adaptive processes, the teacher should strive to maintain control over educational design; without control teachers will lose out to professional designers who will turn them into instructors or presenters as part of an "instructional delivery system." If societies are to avoid the centralization and standardization of "knowledge" (with their totalitarian overtones), educational design should not be entrusted to monoliths, state or private.

Ted Nunan, 1983

The reality is that creativity is a rare commodity among teachers, and we need to identify the really creative teachers and, whenever possible, extend the range of their talents by incorporating their skills in mediated forms, thereby benefiting students. A word to instructional psychology: the more we learn about learning and the more sophisticated our instructional strategies become as a result, the less likely it is that teachers will be able to implement those strategies. Carefully designed, technologically based experiences will be our only assurance that the integrity of those strategies, including any that give great control, will be retained.

Robert Heinich, 1984

It is clear that the role of the teacher is being reinscribed by technocentric discourse. For example, during the first few years after the publication of *A Nation at Risk* (1983), reports such as *Tomorrow's Teachers: A Report of the Holmes Group* and *A Nation Prepared: Teachers for the 21st Century* delineated how changes in the economy demanded new skills and roles for teachers. More recently, individual states have established technology standards for teachers, while in the form of federal aid, several specific programs have acted to support teachers' professional development in terms of securing technical skills.[1] However, several elements coalesce, which influence the changing role of the teacher within the current reform movement. For example, teachers' traditional practices are being challenged by the introduction of constructivist-based pedagogy, where the teacher's role is redefined from being that of a "sage on the stage" to a "guide on the side." However, within the context of integrating computer technology with print and oral traditions, teachers need to take a more active role in synthesizing the complex interactions of these various modes and mediums of communication, thus standing on the sidelines may not be an appropriate place for teachers. Also, standing on the sidelines accommodates the role of teachers as technicians within a training-oriented learning environment (Burniske & Monke, 2001).

In addition, teachers must negotiate students who bring to the classroom a myriad of personal and socially based problems while teachers' accountability is more closely tied to students' academic achievement. In general, there has been a vast increase in policies in the form of standards and accountability schemes that increase the control and rationalization of teachers' work (Hargraves, 1994; Greene, 1978, 1986/1996, 1988; de Alba, 2000; Gleeson & Gunter, 2001; Ball, 2001). Within this context, teachers are required to master the integration of new technologies into their instructional practices. Indeed, although many reforms have targeted changes in curriculum and instruction, more recent reforms aim to change the culture of schools with specific emphasis on the relationships between teachers and their colleagues, administration and their students (Hartley, 1999).

As mentioned in the Introduction, the current operationalization of neo-Taylorist scientific management reforms may be characterized as demonstrating an obsession with control in the form of "performance and performity." Increasingly, the work of students, teachers, and administrators are subject to management and measurement. Indeed, as a policy device, performance management affects both the micro level of education such as the classroom, as well as the macro level, in terms of state and federal standards and assessment programs. Gleeson and Gunter (2000) have found that the discourse of performance "obscures a discourse of power, masking deeper issues of regulation and control of teachers and learners" (p. 154). The outcome is that relationships between the teacher and students and among teachers and administrators are governed by an ethic of exchange and thus become commodified as all parties engage in a depersonalized self-regulating regime, which reduces being in relation to purposive-rational action. This outcome embodies Jeremy Bentham's panopticon system of surveillance whereby those engaged within the monitoring system's structure internalize the surveillance process itself, thus actualizing Foucault's vision of a regime of discipline. In fact, as noted in the Introduction, the expression of discipline via surveillance techniques has been augmented by control technologies such as database systems and the performance report. Indeed, partnership and collaboration must remain only at the operational level, for to truly embrace teachers' decision-making power might ultimately threaten the legitimacy of the system of control itself (Gleeson & Gunter, 2000).

The reduction of teaching and learning to performance outcomes is necessary in a managerial or commodity-based approach to education because as monitoring systems they function in the form of control technologies whose purpose is to generate performance data. These data in turn create a virtual signification of the process of teaching and learning. In effect, this reification process transfers the essence of schools from the reality of place in a geographic sense to that of a virtual representational space of information—a condition that generally characterizes post-modernity. In terms of how this situation affects the work of teachers, Ball (2001) argues that the ideology of performance is fundamentally changing the nature of teacher identity—indeed, the identity of students as well. He also relates this factor to the general postmodern condition rendered by Lyotard (1984) in which Lyotard describes the effects of the "exteriorization of knowledge" (p. 4) or the commodification of knowledge. Thus, individuals within such a regime of discipline and control engage in the process of fabricating self in order to meet set criteria of control technologies in the form of standards and accountability programs. This process of "regressive self-regulation" as identity construction discounts "claims to authenticity and commitment" while encouraging "an investment in plasticity," whereby the fabrication becomes paradoxically the real. Thus, "the discipline of the market is transformed into the discipline of the image, the sign" in terms of constituting the professional (and to some degree) personal identity of teachers (p. 217). Thus, "knowledge and knowledge relations, including the relationships between learners, are desocialized" (Ball, 2001, p. 222). This situation, as Ball (2001) envisions, "is part of a larger process of ethical retooling in the public sector," whereby the space for "autonomous ethical codes based on a shared moral language is colonized or closed down" (p. 223). In effect, what has occurred is that education has been dislocated from its sociocultural base (Morley & Rassool, 1999). As a result, the elements of current educational reform policy characterize a *culture* of performity and arise from a generative technocentric framework driven by efficiency and control. The infusion of electronic technologies is another expression of this generative framework.

Within this context, it should come as no surprise that teachers have had very little participation in the development of policies that directly affects their work and the instructional experiences of their students. Reid (1979) believes this is so because teachers are thought to be incapable of making rational decisions, a position which, he believes, raises serious moral and ethical issues for reformers who act on this assumption (p. 333). Although Reid does not address this factor, such an assumption may arise from the feminization of the teaching profession. Indeed, the marginalization of teachers' roles coincides with the increase in management of their labor. This point is raised by Tyack (1974) who explains that historically the feminization of K–12 education occurred simultaneous to increasing bureaucratic controls and lower pay. In addition, occupations held largely by women have been subjected to bureaucratic controls. In the particular case of education such controls have resulted in the intensification of teachers' labor (Hargraves, 1994) and the deskilling of teachers (Apple, 1993). The deskilling of teachers' labor is complex and related to many structural elements such as the bureaucratization of management and the development of hierarchical systems, the artificial division between the development of curriculum and the practice of teaching (Nunan, 1983) as well as the dependence upon prepackaged curriculum in the form of textbooks and computer-based instruction (Apple, 1987, 1993). Indeed, Gleeson & Gunter (2000) indicate that prescriptive controls on teachers' work and the general context of performance culture limits teachers' professional judgment specifically in terms of limiting and controlling argument and debate even while teachers' labor is intensified. They also explain that while the performance-based managerial model of standards and accountability is more economically efficient, the trade-off is a loss in teachers' professional development and diminution of intrinsically based engagement within a school environment. This is an important point because not only does it underscore the deprofessionalization of teachers, it also means that the contextual and critically based approach to educational reform, which is necessary to address the complexity of education within postmodern society, especially in terms of adopting electronic technologies (Christal et al., 1997), is also not being acknowledged within this delimited framework.

Although performance-based reforms appear to be bottom-up in terms of instituting decision-making authority, in actuality they can often be a shadow play of active engagement in decision-making while simulateously imposing an elaborate system of feedback and control. This point is interesting given the fact that, historically, according to feminist Sandra Harding (1986, 1991), women's traditional labor (e.g., housework and childrearing), being less valuable in our culture than males' labor, has thus been made invisible. Therefore, in one sense the commodification of teachers' labor via bureaucratic controls, which has escalated within the context of the current reform movement, acts to further the invisibility of teachers' work while it simultaneously serves to redefine its meaning in the form of the technical. Consequently, the performance-based approaches to reform act to nullify the humanistic and artistic expression intrinsic to the act of teaching. This same factor applies to typical approaches taken to infuse various technologies into educational settings. For example, Cuban (1986) explains that any type of medium or technology that acts to mediate, displace, or minimize the social interaction between teacher and student is problematic for teachers because "so much of teaching is imagination, improvisation and pacing combined with student rapport, that shifting the center of gravity to machine-student exchanges lessens greatly the joys inherent in the art of teaching" (p. 90). He also suggests that it is this very issue, though often unarticulated, that has influenced the slow pace of the mechanization of teaching over the last century. In addition, given the central position that technology infusion holds as a catalyst to restructure education, it is important to remember the lack of voice which teachers have had in terms of past and present technologically driven reforms (Cuban, 1986, 2001; Tyack & Cuban, 1995).

Despite these factors, it may be argued that current reforms aim to further the professionalization of teachers and more fully engage them in decision-making processes. To be sure, there are specific schools that embrace the democratic spirit of site-based management and invite and act on teachers' inputs and concerns as with Central Park East Secondary School of New York City (Harris, 1996). However, although current reforms in the management structure have ostensibly been designed to augment the professional position of teachers, Hargraves (1994), for example, found these reforms paradoxical: Despite some positive changes, current reforms, which enhance site-based management, also produced intensification of teachers' work and consequently increased burnout. In addition, Hargraves (1994) found, as did Ball (2001), that collaborative cultures become reconfigured as "contrived collegiality" through "safe simulations" characterized by compulsory, not voluntary, interaction, which are "administratively regulated and therefore meant to be predictable rather than unpredictable in its outcomes" thus signifying teachers' lack of control over the process versus their professional power as decisionmakers (p. 208). These attempts to simulate spontaneity and creative social interchange, embody "many administrative devices of change [that] do not just undermine teachers' own desires in teaching. They threaten the very desire to teach itself. They take the heart out of teaching" (p. 3). Thus, as noted above, although teachers may gain some autonomy under the guise of greater professionalism, their potential autonomy is offset by closer monitoring and regulation of their work as both teachers and students are configured by an imposed performance-based culture.

In fact, the current reform movement is beset by paradoxes that reflect a particular confluence of sociocultural and economic forces that characterize postmodernity. For example, Hargraves (1995, pp. 14–20) cites the following five paradoxes, which characterize what he describes as postmodern education. (1) "Many parents have given up on responsibility for the very things they want schools to stress." Hence, there exists zero tolerance policies against violence in schools while "Mortal Combat" is the top computer video game. (2) "Business often fails to use the skills that it demands schools to produce." Despite rising literacy and high school graduation rates for blacks, jobs in inner cities have diminished. (3) "More globalism produces more tribalism." Therefore, in a global economy increasingly dominated by transnational corporations, educational systems demand national curriculum and standards. (4) "More diversity and integration is accompanied by more emphasis on common standards and specialization." Thus, while society and business demand that students acquire flexible work skills, multiple language, cooperative learning, and critical thinking skills, an "obsession with national strength and identity" have created standardized tests and international and school-by-school comparisons. And (5), "Stronger orientation to the future creates greater nostalgia for the past. Complexity and uncertainty are leading many people to long for golden ages of traditional subjects, basic skills and singular values in a world of clear moral certainties." Therefore, outcomes-based education precipitates fundamentalists, insistence on Christian values in curriculum and multicultural diversity precipitates privileged classes to favor private or charter schools that feature traditional values.

Because such paradoxes are not addressed within the context of official reform policy, these reform proposals seem blandly transparent in their attempt to maintain the status quo. Goodman (1995), for example, is suspicious that proposed reforms in the management structure of schools will create a broad base of individuals working collaboratively in a manner that supports an idealized bottom-up approach to change. Rather, he suspects that these management reforms are "a continuation of the expertism that has dominated school reform in this country for over a century" (p. 22).

Michael Apple (1986) also believes that despite the rhetoric of teacher professionalism, current educational reforms in the United States and elsewhere aim to control teachers' work through elaborate management procedures.

> Currently, considerable pressure is building to have teaching and school curricula be totally prespecified and tightly controlled by the purposes of 'efficiency,' 'cost effectiveness' and 'accountability.' In many ways, the deskilling that is affecting jobs in general is now having an impact on teachers as more and more decisions are moving out of their hands as their jobs become even more difficult to do. This is more advanced in some countries than in others, but it is clear that the movement to rationalize and control the act of teaching and the content and evaluation of the curriculum is very real (p. 21).

Maxine Greene (1986/1996) specifically questioned the implications of *A Nation at Risk,* in terms of how its recommendations would affect the lives of teachers and the nature of teaching. Greene suspects that the focus on teachers and their work is due partly to the fact that teaching "is most susceptible to management and repair" (p. 419). Thus, the particular discourse of official reform policy narrowly defines the role of teachers and the definition and purpose of the teaching act. Citing how educational reformers often adopt the technical language and techniques of business and industry, Greene (1986/1996) wonders about "the impacts of positivism and technicism on the discourse and the practice of 'educational reform'"

(p. 420). She believes that such a perspective on education diminishes the complexity and nuances of schools as communities, which she suggests are defined by John Dewey as being inherently social institutions. Therefore, according to Greene (1986/1996), defining learning and teaching via a discourse of technical rationality dissolves the uncertainty, spontaneity, and complexity of the social reality of teaching and instead reinterprets "intelligent practice as a sense of instrumental decisions which we try to make more and more rigorous by application of scientific theory and practice—in our case, in the guise of various psychologies, certain of the social services, or the instructional and computer sciences" (p. 420) Greene (1986/1996) interprets this rationalization of the lived experiences of teachers and students as creating an artificial distancing between the teacher and her students—a distance arising from an imposed sense of objectification where teachers see themselves and their students as objects of "information machines" rather than subjects. This is a lifeless and dispassionate perspective, which forces one to think in terms of behavior rather than action, where behavior is determinable and measurable, and action invites the unpredictable (Greene, 1986/1996, p. 426).

In addition, Shapiro (1990) perceives that the dominance of a positivistic perspective in official reform discourse has reduced the lived experiences of teachers and their students to quantifiable elements or "linear progressive rationality." This reductionism accommodates the desire to further control the work of teachers. Thus, the logic of "instrumental rationalism" or a positivistic framework, according to Shapiro (1990, p. 14), acts to "discount alternative visions of pedagogy—critical and reflexive, aesthetic and imaginative, democratic and empowering." Shapiro (1990) perceives that a positivistic perspective exists as common sense and "makes it the natural and the only possible version of educational practice" (p. 14). Given the "restricted and narrow concerns" expressed in educational reform rhetoric, Shapiro was not surprised to find "a paucity of attention given to the relationship between schooling and democratic values" (p. 14). He expressed dismay at the fact that there has been little attention given to "the enhancement of the capability for self-determination or the empowerment of human beings with respect to the social and institutional environment—a striking omission in view of the increasingly penetrating capability of the mass media to manipulate information and knowledge . . ." (p. 15).

Also, Fred Newmann (1993) believes that the dominant discourse of educational reform is foremost "technical, functional and individualistic" with a task to deliver as many services to students so they may contribute to national productivity and "exercise full choice in personal consumption" (p. 7). He believes that current teacher professionalization discourse emphasizes similar values.

Similarly, discourse on professionalization of teaching emphasizes providing each teacher with continuing technical training, new standards of competence, opportunities to advance to higher status roles within teaching, and the authority for discretion and empowerment in the conduct of one's daily work. This orientation has deep roots in modern Western philosophy, religion, economics, and politics. It has led to designing schools as corporate, rational bureaucracies and conceiving their missions as analogous to shopping malls, restaurants, clinics, or private clubs where the main purpose of the organization is to serve individual, private needs and wants (p. 7).

Newmann (1993) adds that despite the well-intentioned goals for human betterment, "individualistic bureaucracies tend to breed alienation that suppresses learning and creative spirit" while a preoccupation with competitive performance and administrative efficiency "sanctifies function-alism and instrumentalism that undermines an ethic of cooperative care." In effect, these tendencies "weaken both teachers' and students' investment in the constructive use of mind" (p. 8). Newmann (1993), as does Nell Noddings (1992), Michael Apple (1986), and others, reminds us that a community that strives to express care and humanistic values "communicates a vision of human dignity and the public good that transcends the pursuit of individual interest, competence and choice" (Newmann, 1993, p. 8).

The Construction of Teachers' Resistance to Technological Innovations

In terms of the nature of teachers' labor and adoption of technology, Larry Cuban's 1986 seminal work on this topic is still relevant today. Cuban describes the nature of teachers' work in relation to the history of the diffusion of various technologies from radio, film, television to computers. He describes a historical and cyclical pattern of hype and disappointment that arises from three factors—a cultural bias which emphasizes the transformative power of technology, a mistrust of teachers, and the eternal quest to change schools. However, the technology adoption process, historically, may be characterized as "constancy and change" and Cuban specifically questions our cultural bias toward assuming that change is inherently good; just as we assume that all technological innovations are good and necessary. C. A. Bowers (2000) also questions our cultural bias, which associates change with progress. Progress, a root metaphor which exists as a commonsense perception that is rarely critically examined, is also associated with technological innovation. This helps to explain the association between various reform efforts to change education and the diffusion of technological innovation. Bowers (2000) suggests that until, as a culture, we decide what we want to preserve, it is unlikely that we will question technology. Similarly, Cuban also explains that to question whether or not computer technology should be in schools is to raise philosophical questions about the nature of education itself. However, most educators do not think about technology and education in this context.

Cuban's analysis of technology infusion into educational settings foregrounds the practical realm of teachers' work. In doing so, he emphasizes not only instructional and curricular issues, but rather more fundamentally, the moral reality of teaching and the understanding of teaching as an art versus a technical skill. As previously mentioned, Cuban underscores the fact that the essence of teaching is relational knowing, especially the relations between teachers and students, and that the school, ideally, is a community, a place that fosters and nurtures strong social ties. Whereas teachers have been labeled as obstructing technology-based reforms due to fear of the technical, sheer laziness, or lack of imagination, Cuban argues that teachers resist any changes that may impede or mediate, and thus fundamentally alter, the experience of social relations within educational settings. Thus, technology, because of its power to mediate and thus transform the nature and experience of the communication process, is approached with caution, which arises from the realm of teachers' tacit knowledge about children and instruction, what Connelly and Clandidin (1988) describe as teachers' personal practical knowledge.

Also, as explained in the previous chapter, an apolitical artifactual understanding about technology accommodates a simplistic perception about the adoption process. However, Cuban (1986) and Tyack and Tobin (1993) explain that the history of the adoption of technological innovation into educational settings provides evidence that the adoption process is highly contextual and situated. For example, when considering the infusion of new technologies, the existing culture of schools is often seen as something to be eradicated rather than negotiated. This is not a productive approach because the commonsense understandings that our culture holds about what schools "should be" runs so deep that Tyack and Tobin (1993) describe them as the "grammar" of schools, and thus function at a systemic level. Also, innovations are adopted within the contextuality of certain commonplaces, which includes how time and space are defined (i.e., structural elements such as the self-contained classroom). Thus, teachers, positioned to negotiate the reality of structural elements over which they have little control, make "situationally constrained choices," which Cuban (1986) describes as erring on the conservative side. Indeed, teachers' resistances often reflect decisions arising from their tacit and practical experience and not necessarily from a general fear of the technical. Also, teachers may reject the use of a technology as a medium for delivering curriculum because the pedagogical assumptions inherent in the software (i.e., drill and practice) may be incongruent with their personal philosophy about instruction and learning (Christal et al., 1997). In addition, the learning curve for mastering computer-based and information system technologies within the context of teaching is very steep and thus requires much training and time spent working with such technologies over an extended period of time. One national study described teachers' chronic lack of adequate time to complete traditional instructional tasks, much less mastering new instructional technologies, as making teachers literally "prisoners of time" (National Education Commission on Time and Learning, 1994). Teachers often do not have adequate and consistent technical support and training as these are often afterthoughts in most school's technology plans (U.S. Congress, Office of Technology Assessment, 1995). Finally, as mentioned above, teachers are seldom invited into the decision-making process when it comes to setting priorities and initiating policy, including the adoption of materials and technologies they will be expected to use in their classroom (Cuban, 1986, 2001; Tyack & Cuban, 1995).

More recently, Cuban (2001) reiterates that the nature of technology adoption in educational settings is characterized by historical and contextual factors as well as teachers' motivations, which includes the love of children and the relational nature of teaching itself. In terms of broader contextual factors, Cuban perceives that current technocentric reform policy rejects an historic civic idealism and instead emphasizes economic needs and personal gain versus concerns related to the public good. Cuban warns that the lack of emphasis on supporting social capital essential to civic society "underscores the barrenness of the popular rationale for computers in schools" (p. 191). Such barrenness in policy is also reflected in how proponents of technology-based reforms lack respect for teachers' labor and ignore the fact that the essential nature of teaching is a nonrationalizable process. Indeed, like other critics of current reforms, Cuban (2001) cites the need to abandon the technocentric dream that technology will solve our social problems and that access to information via the Internet will automatically (and instantly) make students knowledgeable (p. 188). These false ideals are especially disturbing given the socioeconomic reality of many poor children and the absolute lack of support for teachers and the actual fiscal needs of public schools. Cuban invites educators to ask whether continuing to spend limited funds on technology "will bring us closer to the larger democratic purposes that are at the heart and soul of public schooling in America"? (p. 194). Thus, the underlying question about education and technology is: "Toward what ends?" (p. 193). From Cuban's perspective, "computers have been oversold by promoters and policymakers and undervalued by teachers" (p. 195). However, while the charade continues, Cuban (2001) warns that "to ignore the civic and social roles of education in a democracy will lead to trivialization of our nations core ideals" (p. 197). Even with this dire prediction, he admitted that it was futile to suggest, which he does, a moratorium on infusing K–12 schools with more computer technology as the wisdom behind this recommendation is overdetermined by powerful ideological and economic forces (p. 192).

Given the fact that a technocentic perspective on teaching lacks acknowledgment of its essential relational-based nature, it is not surprising that the resistance of teachers to technological innovations has been characterized in a pejorative sense as a personal, psychological failing. Those who do not choose to use computer technology, for example, are labeled as possessing "computer phobia." Educators who express concerns about possible dehumanization or trivialization of the learning process through the use of electronic technologies are thought to possess "technopathology" (Weston and Ingram, 1997). In addition, within the context of typical top-down diffusion models, problems attributed to resistance to technological innovation are dismissed because "to a large extent, resistance has been reduced to financial and quality issues, rather than philosophical ones" (National Task Force, 1986, p. 59).

Indeed, typical diffusion models and top-down approaches to the management of change easily accommodate the role of the teacher as a mere "delivery system." These elements work together to further the invisibility of teachers' work, a factor epitomized by the creation of "teacher-proof" curriculum materials. To overcome this invisibility, teachers may secure greater legitimacy in the eyes of technical and political elites if they adopt a more overt technically based practice or approach to instruction that supports the stance of the "expert." However the expert, by its very definition, signifies distance and hierarchy, utilizing position and knowledge to establish and maintain their expertise. This stance is oppositional to the traditional role of the teacher as a mentor and nurturer (Tom, 1984). Even so, a cursory review of the signifiers portrayed in computer technology advertisements in educational journals that present the image of the "good teacher," typically feature a female teacher who demonstrates her (pseudo) control over the technology by pushing a button or two. This popular image may offer teachers more esteem in terms of technical expertism, but it is an image largely reflecting corporate ideals and may lead to the loss of the essential nature of teaching itself.

> For if specialization wins for teachers the public regard and economic standing they have historically lacked, it may do so at the risk of falling into the same traps of technological dependency and public apathy that have been associated with expert relations in other fields. Teaching also could come to be seen in a more technical light rather than a field particularly dependent on decisions about the social ends of education (Welker, 1991, p. 8).

Welker (1991) is reiterating what Nunan (1983) predicted in the quote featured in the opening of this chapter. Nunan explains how the field of instructional systems design or instructional technology (IT), a field whose genesis arises from a post–WWII military training paradigm and thus emphasizes a training-based approach to teaching, has greatly influenced education and the role of teachers. For example, the traditional IT's techno-rationalist orientation to teaching artificially separates development of curriculum from the teaching experience and thus deskills teachers by constructing their role in a reductionary and apolitical manner as mere "delivery systems"—which could just as easily be a computer or video-based system of content delivery. Therefore, as explained in the previous chapter, the emphasis, in terms of the act of teaching, is not on communication as ritual and the experience of social relations, but rather as transmission or transportation of mere information (Carey, 1989). In addition, the other quotation featured at the beginning of this chapter by Robert Heinich (1984) epitomizes the logical outcome of such a technicist framework, although not all practitioners of IT share such sentiments. Heinich's utilitarian perspective on teaching is insidious on two levels: (1) the complacent attitude toward replacing humans with machines, and (2) the will to commodify teachers' craft to ultimately digitize their knowledge and experience in order to reanimate it in the form of artificial intelligence-based expert systems (i.e., Intelligent Tutoring Systems). Such utilitarian-inspired efforts epitomize Jacques Ellul's notion of *technique*, which as mentioned in the previous chapter, describes an approach to reification of social processes toward the end of ultimate efficiency. Indeed, whenever *technique* exists as commonsense, control over social processes arise, as in the case of teachers' roles, which then become both redundant and simulated, indicating a hidden absence of the real. Therefore, the outcome of Heinich's (1984) vision surpasses the 19th century expression of technology as automation and rather embodies a 21st century postmodern expression of simulacra.

The Meaning of Teachers' Resistance

Although not typically acknowledged as a part of a teacher's role, the teacher as gatekeeper holds a privileged position as one who has the power to resist current reform policies. Specifically, a teacher's agency may be characterized as a form of trusteeship (Sergiovanni, 1994), in terms of citizens serving the public interest (Reid, 1979), or as citizens acting as "public intellectuals" (Aronowitz & Giroux, 1991, p. 108) as well as that of initiators of social change (Greene, 1986; Bowers, 1988; Hargraves, 1994;

Nunan, 1983). However, Apple (1995) asks "not whether such resistances exist . . . but whether they are contradictory themselves, whether they lead anywhere beyond the reproduction of the ideological hegemony of the most powerful class in our society, whether they can be employed for political education and intervention" (Apple, 1995, p. 146). Apple's (1996) ideal of "contradicting resistance" is associated with his notion of "non reformist reforms," where educators are understood to "transform the practices of schools and defend democratic practices from economic logic—such reforms are self-consciously linked to a larger social vision and social movement" (p. 109).

Thus, certain critics of the dominant reform discourse provide descriptions of teachers' roles, which underscore the potential of "contradictory resistance" and assume that teachers can therefore exercise a critical stance toward current functionalist and technocentric reform policies. For example, Andy Hargraves (1994), who understands that the traditions of education are being threatened by particular elements of postmodernity, believes that teachers are challenged to "engage effectively with the images and technologies of the postmodern world" while also maintaining "the cultural analysis, moral judgment and studied reflection they threaten to supersede. Teachers must be both competent users and innovators with technology and moral guardians against its most trivializing effects" (p. 76). Hargraves' (1994) conceptualization of teachers' roles, however, requires a critical awareness in relation to power, media and technology. It also assumes that our commonsense understanding about technology embraces a dialectic perspective, when in reality, as discussed previously, the bias is to construct it in a singular, uncontested fashion as a neutral artifact.

In addition, C. A. Bowers (1988, 1995), who has written extensively on problems related to technology-driven reforms, envisions teachers embracing not only a critical stance toward the current technology-based reform effort, but also to adopt an ecologically based political framework. Bowers (1988) argues that our drive to infuse schools with technology as the solution to education's problems blinds us from the real issues facing schools and that teachers are obliged to awaken from this illusion and reclaim their responsibility as educators.

> Until teachers reclaim their moral and intellectual responsibilities to students, and educational computing experts recognize that the nontechnical educational issues are the primary ones yet to be addressed, it is likely that educational use of computers will be driven by the forces of the marketplace and by the cultural myths that put out of focus what we are doing to ourselves and our environment (1988, p. 115).

However, the privileged position given to teachers' agency and their capacity to engage in "contradictory resistance," may seem naive, especially since teachers do not stand outside their own culture's bias about technology and many generally perceive that they have very little power within the educational institution. Indeed, the question arises if whether or not teachers can be further empowered (or indeed emancipated), and in turn empower their students, through these new technologies if they do not possess a critical perspective regarding technology in general. Opposition and resistance becomes moot if teachers perceive that electronic technology is a mere tool and therefore unquestionably accept the policy of rapid infusion as not only necessary but "inevitable" to meet the needs of the Information Age.

Even so, Hargraves (1994), Bowers (1988), and others envision teachers uncoupling themselves from commonsense socioeconomic assumptions. This act, nevertheless, requires a great amount of critical awareness, a sense of agency to exercise one's social imagination and a level of civic engagement to which teachers are generally not called to nor actively encouraged to address. Even so, not to engage a critical stance, according to Maxine Greene (1995), precipitates an inability to conceive an alternative order of things, which can give rise to "a resignation that paralyzes people [and that] an accompanying ebbing of the sense of personal and communal efficacy may submerge people in the given, in what appears impervious to protest and discontent" (p. 19). It may be that because of the axiomatic assumptions our culture generally holds about technology's relation to material and social progress that even educators are unable to critically imagine how these technologies may influence the lifeworld of schools, at least not beyond the visions offered by technical-utopian rhetoric.

However, teachers are not *wholly* without independence and do possess the ability to practice rational decision-making (Reid, 1979). The history of the diffusion of technology is a testimony to the power of teacher's resistance and to the fundamental role that teachers' practical and tacit knowledge play in their decisions about adopting new instructional techniques and technologies (Cuban, 1986, 1996). Indeed J. J. Schwab's (1983) and Cuban's (1986, 2001) work, specifically in terms of technology adoption, indicate that teachers' decision-making resides within the realm of "the practical" meaning that all innovations must meet the criteria of serving the necessary institutional goals and instructional outcomes established for teachers by society-at-large and their school's administration. In addition, there are inherent moral conflicts within the context of educational reform endeavors (Hargraves, 1997). Teachers often struggle to negotiate the power of official knowledge dictated by policy elites and school administrators with their own moral reasoning and tacit and situated experiential knowledge (Clandinin & Connelly, 1995). Also, it would not be surprising for teachers' attitudes to reflect the conservative culture and values of K–12 education which in turn reflects the common sense of the community (e.g., computers equate only to progress).

Therefore, teachers' relative power of resistance against structural elements and the force of official policy may be characterized as resigned acquiescence or covert rejection and withdrawal. As noted earlier, within the context of performance-based culture, even when teachers participate in decision-making, the process may be structured by an administrative framework, which does not guarantee establishment of an authentic forum for teachers' input and agency. Therefore, although teachers' power of resistance certainly exists, it could be understood that it is generally without voice. Without articulation of voice, a position of resistance remains oppositional but does not yet have the power of transformation or praxis. This is what Apple (1996) means by resistance having a "contradictory" function, leading beyond the hegemony of the dominant power structure. Without a place to stand, without a voice, teachers' resistance may arrest the successful implementation of technocentric-based policies. Even so, by its very nature, teachers' work is immersed in the invisible world of tacit knowledge and therefore continues to become more invisible within the context of a functionalist-based political and institutional framework. This condition is demonstrated by policies that emphasize control through standards and accountability. Thus, teachers' work becomes subjected to increased processes of monitoring and performance-based standards, which further inscribes the rationale of instrumental rationalism as the framework that guides reform efforts (Hargraves, 1994).

Thus, Greene (1986/1996) reminds us that if educators and especially teachers are to become what John Dewey (1954, p. 184) described as an "articulate public," they need to break out of the given reform tautology and envision other possibilities—possible visions that enjoin the purpose of education with traditional utopian-based goals and democratic principles. Greene (1986/1996) acknowledges the difficulty in generating an alternative vision to that which is offered by current reform discourse. But even so, she finds the silences deeply troubling, signifying a loss of imaginative thinking as a possibility.

> What troubles me is the lack of concern I feel around me, the routines and automations that have replaced the investment in possibility. What troubles me as much is the neglect of freedom in its active sense, the freedom linked to an awareness of the unpredictable, the possible (p. 423).

Therefore, teachers' resistance within the context of current educational reform creates a space of ambivalence within which teachers' power and agency is negotiated. On the one hand, teachers, positioned by political and structural factors, are left with silence and acquiescence. On the other hand, because such factors grate against their moral foundation and pedagogical beliefs, they engage in practices of resistance. Thus, teachers are caught between the two major philosophical frameworks driving educational reform policy. Indeed, the aim of the study, a comparison between the discourse of policy elites and their critics and that of the situated and contextual perceptions of teachers, inadvertently creates a contrast between the abstract realm of the political/theoretical and that of the teachers' experiential and personal realm of knowing. The research of educational theorists Clandinin and Connelly (1988, 1995) was helpful in delineating this dialectic and is discussed in the following section.

Understanding the Work of Teachers Within Performance Culture

In their earlier work on teachers' relational and autobiographical knowledge, Connelly and Clandinin (1988) focused on individual teacher's "personal practical knowledge." In their more recent work, Clandinin and Connelly (1995) compared the personal, moral realm of teachers' personal practical knowledge to that of a broader context of influence which they labeled as teachers' collective "professional knowledge landscape." The realm of teachers' personal practical knowledge, according to Clandinin and Connelly (1995), is anchored by teachers' experiences with students within the safe and private space of the classroom. A teacher's personal practical knowledge is expressed in the language of story as it reflects how teachers come to know themselves as "intimate social and traditional" storied individuals through their experiences with students. Clandinin and Connelly (1995) explain that personal practical knowledge "is a kind of knowledge that has arisen from circumstances, practices, and undergoings that themselves had affective content for the person in question" (p. 7). Because it is based on relational knowing, teachers' personal practical knowledge is inherently moral in character.

In contrast, teachers' professional knowledge landscape exists within the realm of the public and thus is subject to review. It is not characterized by a language of personal story, but rather a "landscape of abstractions" dominated by theoretical knowledge that has collapsed into "codified outcomes of inquiry" or what J. J. Schwab (1962) refers to as a "rhetoric of conclusions" (Clandinin & Connelly, 1995). This "rhetoric of conclusions," according to Clandinin and Connelly (1995), is then packaged for teachers as textbooks, curriculum materials, and professional development workshops (p. 9). Standing as official reform policy such knowledge claims become "stripped of a public deliberative process that gives rise to them" (p. 8). Thus, the professional knowledge landscape of teachers is "embedded in a sacred story," meaning that the policies and curriculum reforms are delivered to teachers through a "funnel or conduit" and configured as a "rhetoric of conclusions" and thus are seldom questioned. Therefore, such rhetoric is neither theoretical or practical, "rather the material and language are abstract. Abstract diagrams, assessment plans, . . . policy prescriptions, and so forth, fill the landscape" (Clandinin & Connelly, 1995). In this sense, they are not grounded in practical knowledge. "There are few, if any, links between the abstract statements of policy and research coming from the conduit and the phenomenological world to which they refer" (p. 10). Moreover, because the rhetoric of conclusions is uncoupled from their narrative contexts, it exists as a received and prescriptive "conduit of shoulds" (Clandinin & Connelly, 1995, p. 11).

Indeed, Clandinin and Connelly (1995) believe this prescriptive element reflects how an "entry point for debate and discussion of the funneled materials" does not exist. Teachers, therefore, "are screened from the subjectivity of human agency that gave rise to the material in inquiry and in policy deliberation while being taught that their own agency with regard to the decontextualized and denarrativized material would amount to incompetence or disobedience" (p. 11). Because the abstract rhetoric of conclusions is characterized by conflicting moral admonitions, a factor also noted by Hargraves (1994, 1995), administrators and policymakers "often find it necessary to formulate vision statements in attempts to give moral shape to the professional knowledge landscape" (Clandinin & Connelly, 1995, p. 11). Although these offer a degree of moral unity, they are often prescriptive and not negotiated and thus furthers a performance-based culture within schools.

Clandinin and Connelly's (1995) framework of teachers' professional knowledge landscape and personal practical knowledge is helpful on two levels. Firstly, their understanding of teachers' personal, practical knowledge reflects my effort to address how teachers experience educational reform within the context of their school. Specifically, their work helps to situate how, and to what degree, the dominate discourse of official reform policy as part of teachers' professional knowledge landscape influenced an informants' personal practical knowledge. Clandinin and Connelly's framework, therefore, provides a dialectic between the realm of the practical and that of policy discourse.

Secondly, Clandinin and Connelly's (1995) understanding of the construction of teachers' professional knowledge landscape parallels certain perceptions offered by those who criticize the dominate discourse of reform policy. For example, their reference to Schwab's notion of "rhetoric of conclusions" as a means to characterize the content of the professional knowledge landscape and metaphors such as "conduit" and "funnel" to characterize the means through which such knowledge is communicated to teachers, and Clandinin and Connelly's reference to the lack of conversation and deliberation, reflects the concerns of those who criticize the current reform effort as being built upon certain "inevitabilities" and whose discourse constructs a particular singular technocentric vision of education.

Regarding this broader context of teachers' perceptions (i.e., professional knowledge landscapes), Clandinin and Connelly's (1995) research indicates how this landscape has fundamentally changed over the years. For example, they refer to teachers' sense of a "multiplicity of competing moral positions that reflect the modern complex of forces that influence the professional knowledge landscape," which ultimately shapes teachers professional and personal lives (p. 32). This study expands what Clandinin and Connelly (1995) refer to as teachers' "knowledge context," by examining how teachers interpret current reform discourse that reflects the "modern complex of forces," especially regarding the sociocultural narratives driving current educational reform policy.

In addition, Clandinin and Connelly's (1995) findings indicted that part of the complexity of teachers' work arises from the fact that their "crossing back and forth between the two parts of the professional knowledge landscape [the rhetoric of conclusions and their narrative knowing] creates epistemological and moral dilemmas for teachers" (p. 14). Teachers accommodate this "boundary crossing" through creating "cover stories," or speaking "the language of the conduit," or of plans, results, and policy implications (p. 14). However, this "language of the conduit" does not allow teachers to express what is of most importance to them—the stories of children and classroom events. The process of teachers negotiating between the two spheres—the rhetoric of conclusions and their narrative-based knowing—was evidenced in my interviews with teachers.

Finally, Clandinin and Connelly (1995) also acknowledge the importance of which context plays in terms of understanding schools as communities. They indicate that schools possess "a kind of organic integrity" that arises from a collective life history (p. 28). This study sought to underscore the importance of context and the understanding of schools as communities by reporting the data in the form of a narrative, specifically the stories of two individual case study sites. Thus, the situated position of each informant, their individual stories about their work, and their school's reform program is further contextualized within the life history of the school as a whole. Indeed, in the next two chapters, we shall examine the narratives of Shelton Valley Middle School and Zepeda Elementary.

Note

[1] Some specific programs developed by the Department of Education which addresses the need to support teacher training in technology and professional development in terms of technology integration are as follows: (1) *Preparing Tomorrow's Teachers to Use Technology* (1999); *Technology Literacy Challenge Fund* (1996); *Regional Technology in Education Consortia (RTEC)* (1995), and *Technology Innovation Challenge Grant Program* (1995).

CHAPTER FOUR

The Story of Shelton Valley Middle School

We will be connected and we'll have more computers but I think we are going to be about where we are now with the kids.
Roger, Shelton Valley Middle School teacher

In the future, education will be totally different. You can have interaction through teleconferencing and you'll have some personnel on duty, but it won't be to the extent that we have personnel now—teachers.
Mary Jane, Shelton Valley Middle School librarian

Shelton Valley serves approximately 780 middle school students, grades seventh and eighth, and resides within a rural setting of central Texas surrounded by large ranches. Shelton Valley's district is one of the largest in the state and covers over 500 square miles. Looking out over the school's athletic field, for example, one's gaze meets a panoramic vista overlooking a beautiful countryside of rolling green hills. The setting is very peaceful and serene.

Throughout its history the school has served rural, white students from low to medium income families. However, Shelton Valley's rural setting and heritage was being transformed by a rapid increase in population and economic growth throughout the district. Wealthy suburbanites, fleeing the problems of surrounding large urban areas, had moved into the school district upsetting the traditional local community. This situation coincided with an increase in discipline problems, a higher ratio of students to teachers and general overcrowding in classrooms. Several teachers expressed concern about certain issues, such as the shift in the homogeneous social economic status (SES) of the school's culture, concern about student behavior and discipline problems, and the general qualitative changes that the current rate of growth engendered in their community—many of which were seen as a direct consequence of the influx of wealthy "city people" whom they perceived to have different values and standards of ethics.

The influx of more students had also exacerbated the district's chronic fiscal problems. As one of the largest districts in the state, it is both sparsely populated and has relatively low land value. Despite these factors, the district, based on its extensive area, was reassigned to qualify for the same tax base categorization as some of the wealthiest of school districts in the state. The principal, David, noted that "although the district almost covers 600 square miles, they [state officials] don't seem to understand that all that's out here on this land is a few dusty cows and some old mobile homes."

Also, the district's technology coordinator reported that, although once on the "cutting edge of technology," the district's reclassification of Shelton Valley as a "wealthy" school disallowed its qualification for many state and federal technology grants. In addition, although growth had caused a rise in property taxes and thus could alleviate some of the district's financial strain, certain local taxpayers filed a suit against the school district in which they contested an $18 million bond issue for building permanent high school and middle school classroom additions. David was dismayed by the lack of support demonstrated by certain local citizens and was also concerned about how this suit might impede the district's ability to acquire funding for building a state-supported fiber-optic Wide Area Network (WAN) system that required district-based matching funds.

Changes to Curriculum and Instruction

According to David, the school had changed its administrative policies to accommodate site-based management. He mentioned how the development of interdisciplinary teams was at the center of their reform effort. Each team had a core of five teachers and approximately 130 students. The teams operated as a school within a school to support teacher collaboration and more effective and personalized education for students. The teams consisted of teachers from science, math, history, English and reading. Team members collaborated in the development of thematic-based curriculum.

David explained how the school's mission statement was based on eight educational principles adopted from the Carnegie Council on Adolescent Development. A school brochure describes schools as "small communities for learning," that "empower teachers and administrators to make decisions," and "strive to re-engage families in the education of young adolescents by giving families meaningful roles in school governance." In addition, the principal was very committed to cooperative learning and, according to many of the teachers, insisted that all teachers incorporate it into their instructional practices.

Most of the teachers expressed positive comments about the teaming structure because the opportunity to work collaboratively helped to establish collegiality as well as a consistency in expectation and standards among teachers for their group of students. However, the notion of cooperative learning, for many, seemed to be equated to simply rearranging the desks into clusters or groups. Many expressed frustration about the principal's insistence on its usage and the numerous in-service training programs on cooperative learning. Also, little evidence indicated that parents were given "meaningful roles in school governance" as promised in the official school documents. In addition, many teachers thought that site-based management decision-making, as discussed later, was in actuality an empty gesture.

The Uses of Electronic-Based Instructional Technology

To the observer, Shelton Valley appears very organized, tidy and clean. The classrooms have only a few posters on the walls and the desks are arranged in rows. There are no computers in the regular classrooms. However, the special education classrooms have a few computers that are used primarily for drill and practice programs. The school has two classrooms dedicated to the instruction of computer literacy and computer programming. There is also one computer lab that was designed to accommodate an Integrated Learning System (ILS), specifically one developed by the Jostens Corporation. An ILS provides all aspects of instruction, remediation, and assessment. The drill and practice instructional approach embodies a behaviorist understanding of learning theory and is designed as a form of basic skills remediation. It carefully tracks the progress of students and provides performance feedback to teachers. However, ILS as a particular application of computer technology is questionable because it can severely delimit the learning experience of students because it frames instruction within predetermined, discrete learning objectives and matching criterion referenced testing. This narrow application of computer-based instruction has been criticized, considering current aims to introduce constructivist and social constructivist learning theory into practice (Duffy & Jonassen, 1992). Also, such applications are often targeted to disadvantaged, low-performing students. Although Shelton Valley had been using the Jostens ILS system for remediation in math and reading for both general education and special education students for approximately seven years, the principal had recently decided to discontinue its use and planned to invest in another vendor's ILS.

The library, a relatively small facility, offered students access to computers for word processing, games, and CD-ROM research sources. The librarian had just completed the task of automating the library's inventory and was in the process of gathering information about expanding the library's Local Area Network (LAN) to incorporate the school's two computer literacy labs. This endeavor, however, proved to be a technically difficult task, and caused much divisiveness between the librarian, the principal, and the two computer literacy teachers. Many conflicts surrounded the process of technology adoption at Shelton Valley and thus compose the central narrative plot of Shelton Valley's story. This story is discussed in the following section.

Negotiating Technology Adoption: A Missed Opportunity

Shelton Valley, in conjunction with the district, developed a technology plan for building a LAN and a WAN telecommunications infrastructure. Shelton Valley's librarian, Mary Jane, was also a member of the district long-range technology planning committee, a consortium of teachers from the district's schools, administrators from the central office, including the district technology coordinator, parents and members of local businesses as well as technology consultants. Mary Jane explained that the district's Technology Plan outlined specific technology diffusion goals for the next several years and would cost the district an estimated $8 million.

The plan, according to Mary Jane, was based on extensive site visits to schools in other districts. Its main objectives were: (1) build a telecommunications and network infrastructure (LANs and WANs), (2) setup a computer lab for every 300 students on the campus level, (3) build teacher's stations where each teacher would have a computer, CD-ROM, and telecommunications access, and (4) implement a curriculum in which computer skills, including the use of the Internet, would not be taught as a separate computer literacy course, but rather integrated throughout the curriculum. Presently, students were required to take a one-semester computer literacy course in sixth or seventh grade. Shelton Valley had two instructors who taught such courses.

Other goals listed in the district's technology plan's vision statement referred to students engaging in "collaborative and interactive learning" as well as both students and teachers successfully participating in the "electronic exchange of global information" while preparing all students for participation as responsible citizens in a "democratic, technological society." Indeed, in the stated rationale for their plan, the authors note how the world has radically changed because it is "already information oriented and is increasing in geometric leaps." Indeed, reference was made to the pragmatic needs of corporations in that "global pressures put a premium on American industry" and how schools must change to meet corporate human resource needs specifically via the use of electronic technologies. This stance clearly reflects the dominant educational reform perspective.

The technocentric reform rationale envisioned in the district's technology plan was also supported by both district-based teacher and parent surveys conducted by the district technology committee. Parents envisioned that the primary application address their children's need to acquire computer literacy skills, for college and a competitive job market. However, parents' greatest concern regarded students gaining access to inappropriate materials on the Internet and that the expanded use of computers would not be used as a substitute for learning traditional academic skills. In addition, parents reported their children's home computer usage was dominated by playing games or for entertainment purposes versus school work. In some of the written responses parents indicated the inevitability of computer infusion into schools and elsewhere such that everyone's life "will revolve around computers."

With only a few exceptions, the teacher informants at Shelton Valley adopted the assumption that the diffusion of electronic technologies into schools was "inevitable" given the fact that electronic technologies seem to be a part of our everyday lives and are integral to the business environment. For example, Cheryl, an eighth-grade English teacher, stated that computer technology is the "tool of the 21st century. . . . It's the single most important purchase we've made for the education of our children." Some of the teachers and the principal believed that access to the Internet was essential to students attending rural schools such as Shelton Valley because it offered a means to expose isolated children to the world (although most did not distinguish it as a virtual experience). David stated that access to information was a matter of equity: "My dream is no matter how humble the circumstances children come from, when they come to school, they can access the world."

However, despite the perception that access to information would level the playing field, the school's struggle to negotiate the technical complexity of their endeavor to integrate telecommunications and computer technology into their campus was further stymied, ironically, by a lack of communication and consequent factionalism, a divisiveness that appeared to be rooted in fundamental differences regarding pedagogy. One example is related to the endeavor of hiring an outside consulting firm to direct the development and implementation of a district WAN telecommunications infrastructure and is examined later in this section. Another example is the confusion that arose surrounding the fate of the school's Jostens ILS lab. During the timeframe in which the interviews were conducted, the principal had decided not to use the existing Jostens ILS and was "shopping around" for another vendor. Perhaps because of the confusion surrounding the decommissioned ILS and its relationship to the building of a LAN at the school, he referred me to the librarian to answer any further questions about the issue. The following section examines the confusion surrounding the ILS and a related issue, the implementation of the school's LAN system.

Jostens' ILS and the Building of a LAN System

Roger, who taught seventh grade computer literacy, questioned the school's technology program. Some of the teachers who were interviewed related general confusion and, in a few cases, cynicism about the management of the school's "technology problems," but only Roger had direct experience that substantiated his claims of what could be described as mismanagement. Roger was not one of the teachers selected by the principal to participate in the study. However, because his name was mentioned by many of the informants—he was described as a "former coordinator" of the school's technology committee—I felt it was important to offer him the opportunity to share his side of the story.

Although many of the informants at Shelton Valley expressed some level of critical awareness about the pros and cons of diffusing electronic technology into educational settings, Roger actively sought to move the process of planning the uses of technology from one of infusion (a top-down orientation) to that of diffusion, where adoption arises primarily from pedagogy and curricular-based considerations. For example, Roger explained that a lack of planning and understanding about how electronic technologies are to be integrated into a curriculum plan often leads schools down the wrong path. He cited Shelton Valley's decision to continue using an ILS as a case-in-point.

> Just having a little bit of money, lack of any kind of visionary leadership, things kind of get frittered away on inconsequential expenditures—Jostens lab is a case-in-point. Jostens and others like them are pretty much slammed in the literature that I've read. Drill and practice; it seems that everything I read says that it is *not* the way to use this technology. It is a use. It has *some* applications, but it is certainly not anything that will produce long-term results. It is *not* going to foster in-depth learning. It's just electronic flash cards. We could use cardboard paper and tape for that. We don't need electronics for it.

Roger's position raised issues related to pedagogy and learning theory, questions that few other teachers directly addressed with regard to the use of an ILS or any other technology-based instructional application. Despite the fact that Shelton Valley's technology decisions did not associate the selection of particular computer applications to curriculum decisions, the forty percent of students classified as "at risk" (based on a combination of students classified as low SES and underachieving) served as the rationale for investing in an ILS. Not only is the decision to use an ILS popular in schools that serve poor and low-performing student populations, the sale of such systems is often linked to improving standardized test scores. For example, the ILS that was under consideration to replace Jostens was specially designed to teach the state's curriculum essential elements and was tailored to support student's performance on the state's mandatory standardized tests (TAAS).

Mary Jane, the librarian, made the decision to discontinue the use of the Jostens system based on pragmatic reasons—the system was designed for a DOS-based platform such as IBM and the school's lab had Macintosh computers and thus the system was very slow and ultimately this factor impeded its instructional aims. Mary Jane explained the situation as follows.

> It turned out to not be a really good situation. The kids got to the point where—'oh, do we have to go to the lab?' They were really impressed with it at first and then they got where they weren't. It was not really the material, it was just the networking set–up that we had just hindered it so much that it sort of defeated its purpose.

To address this situation the school had originally decided to invest precious funds to change the system's AppleTalk networking to Ethernet cabling in an attempt to improve the system's processing speed. Because they had "seen other systems that seemed better," Mary Jane reported that, "at this point the principal intends to go with IBM or Plato, or we're going to look at some other system." Therefore, all of the money invested in upgrading the Jostens system was wasted. She added that special education and "at-risk" students were to be the likely users.

Despite the fact that Mary Jane did not question the pedagogical validity of an ILS or how its usage was directly reinforcing the tracking of students, she did recognize how its design may be a "turnoff" for teachers because it is designed to stand alone and does not require the involvement of the teacher either as an instructor or as a curriculum developer. Mary Jane compared the use of ILS to surfing the Internet. In the latter, a teacher has several options in terms of the direction one's interest may evolve, whereas with an ILS, "you don't have options when you are working on a program and basically the kids don't need a teacher once they get into it. They just do what the program tells them to do."

Satie, a seventh-grade social studies teacher with 34 years of teaching experience, had extensive experience with the use of Jostens in her instruction and was also directly involved with the initial selection of the Jostens system for Shelton Valley and the district. Her recollection of Shelton Valley's and the district's adoption of the Jostens system indicated that an ILS would meet the educational needs of students and that the behaviorist–based pedagogy of the system sufficiently matched the instructional approaches of the district's educators. Satie expressed that the Jostens system was "very well set-up and well run" and "was very good for certain students who were low level readers, but was a total waste of time for students who were on or above grade level." She admitted, however, that even low level students "eventually grew bored with the system." But she felt that the student's boredom did not arise solely from repetition of exposure or the repetition of the drill and practice format, but rather, the students' age, "their learning disabilities, their inability to concentrate on any one thing for a very long time. They need a lot of different kinds of teaching methods to be used rather than just the computer." This response was puzzling, for if such students need variety in their instruction, why invest in an expensive instructional system for them which offers only a static form of instruction (i.e., drill and practice)?

The lack of critical understanding expressed by the teachers about the pedagogical issues surrounding ILS simply may arise from a less informed position about the technology itself. For example, Satie was not aware that the system's slow response rate was inappropriate, and stated that "I didn't realize that it was not supposed to be slow." Satie also admitted how using the Jostens system allowed teachers to group and track the performance of students, stating, "Well, we did and that's what it was. But they are no longer using it." Despite the technical flaws and the negative reactions of many students, Satie did not express a critical understanding or interpretation of the uses of the ILS. In fact, when asked if she had any misgivings about bringing electronic technology into education, she replied, "at this point I do not have any misgivings about it. All that I have seen, the way that technology has been used in middle schools, has been beneficial." It may be that her lack of technical knowledge about computers, in addition to her being one of the teachers to have selected the Jostens system, framed her perspective about using an ILS to the extent that she was unable to assume a critical position. Satie clearly supported the decision to use an ILS and believed that problems arose from the fact that some teachers failed to understand the needs of students with learning disabilities. As pointed out earlier, the fact that the instructional design of an ILS may exacerbate their learning disabilities (i.e., the need for variety in instructional strategies) was not addressed.

The special education teacher, Susan, believed that the failure of the Jostens ILS system arose from too much frequency in scheduling where the repetition of exposure led students to "reach a state of burnout from being on the computer all the time." Susan also found that the student performance feedback provided by the system ironically indicated that the students were not actually reading the materials but rather simply guessing. She seemed confused as to whether or not the reaction of the students was caused by the frequency of exposure or perhaps the design of the system itself. "I think that it would have been more effective if we had it once a week or maybe Monday and Friday but back-to-back was not good. . . . Or maybe it was just the nature of the program." She also explained that the program was text-based and that today, students need variation in the modality of their instruction, which may include alternatives to text. "I hate to say it but kids nowadays are so bored so quickly and trying to keep them motivated is the biggest challenge we have. They have been on that program the whole previous year. Who knows, maybe they were just tired of that drill and practice set-up." Susan had also observed that children tend to relate the use of computers to playing games, indicating that their expectations may have negatively affected their willingness to interact with any ILS. "I don't know if there is any truth to it or not but kids are hooked on TV and Nintendo which has so much movement so that when they sit down to the computer they want to play a computer game."

Susan, who has very little experience with using computers, did not mention the slowness of the system as being a problem. None of the other teachers discussed the use of the ILS system, either because of the subject matter they taught (it was used only for remedial instruction in math and reading) or they were new to the school. However, although Roger had never used the system, he was the only teacher interviewed at Shelton Valley who expressed a critical perspective about its use on the grounds that the learning theory and pedagogy the system embodied was inappropriate and thus investing in such a system countered the progressive reform efforts of the district.

The principal, who had decided to invest in another ILS, did not directly discuss his decision during our interviews. Rather, he referred me to the librarian. David did, however, offer some insight into his perception about computer-based instruction (CBI) and his understanding of sound pedagogy. He described how the typical use of computers by students as being superficial—"electronically shuffling information around with their fingertips"—a "very passive" process. He believed it was this very reason that made working with computers attractive to children. "That's one of the reasons that I think kids love to sit down and play with computers. You aren't required to really learn all of that [about algorithms or the internal logic of computer software] but you can be a whiz and manipulate it all around and move it around and play with the bells, baubles and flash." David concluded that this is not a reflection on a student's lack of intelligence but rather, "I think the temptation is not to delve below that level of passivity. It's there every time you turn on the keyboard." David did not, however, relate his perceptions to questioning the pedagogical validity of maintaining an ILS at Shelton Valley. Nor did his perceptions guide his decisions about Shelton Valley's or the district's policy development in terms of the adoption of electronic technologies.

David's decision not to use the Jostens lab left its hardware facilities in limbo. There seemed to be several stories as to the fate of the lab. Some teachers heard that the lab's computers were going to be dispersed throughout the school. Others reported that the majority of the computers were to be given to the special education teachers. Because the Jostens lab was not running, Susan reported they had no form of remedial training for the special education students. Susan also mentioned how decisions about the uses and allocation of technology seemed arbitrary at best.

> Here's a true confession: We never know. In fact we did not understand why the program [Jostens ILS] was not up and running this year. Then we got a memo that there was not going to be access to any computers, and that's kind of where we are. Then somebody came down, some computer technician, to our department and said that we are going to be getting about four of these computers and where do you want to put them? That was the first we heard that we are going to be hooked-up to anything new or old or different or anything. . . . We are still trying to figure out why we are getting them and academic teachers are not getting them and are concerned about some hard feelings. We certainly don't know where to put them.

Other teachers expressed confusion about the fate of the Jostens lab. Lisa, an eighth-grade science teacher who had been teaching science at Shelton Valley for two years, explained how the resolution of the computer lab issue had taken several twists and turns.

> That's been a big problem [the Jostens lab]. . . . You know that a lot of money was invested in it and we are kind of in the process of trying to get that brought back up to par and the networking done so that those things will be available to us again and maybe a little bit better software system. A lot of money was spent on things last year that just didn't pan out. So we are in a real state of flux right now with that and trying to figure out exactly [what to do]. . . . the last thing I heard—this is not official, I kind of got it from another team leader—is that we were *probably* going to go ahead and continue with what we have and open the computer lab back up.

Although Lisa felt that her science classes would be greatly enhanced through the use of computers, she pointed out how with a school the size of Shelton Valley with only one lab, the likelihood of her students having weekly access was not very high. Lisa preferred having computers in each classroom versus having students visit a separate room or computer lab. As a member of the district planning committee to design a new middle school, Lisa pointed out how the distribution of computers within and between districts was not equitable. She also believed that the key element to successfully incorporating computer technology into a learning environment is planning.

> One of the things we did at my previous school is when our test scores went up we got a grant from the state for campus improvement of $12 thousand and we spent it all on campus networking. So a lot of it is just how you plan and what you truly want in your school. I think that has been the problem here in the past—no one has truly pushed the issue.

The lack of communication and deliberation about technology-based decisions was epitomized by a statement made by Cheryl, an eighth-grade English teacher. Although she had experience with using computers in her instruction and had written technology grants for the school where she had previously taught, she seemed to lack basic information about the schools' technology-related activities and decisions.

> This school is not as advanced technologically as it should be or as I would like it to be. And that was something I would like to work toward. So to my knowledge we do not have a technology committee, at least we do not have an active one. I wish we did. I think we just need some more leadership in that area.

Cheryl's comment is interesting given the fact that Shelton Valley did have an active technology committee, but it was severely weakened by factionalism. Satie explained that Shelton Valley had a technology committee but admitted that "I'm not aware of who are members. I was [a member] for several years but not for the last couple of years and I don't know who the chairman is right now." Satie suggested that the librarian, Mary Jane, would know more about the school's technology plans and the technology committee. Because of her past experience with acquiring the automated library cataloging system, Mary Jane emerged as the most technologically knowledgeable person at the school. However, according to Mary Jane, it was not only her past technological expertise, but also apathy on the part of the teachers that brought her to the position of being a leader and decision-maker in terms of the school's technology planning. Mary Jane explained that although she likes computers, "we got a lot of teachers who don't ever want to get on a computer at all. They're just totally opposed to it." She was unaware of other teachers who wanted to get involved and decided that if the entire school was networked and computerized "the teachers would be forced to use it, just by doing attendance and recording grades on the computer." She realized that the closing of the Jostens lab left some teachers angry and disillusioned but this was a necessary sacrifice "in order to get where they want to next year." In the meantime, students could use the computers in the library for word processing.

The projected technology plan developed by Mary Jane and the principal was to have a LAN configuration that would also include a computer with a CD-ROM, modem and television satellite capabilities and a printer for each teacher. The classroom computers would be networked to the library data bases. In addition, the two computer labs dedicated to teaching computer literacy courses would also be networked to the library. These two computer literacy labs would become the school's open computer labs. In fact, the teaching of computer literacy would be eliminated. Instead, the uses of computer and telecommunications technologies would be integrated across the curriculum and not be taught as a separate subject. Naturally, according to Mary Jane, the computer technology teachers in particular were resistant to this plan.

Mary Jane believed that "technology-based teaching" was necessary to assuage the boredom of students—"we're having a lot of problems in education and that's because kids are bored." Essentializing technology as an instant motivator was equally matched by Mary Jane's emphasis on access to information as the basis of education itself.

> The gist of it in a nutshell, its just like where you read everywhere, that our knowledge base is expanding so rapidly that there is no way that students can learn even a minute portion of the information that is available and I think we will go into a total idea of learning access rather than learning knowledge. So if you can put your fingertips on it that's all you need.

Mary Jane's philosophy of learning, in that it involves "learning access rather than learning knowledge" was unique within the context of Shelton Valley, for no other participant placed so much emphasis on access to information as a framework for learning and instruction. In fact, she admitted seeing education as "being totally different" than it now exists, and predicted that "you can have interaction through teleconferencing and you'll have some personnel on duty, but it won't be to the extent that we have personnel now—teachers." Mary Jane's perspective on the reform of education was fundamentally technocentric for she not only equated the instructional process to a mere delivery system but also seemed comfortable with the idea of using distance education and telecommunications as a means to replace and/or reduce the number of teachers. She did, however, concede that elementary students required the nurturing of an actual teacher.

Mary Jane's uncritical acceptance of technology-based reform was sharply contrasted by one of the computer technology teachers, Roger. Indeed, their philosophical differences resulted in professional antagonism toward one another. Mary Jane ascertained that Roger's questioning of campus decisions related to the uses of technology arose from the prospective cancellation of the computer literacy classes. However, Roger's actions contradicted this assumption, because he actively tried to engage teachers in the integration of technology into their instruction and offered to assist and train them to use technology—activities that would be his main duties if the computer literacy classes were to be eliminated from the curriculum. His efforts, however, were often thwarted by the practical constraints of teachers; specifically the constraints which TAAS had on teachers' instructional practices and curriculum development. He pointed out that if such issues were not addressed, the creative potential that electronic technologies could offer to instruction would be left undiscovered. Thus, the resistance Roger had encountered seemed to arise from contextual constraints rather than fear or lack of interest.

> The core teachers are driven by TAAS, especially in seventh and eighth grades. Everybody is just frantic. It's a top-down thing. I have gone out of my way to entice them and set aside time to let them bring their students in, to help them prepare a lesson, show them the software, be there on my time-off to facilitate for them. It's not that they are not interested. They are polite. It is intriguing. Some of them have even sat down at the computer and think it's great. But they just don't have the time.

According to Roger, teachers who are most enthusiastic about electronic technologies are generally younger and had technology training in their preservice education. Teachers who lack past exposure find it difficult to imagine technology's potential as an instructional aid. Even for teachers who had past experience, the inherent complexity of electronic technologies demands not only time but genuine interest in the technology itself. "They [computers] are not organic. You just can't go to the pencil sharpener and come back with a fresh point. You got to spend a few hours studying the manual." Fortunately, Roger's attempts to reach out to his colleagues were not all in vain as he was able to collaborate with the science teacher and her students successfully integrated the use of graphics and the program SimCity into a multimedia presentation on earthquakes.

Roger's perceptions about why teachers did not integrate technology into their instructional practices were corroborated by comments made by other teachers. Most pointed out that teachers in general lacked the time to become comfortable with the technology. Every participant mentioned teachers' fear about electronic technologies but explained that fear arises from lack of training, adequate technical support and familiarity with the new technologies, not from an innate fear of technology per se. Many of the teachers referred to the issue of age, indicating that younger teachers have more training and familiarity, thus are more apt to feel comfortable using technology. For example, Janet, a new teacher and the youngest of the teachers interviewed, had an extensive background with using computers and was highly enthusiastic about their infusion into schools. Having attended a rural high school and experienced distance education, she was grateful for the learning opportunities this technology brought to her school that otherwise would not have been available. Whereas Roger, who was both older and an experienced computer user, expressed suspicion about what he described as a "teacher in a box" approach to instruction.

Lisa was relatively comfortable with using computers as an instructional tool and believed that teachers were resistant to using technology because of inadequate technical support—a situation she had personally experienced in the past. Also, her experiences with computer technology demonstrated the complexity and often contradictory perceptions, which many of the individual teachers brought to the subject of technology and educational reform. For example, Lisa believed that through district and administrative policy and typical advertisements for computing technology, teachers are made to feel they are "behind the times." This reconfiguring of a teacher's identity creates an ideal image of the "good teacher" who is savvy with technology. Such an idealization generates guilt and perceptions of inadequacy among teachers. She further explained how a teacher is positioned to assume that "if they are computer-driven in their activities, then you would *really* be doing something special and important than what you've been doing." Lisa explained that she knows many teachers "who buy into that and think, 'well, if I was any kind of teacher, I would be able to do all these wonderful things.'" Lisa explained that she had not personally bought into this perspective. Despite her enthusiasm for computers in the classroom, she turned down a very desirable science teaching position because the school had adopted a computer-based science curriculum and completely replaced hands-on activities with a computer simulation software.

> Their department head took me around and showed me the school and they were so pleased that their chemistry labs had all gone to computer-driven labs and a lot of their biology labs were computer-driven. They no longer did dissections or actually performed the experiments—that was done on the computer. They had all this high tech equipment they were very proud of. I was *not* happy to see that at all because I just feel like there is a lot of value to actually performing yourself rather than sitting in front of a screen and seeing things flashing before you. I didn't like it at all. I think it is wonderful when you have that kind of resource available to you, but to be dependent upon that and to use that as your teaching mechanism all the time is very disturbing to me.

Lisa explained that the adoption of this type of simulation software makes teaching easier because "when you do labs two or three days a week like I do, it really is time-consuming. I just think that they were taking the easy way out on that." Lisa believed that having children sit in front of computers all day in school when they "sit in front of the TV now and go home and play video games" which, she added, is why homework never gets done, is only exacerbating an already bad situation for learning. Looking over at the disarray of materials left behind by the last science class, Lisa explained the moral issue this situation offers teachers. "I think we need to discourage that kind of teaching in school. I hope that doesn't become commonplace. I do think in that case teachers are giving up their responsibility [to students]."

However, like many of the teachers, Lisa's perceptions about technology and media were contradictory. Despite her sensitivity to market forces driving the infusion of technology into schools and her awareness of problems related to children's exposure to media and computer-based entertainment and instruction, she felt that adoption of Channel One programs (controversial commercially based cable television programming designed for classroom use, which provides hardware to the participating schools and demands mandatory viewing by the students) was acceptable, especially for students in rural areas, such as Shelton Valley. Lisa's cavalier attitude toward Channel One's commercial aims was rationalized by the fact that students "get so much anyway [advertising] that a little bit more commercialization is not going to hurt them." However, she also admitted that most educators buy into Channel One simply to acquire the hardware without giving consideration to what, if any, educational value it offers.

The informants' perceptions about the meaning of the term "Information Age" also offered some interesting contradictions. Whereas Roger and the principal expressed skepticism about the Information Age rationale as a basis for reforming education (i.e., "Information [Age] is terrific marketing" and "It's a meaningless hype term that's something somebody invented in order to sell computers," respectively), some of the teachers, such as Satie and Susan, had no idea how to describe or define the Information Age. Even so, Satie, who had no misgivings about educational computing, felt that children were already overloaded with too much stimulation and information from media, and that the growing use of computer games as entertainment only added to children's alienation and avoidance of "real people relationships." Cheryl expressed similar concerns and sensed that a relationship existed between ADD (Attention Deficit Disorder) and our media and information saturated society, a factor which in fact has been proposed by educational psychologist Jane Healy (1990, 1998). Ironically, Cheryl wondered if there existed a way that educators could harness the attention children put into video games (utilize the gaming aspect as an effective teaching strategy) to secure their attention. Similarly, Janet perceived computers as a great motivator and imaged how the gaming aspect of entertainment software could enhance the play theory of learning. Janet foresaw how ADD children could be given a school version of Nintendo and "be fascinated for hours." Cheryl did perceive the paradox that media and computing technology presented to educators and parents, whereas Janet, a much younger teacher and user of computers since the age of eight, did not seem aware of this subtle factor.

Most of the teachers defined the Information Age as our present time characterized by rapid expansion of easily accessible information. Lisa and Mary Jane related the characteristic of easy access to information to curriculum and instructional concerns, a factor that indicated a deeper level of internalization of the official discourse of reform. Lisa, for example, expressed how the Information Age signaled that teachers need to rethink curriculum and their instructional practices and no longer teach content but rather focus on thinking skills and finding information while being the "guide on the side." Mary Jane's perspective clearly paralleled that of Lisa's with one important exception—Lisa had some misgivings about computing technology whereas the only misgiving expressed by Mary Jane reflected the purely technical concern about the rapid obsolescence of computer technology and the incompatibility problem this often created.

Perhaps because of his past professional experience in graphic design and marketing, Roger expressed a very complex understanding about the effects that computer-based technology could have on the learning process. Whereas Mary Jane emphasized the power of the new technology to deliver more information Roger seemed very concerned about its social effects. He wondered "whether civilization shapes tools or if the tools shape civilization," and answering his own question, described the relationship as "a process. It's a loop. We built a car and it changed the way we live. We built a PC and it's changed the way we think." Roger used an example to explain his perception that tools ultimately shape civilization.

> There are valuable aspects to both pen and paper and the computer as a tool of composition but when I read the screen and read the page, being where I am at my age, because of my training, I see something different. I don't know that children do though. And so does the tool shape the culture? I think so. When what I write is printed out, I want to hold the print in my hand and then I want to scribble on it. If I want to understand the context and the content, I want it on a piece of paper.

Roger's framework for understanding technology, one which recognized how it exists not only as a tool or artifact but also as a process of social shaping, might have also enabled him to turn a critical eye toward the school and the district's plans for technology adoption. In effect, he was critical of what appeared to be a thoughtless or technocentric approach and his opinions only led to his being criticized by those who perceived his objections as perhaps too abstract or theoretical. Or worse, that his opposition simply arose from a self-serving perception that the proposed changes to the curriculum (the integration of computer literacy across the curriculum) threatened his current position. Thus, ironically, his resistance was rationalized as simply protecting the status quo.

For example, Roger was very concerned that "the people who are now teaching were not exposed to these new technologies and don't know the power of it." He was not only making reference to the medium's power to engage or mesmerize, but also to mediate and shape consciousness. Roger explained how the use of electronic technology acts to mediate the process of instruction and in that process of mediation, something is lost. Indeed, the effective use of electronic technologies arises from a sensitivity to the qualities of the medium, which most teachers do not possess. Consequently, the use of electronic technologies may have unintended instructional outcomes.

It [computer technology] solves a lot of problems but there is a diminishing return point. With high technology there is high risk. . . . If I sit there and I am talking students through a lesson at my computer and I am using the large monitor as a point of reference, there is a certain loss. As a visual aid, it's okay, but it's a layering. The more layers you put between you and the immediate contact you have with an individual the less impact you have. What is the best class size? One student. That's why distance learning gives me the chills. I like to watch TV just like everybody else, if it's good programming. It is the same with connectivity. . . . It is hard to understand but most students don't like to read, and if I load up the screen with lots and lots of information—that's great. The information is there. But are they digesting it and internalizing it and utilizing it? I don't think so. I don't think most teachers give much thought to that.

Roger's sensitivity to the medium, in terms of how it acts to shape the message, was unusual in its sophistication so that asking his colleagues to consider the use of technology from such an informed perspective was perhaps much like asking a fish to take a different look at water. Remember that understanding technology as a mere tool is the commonsense way that our culture generally understands technology. Our cultural bias is not to consider how our technologies shape the way we think or relate to others. Considering Roger's position toward the nature of technology, it is no surprise that he believed that access to information is not an end in itself, in terms of an educational objective. "Knowledge. Information. Wisdom. Information is the tinker toys in our mind. You can access information all day long, but doing something with it, that is another thing entirely." Roger also stated that "the ability to control [information] through sophisticated software does not provide any greater understanding of what you are doing." Roger's position on questioning the assumption that access to information acts as a guiding principle for leading education into the next century stood in stark contrast to the position offered by Mary Jane, who believed that access to information resources via the Internet was central to reforming education.

I think right now we limit education by the way we teach or limit information. Once we are on-line with the world we should be able to overcome that. . . . We need a way to access information. We need a way to obtain it and send it out, so it's the coming and going of information.

Possibly, Roger's background in media production made him sensitive to the nuances of electronic technologies whereas Mary Jane's concern for open access to information arose from her background as a librarian, a role in which she experienced a constant but necessary battle against censorship. However, Mary Jane's technocentric perspective reflected the dominant discourse, which accepts the "inevitability" of technology infusion not only into educational settings but also into every aspect of daily life. She described the relationship between society and technology as "a force," one with such pervasive power that "I think the time will come very soon that no matter what walk of life you're in, you're going to be involved in technology—whether you want to or not. . . . If you want to do banking, purchase something, exist period, it's going to involve technology." Mary Jane was also emphatic about how electronic technologies in education today do not exist "merely as a phase that we're going through. It's a way of life." Mary Jane dismissed the idea of overt marketing of high technology to schools, a point often raised by Roger, and instead focused on the inevitability of technology-based reform and the importance of access to information to schools, concluding that information technology will create "a new era of learning and people can accept it or not. It's not going to stop."

Teachers' Perceptions About Technology and Society

Roger's and Mary Jane's perspectives on the nature of technology neatly fall into a contrast of oppositional ways of understanding technology, but how did the other teachers and the principal conceive the relationship between technology and society? As mentioned earlier, most of the teachers at Shelton Valley believed that the infusion of new technologies into schools was inevitable. However, Janet believed that educators should not totally focus on technology, although acquiescence to its ubiquitous presence and centrality was normative. She predicted, "technology is going to be bonded to society until the bitter end, whenever that may be." Janet equated teachers' expertise with using computing technologies with their professionalization. In addition, Janet did not cast a critical eye on the fact that the infusion of new technologies into education was market-driven. Rather this situation was simply an artifact of our capitalistic society and competitive ideology, one to which teachers needed to acquiesce in that schools have a responsibility "to prepare children to compete in this society."

The principal expressed a more philosophical view about the relationship between society and technology but also felt there was not much one could do about the growing influence of electronic technologies in our lives. As an example of the relationship between the social sphere and technology, David cited the profound influence that the McCormick reaper had on changing the nature of farming from a small, family-owned, labor-intensive enterprise to a largely automated, multinationally owned agribusiness industry. He conceptualized technology as "a complicated tool that we must learn to use wisely." David also felt that the computer is a tool or an aid to society but will "never master my brain" or, in effect, overcome the human element. On the other hand, the principal did acknowledge the possibility of globalized, market-based information systems acting as a threat to individual privacy.

For all his insight into the complexity that electronic technologies pose for postmodern society, however, the principal seemed comfortable in the acceptance of the situation as given. Overt resistance to the expression of power through technological systems was not part of his vision. He concluded that "the system is built ahead of time and if you want to play the game, you have to play it their way. That type of control will be paramount." However, David referenced the story of Ishimal, which depicts a paradox of science and technology as such that if you solve one problem using technology, you create a hundred more. This paradox, according to David, is complicated by the fact that technological changes happen quickly, especially during the past 100 years. On the other hand, the human sphere of beliefs and values does not change so readily. Thus, in many cases, technological change has outstripped our moral and ethical thinking. The principal concluded his discussion on the relationship between society and technology with reference to the growing ecological challenges postmodern society faces.

> I don't generally like to engage in dismal, pessimistic conversation, but we cannot in this nation and in Europe go on consuming sixty percent of the world's wealth and energy. It's going to come to an end. We cannot go on abusing the planet. There are all those doomsday people who tell you it's going to come to an apocalyptic end. I don't think so. I think it will peter out over the long haul in a reverse trend of the way we built it up. But regardless, even if we descend into that—I use to give this famous lecture where forty percent of the students were Native Americans—life was sweet and worked very well with the Cheyenne Indians before Henry Ford ever made his first automobile. And if we have to go back to that we can do it. That does not mean we have to be diminished intellectually to do so. But the gadgets we so resplendently equip our culture with are totally superfluous to life. . . . we cannot go on growing.

David further explained that individuation and privatization are core social and political problems behind current ecological challenges. "Ownership of everybody having an automobile, that's a dominate idea today and we are all choking to death on that concept." David wondered if we have lost control over our creations. "Who owns whom? Does the automobile own you, or do you own the automobile? Well, its beginning to look like the automobile is owning all of us and is going to drive us to an early grave if we don't do something about it." In conclusion, David proposed that humanity needs to arrest the present trajectory of autonomous technologies. "Ultimately the big question is, is man capable of controlling his future? If he's not, Mother Nature will do it for him. Mother Nature won't paint near as pretty a picture as man can paint, but he can control it. Maybe some of the apocalyptic things will come true if we don't manage our affairs correctly."

For Cheryl, the most troubling issue regarding the relationship between society and technology was that "technology can be isolating though it makes things easier—like FAX or on-line communication. You can do it at home, but this leads to less socialization." She believed that the aspect of diminished socialization would pose a challenge for distance education. Cheryl also made reference to the movie "The Net" to explain her concerns about new technologies' potential power of isolation and, in the hands of the state, the power to instantiate a surveillance society and control our lives and identities through manipulation of electronically based personal data. In addition, Satie confessed that she had "nightmares about technology where everything is computerized. What if a computer virus hits every computer in the U.S.? The whole U.S. would shut down—banks, telephone companies, the government. And people would not know what to do. We just always live for the computer."

In terms of how the new technologies may affect education, Cheryl focused on the issue of isolation. For Satie, however, the issue was not so much isolation but the general milieu in which media, computers, and information technologies create for children a coalesce of technological influences that communication scholar Neil Postman (1993) describes as "media ecology." Specifically, Satie was concerned about how such a confluence of various media shapes, if not delimits, children's imaginations. Her assertions arose from her 34 years in teaching where, over the years, she has had to increase the use of visuals into her teaching practices. "Now I have to use so many more visualizations, where I didn't have to use so many before. The disadvantage is that when one reads they have their own picture in their mind, but you cannot do that when visualizations are already provided. And students expect to be entertained." Thus Satie associated a passivity induced by media consumption and how this experience inculcates the need to be entertained to a diminished capacity for imaginative thinking or an imaginative framework that arises from media sources alone.

Satie admitted that she felt sorry for children who never have a chance to more fully use their own imagination, although she admitted that with data-bases, the Internet, and laptop computers, "there really is no need for kids to have to learn all the things I had to learn, cause I had to carry it around in my head and now they carry it around in a laptop computer." However, Satie questioned the assumption that access to information equated to the possession of knowledge: "They have access to all kinds of information, but what do they really know? What does it *mean* to them?" Although Satie reflected a commonsense belief in the necessity of computer-based instruction in schools, she drew the line when it came to the reductionism of the information access rationale. In fact, Satie believed that she and other older and more experienced teachers were "holding the line," standing for "old fashioned ways" of teaching and values and that such teachers gave students a solid foundation of skills and knowledge.

Most teachers, when asked to reflect on the relationship between society and technology, offered a range of interpretations, which, however, were anchored by a commonsense artifact/tool–based understanding. Only Susan, the special education teacher, admitted that she had never before thought about technology in an abstract sense and seemed to lack the vocabulary to articulate any thoughts regarding this question.

The teachers' perceptions about the relationship between technology and society, I believe, opened another dimension through which one may view the school's current technology-driven reforms. Although most acquiesced to the dominant discourse of "inevitability," hidden reservations and fears existed. Many seemed to lack a vocabulary with which to articulate their feelings and reservations. They also seemed unable to relate their generalized vague discomfort with the growing presence of technology in the lifeworld, specifically the infusion of computing technologies into schools. However, as explained later in the story, the informant's fears about the growing influence of electronic technologies also paralleled their concerns about certain social issues that affected Shelton Valley. In addition, the teachers had no forum in which they could voice their fears, hopes, and reservations, especially since the technology committee was weakened by factionalism, and the site-based management process, according to many of the teachers, was simply an empty gesture.

Another example of how the challenges surrounding technology adoption became a divisive issue for Shelton Valley is examined in the next episode, and describes how the installation of the LAN system created more problems for the school than it solved. This episode begins with Roger's assessment of the school's site-based management and decision-making procedures.

The Failed LAN System

At the time that I interviewed Roger, although he had been the chairman of the technology committee during the previous year, he was no longer an active member. However, he was still an active member of the district technology committee. He expressed deep frustration with the manner in which technology-related decisions were made on both the school and district level.

The dissemination of information is erratic. This is my personal opinion. Last year I embraced this position wholeheartedly and was here from seven in the morning until nine or ten o'clock at night. I turned this into my life. Part of that was just the learning curve of being a new teacher. But in addition to classroom duties it was the technology committee for site-based quote unquote schools. And there is no technology committee. I was head of the technology committee but there is no technology committee. That turned out to be pretty much the way this school functions as a site-based entity. It is tacit or only there for show. Now I'm elected to the school's site-based committee and found that to be completely true—so we make recommendations but they are not really acted on. I was on the district technology committee and it was pretty much the way that functions, so its not an isolated thing. . . . After time to reflect I have come to the conclusion that the crux of the problem is lack of long-range planning involving everyone's meaningful input, building a true goal towards which everyone can work towards.

Also, Roger likened the funding process to "a shell game," a situation further burdened by "hidden agendas and some political issues." He concluded that, given the circumstances of "just having a little bit of money, lack of any kind of visionary leadership, things get frittered away on inconsequential expenditures."

Although Mary Jane assessed that most teachers at Shelton Valley seemed opposed to the use of technology, Roger believed that what really influenced teachers was a lack of incentives, support, and time. He explained how membership in the district technology committee was conducted by "drawing straws," with the current members "getting the short ones" and that "everyone had a narrow vision of what they wanted and nobody defined any problems or needs." Even so, as chairman of the technology committee, Roger proposed the use of HyperStudio and SimCity as software for collaborative-based projects and set out to support this curriculum change by configuring six computers, upgraded for multimedia, on a mobile cart so that all classrooms could have access to the necessary technology. The plan, unanimously approved by the technology committee, was rejected by the administration. Instead, the administration decided to spend the money on upgrading the Jostens lab networking from AppleTalk to Ethernet. However, after completion of this network upgrade, the system still did not function satisfactorily. As explained above, the administration then decided *not* to continue using the Jostens system. Roger wondered in amazement why the administration would spend $30,000 on upgrading a system and then decide not to use it. He then explained how the votes of the campus technology committee are not recorded so it is easy to just channel the money in another direction. He also explained that Mary Jane, needed more computers for the library and disbanding the Jostens lab was convenient. Mary Jane then had the two computer technology labs networked to the library via an Ethernet connection, but did not arrange any specifications with the technician, nor was there a contract. She reported that the principal gave the simple directive: "just get it done." As time went on, however, the technician abandoned the half-completed job and had left certain functions of the automated library system completely disabled. Mary Jane reported how the technician could not be reached for several days and that how the last computer serviceman "shafted the district." She was frustrated by the fact that the district would not hire anyone to organize and monitor such high-technology projects "which, in the long run, is costing a lot more money to the district [because of errors in decision-making]."

Several weeks later, Roger reported that the installation of the Ethernet was still unfinished and that, in fact, the technician had attempted to simply leave the networking system incomplete after having run into some unforeseen technical problems that would necessitate expending more time than he had been willing to give. Roger had to threaten the technician with reporting the incident to the district and school board. However, he did not blame the technician, but rather the general lack of communication and cooperation that characterizes the decision-making process at the school.

> The reason is that there was no communication to begin with. They should start with the kids and teachers and try to understand what we need to make learning happen. What are our needs? Well, they would have discovered that, in terms of networking, in our little rooms we don't need anything. We could have used a few machines. But they did not need to spend the money there to do what they did. They decided from the top-down. They did not do their homework to understand what really was necessary to effect what they had decided what we needed. So when they came in to put in what they decided what we needed, they disrupted what we had and they wrecked it so that we stopped being able to deliver what we depended on. That caused more problems than it solved. Then the poor guy who was doing it decided that he was going to get out and just leave it [the inactive networking system] as the ghost in the background that we could turn on one day. It was silly.

At the end of the semester, Roger offered details about how the networking situation had not changed. He explained that because the school had not negotiated a contract with specifications or design plans, there existed no accountability on the part of the technician. Roger was very frustrated by the fact that a needs assessment was not conducted. "This is indicative of the overall attitude toward technology in this school. It's not inculcated into the curriculum, but brandished as a star in our crown. We're networked! But what does that mean? How have these kids been affected?"

To their dismay, Roger and the other computer literacy teacher found that after the technician had announced completion of the network installation, the hardware in their labs would not work. In reality, the machines in the computer literacy labs were not capable of handling a high-speed network. Roger angrily insisted that Mary Jane and the principal were aware of this technical fact but went ahead with the change of networking anyway, despite the fact that they never assessed, in terms of curricular objectives, why the two computer literacy labs needed to be connected to the library. In turn, Roger reviewed the Texas Education Agency (TEA) accounting specifications and found that the money spent installing the Ethernet system was specifically allocated for curriculum, not infrastructure. He explained that in effect, "the school was spending the money illegally, against TEA specification." Also, the lack of understanding about how these electronic technologies may be integrated into the curriculum, much less how they may qualitatively effect instructional experiences of teachers and students for better or for worse, was epitomized by a presentation given by IBM, attended by Mary Jane, the principal, Roger, and several members of the district technology committee, and is discussed in the next episode.

In Search of Direction: Avoiding "Silicone Snake Oil"

Shelton Valley's search for direction, in terms of computer and telecommunications technologies, led the school staff to seek advice from IBM corporation's division, which offers assistance in planning a telecommunications networking system's infrastructure. At the meeting, the IBM sales representative noted that they have both educational and commercial clients and have assisted other school districts with their infrastructure plans. Their proposal of action, which delineated seven phases of district technology planning and implementation, had been adopted by three other districts within Texas. The presentation clearly demonstrated the great complexity involved in the construction of a WAN/LAN network infrastructure. The representative also suggested that Shelton Valley acquire state funding designated for telecommunications infrastructures (HB 2128) as the state would support technology-based reforms that would both "raise your test scores" and basically "force teachers to use computers" and telecommunications technologies.

In addition, the fundamental reason given by the IBM salesperson for building a WAN within a school district was to make the management of information more efficient. The participants were reminded how efficiency would decrease costs. In addition, the "global world demands Internet access" for educators. Throughout the two-hour presentation the issue of how this technology was actually to be used as an instructional resource was not addressed. However, additional information about the provider's software featured proprietary tutorial and drill and practice programs (that would be delivered by the WAN/LAN system) designed to address achievement on state-mandated standardized tests. In fact the only reference to curriculum or instructional issues was made with regard to how HB 2128 demanded that schools address specific needs and outcomes and aligned accountability measures. In effect, the vision of possible applications for networked telecommunication infrastructures supported by HB 2128 funds was similar to that of an ILS, except that processing test score data would be centralized within a district versus a strictly campus-based level of access.

In general, the presentation revealed some troubling assumptions: (1) that telecommunications and computer technologies would involve a top-down mandatory "adoption" by teachers; (2) the curriculum could be conceptualized as being driven by the infrastructure design itself (i.e., ILS configuration); (3) that educators would enable the allocation of scarce educational and fiscal resources to technocentric endeavors without question; and (4) despite the obvious technical complexity of networked systems, the issue of endless costs related to maintenance and upgrades was not addressed and thus remained a hidden factor.

Mary Jane believed that the IBM plan would help the district realize the building of its WAN system. However, in his expressed skepticism Roger referred to the IBM representative's sales pitch as an example of what Clifford Stoll (1995) describes in his book *Silicone Snake Oil* as typical hucksterism of the computer industry and the general marketization of education.

> Oh, you mean the "Silicone Snake Oil"? That guy [the IBM presenter] just reeled off a bunch of buzz words. You know, its like the old used car salesman scenario where the little family is sitting there in the audience saying, 'should we spend the money? Is it really going to get me to the grocery store bigger, better, faster? Cause we gotta feed the kids!' And the snake oil salesman was saying, 'Yes mam!' So we're evaluating it on the basis of a matrix of needs and we can't really understand why we are getting on this bandwagon.

The factionalism that plagued Shelton Valley, in terms of its technology planning, had deeply affected Roger. At one point he confessed that he had abdicated some of his responsibilities as a teacher by not standing up to the status quo. When the principal's and Mary Jane's resistance to his ideas and their criticisms turned to the realm of the personal, Roger backed away from being actively involved with the campus, and later, the district technology committees. He retreated into his classroom and ironically refocused his energies on tinkering with the newest software technologies.

> You have to take a stand and be bold—reclaim your moral and intellectual responsibilities. Well, I had a responsibility to say 'no' and I let it go somewhere. As an educator, I let it slip away from me. [I] did not have the guts, courage, character to keep it, whatever it took. And then I am being swept away by these other things—this marketplace. The computer technology and all these wonderful things it's going to do for me. It has taken the place of these

fundamental educational things that I need, that I am morally responsible to my successive generation [to address].

This level of self-reflection and political awareness was not reported by any of the other Shelton Valley teachers.

Although many Shelton Valley informants expressed confusion or ignorance about the status of technology planning at their school, Roger and Mary Jane seemed to battle for control over the school's rudder while forging divergent paths or directions toward their individual vision about reforming their school and district with the use of electronic technologies. Unfortunately Roger's questioning of what he perceived to be an uncritical approach to the adoption of technology was not appreciated, at best misunderstood. Ironically, the principal was also suspicious of the marketing aims of technology vendors. He stated that his only misgiving about bringing electronic technologies into education was "getting the hucksters out of the way," people who he described as "willing to sell you the Brooklyn Bridge of technology when the Brooklyn Bridge may be the last thing you need." However, the principal did not share these misgivings with Roger. Nor did Roger's appeals for a more pedagogically based approach to technology adoption connect with the principal's fundamental misgivings. In fact, Roger reported that there was very little support from the administration. Roger believed that site-based management was "tacit, the site based management committee makes recommendations but they're never acted on." This experience was also expressed by Susan, the special education teacher, who stated that, "as a faculty we could meet as a group, and I think on the surface it may look like we do. But when it comes down to the final decision, suddenly it appears on paper [from the administration] and its something different. It's just an exercise."

The Culture of Shelton Valley: Holding the Line

As explained above, Shelton Valley was undergoing change on two levels. Its efforts to incorporate telecommunications and computer technology into the school was also paralleled by challenges on a social level. Much of the information pertaining to the culture of Shelton Valley and the teachers' perceptions of the general social reality within which their school existed, arose from their responses to the question about whether or not a crisis existed in education. Many of the informants at Shelton Valley expressed that if schools were in a state of crisis, the cause resided not so much in the schools per se, but rather in society-at-large. This response could be interpreted simply as teachers "passing the buck" but, according to Seymore Sarason (1995), schools inherently are "social barometers" and thus reflect the society's general social milieu. Indeed, this broader perception about the nature of a crisis in education was consistent among the participants of both sites. While reflecting on this matter, several teachers from each site expressed grave concern about diminished family values and increased behavioral problems in children and suspected that the general violence in our culture was being reflected in the lives of children.

Shelton Valley's rural setting and its physical isolation had once acted as a buffer to certain social influences related to the media and the commodification of youth culture. Even though gang violence and physical safety were not major considerations for Shelton Valley teachers or the principal, many expressed that something had changed the relationship between teacher and student and parent and teacher in that an "us versus them" antagonism poisoned the foundation of the school's community. Some teachers sensed that social problems arising from the loss of traditional values and the breakdown of the family structure as well as problems arising from the structure of the public educational system itself posed immense challenges to educators. In effect, although Shelton Valley clearly did not suffer from the social challenges that visit upon more urban schools, the modest rural community was struggling to negotiate and make sense of social changes that arose not only from the society-at-large but also from changes in the community's local population.

Some teachers perceived that a rise in discipline problems and conflicts among students arose from divisions between wealthy and poor students. Others mentioned diminished respect for education in general, the effects of the media and a lack of interest in reading. Many teachers believed that the lack of personal responsibility on the part of the students was exacerbated by parents who blamed the school or a student's teacher for their child's poor academic performance. Frustrated by the sense that they lacked legitimacy in the eyes of certain parents and students, a factor exacerbated by the perception that their "hands were tied" in terms of discipline, teachers related this to the structure of the educational system, specifically the bureaucracy surrounding mainstreaming policies.

The teachers also complained about a TAAS-driven curriculum, which seemed geared toward raising standards to the extent that many children were being setup for failure, a factor which possibly contributed to their lack of engagement. Many teachers expressed that the curriculum reflected a college preparatory bias and that many students' needs were therefore not being met by the curriculum since a fair percentage of students did not desire to attend college. The most insidious aspect of this situation is that many of these students were being labeled "at risk." Some teachers explained that the unrelenting drive to raise standards had been nevertheless thwarted by a necessary dilution of the curriculum to avoid massive failure rates. The "dumbing down" of curriculum in turn negatively impacted the more advanced students.

As discussed in the previous section on technology adoption, when teachers attempted to develop solutions to address some of the school's problems, the school's administration did not act to support their efforts, thus undermining the site-based management system.   Also, in one particular situation, which involved a special education student who broke the school's no drinking rules but was nevertheless readmitted into the school because of a threat of a legal suit, the integrity of the school's institutional authority was called into question.   For many teachers, this incident epitomized the dramatic changes in the school's culture and added to their sense of helplessness in the face of such changes. Therefore, the teachers' frustrations with the societal challenges over which they had little control in combination with structural barriers, such as the ineffectiveness of the site-based management process, only served to further their sense of demoralization and resignation. Fortunately, many teachers did seem to find solidarity and strength through working collaboratively with their teams.

Based on the informant's perceptions, the elements affecting Shelton Valley's culture can be divided into two broad levels of influence—societal and structural. The specific outcomes and responses to these two areas of influence are detailed in Figures 4.1 and 4.2.

Figure 4.1: Levels of Influence: Social Problems

Influences	*Outcomes*	*Teachers' Responses*
Changes in family structure and economic disparity	discipline problems	"holding the line" teaching morals and values
no parent/student support	loss of interest in education and no accountability	demoralization and "us versus them"
negative influence of media	boredom	decrease in reading and critical thinking skills

Figure 4.2: Levels of Influence: Structure of the Educational System

Influences	*Outcomes*	*Teachers' Responses*
current mainstreaming policy	discipline problems	frustration "hands are tied"
labeling students "at-risk"	dilution of the curriculum and rising standards	"hands are tied"
standards-driven curriculum	cycle of student failure	demoralization
site-base management	top-down and ineffective	withdrawal from decision-making

The remainder of this chapter examines some of the societal and structural influences indicated in these figures.

Social Influences

Satie, who has approximately 34 years of teaching experience with 26 years in the local district, believed that the economic disparity that characterized the local community had negatively impacted the school's culture as well as the academics of students. "We have quite a number of haves and have-nots and it does make a difference in their school work." Cheryl, who was fairly new to the school, explained that the influx of more wealthy families and their particular set of norms and values had challenged Shelton Valley such that, ironically, this small, rural community could lose the very qualities that had originally attracted urban parents.

In fact, the teachers' perceptions about the influence that general social problems had on the current "crisis" in schools—specifically the lack of "family values" and personal responsibility; a general change in lifestyle which has weakened family ties; and media's influence on youth culture and consequent peer pressure—is reflected in the following comments made by Satie and Cheryl.

> Satie: Several decades ago I believe that more people went to church. Families stayed together more often. . . . Like they say, it takes a whole village to raise a child. Well, we don't have those villages anymore. A kid leaves this school and goes out to his subdivision and gets in all kinds of trouble. There's nobody there. The preacher isn't there. The teachers aren't there looking at him.

grandma's not there looking after him. He's free to do what he wants and nobody knows unless someone, the police, catches him. . . . The social level has become the way it is because of the things they [children] see on TV and movies.

Cheryl: We need to do something in the next five years or we will lose them completely. There are problems related to family breakdown and there is no support from parents. Teachers have no credibility. Kids are influenced by other kids—their peers and from TV. So there is no motivation to do well in schools. . . . You know, probably years ago people were more religious and the values were taught within the religious setting. The students who still have religious influence in their life, you can tell it in the classroom—in the way they treat each other. That's another thing that's missing in our society in that the values aren't being taught at home or anywhere.

Susan, the special education teacher, noted that although most children are bored with school it is not only the influence of peers or the media that affect their motivations, but rather very serious social problems that situate the meaning of school within their lives.

I hate to say it but kids nowadays are so bored so quickly and trying to keep them motivated is the biggest challenge we have. . . . We forget that most of the kids are coming from broken homes with drugs and alcohol, emotional and sexual abuse. That constitutes the majority of kids we are dealing with. So when they come to school they are not real concerned about whether they passed the TAAS test or not. That is not a priority in their lives. Survival is a priority. . . . They are dealing with experiences that I had never heard about when I was a kid let alone had to deal with. But times are changing.

Indeed, the alleged absence of academic responsibility and growing cynicism demonstrated by students complicated certain behaviors directed towards teachers. For example, Janet, a first year teacher, related how students' back talk was difficult to negotiate and was her "single largest problem."

The school's principal also expressed concern about the general lack of values within the society-at-large. "I would say that if the nation is in a crisis, that's where it's at—crisis. We've lost our way and our values." Also, while many of the teachers made reference to the negative effects of media on youth, David believed that our age of television and "push-button information culture" had negatively affected children's imaginative thinking and interest in reading. He concluded that "its frightening to me that children we have coming up don't want to do that [use their imagination]. And they don't want to pick up a book and read. They don't want to burn the energy. I know that's a negative generalization, there are lots of kids that do like to read, but I'm afraid that there is a trend in that direction." Two other teachers, Satie and Janet, theorized that diminished imaginative thinking or according to Satie, "their ability to think in pictures in the mind," was directly related to constant exposure to media, specifically visual imagery such as television and film. As an experiment aimed to foster more imaginative thinking, Janet planned to use old radio broadcasts from the 1930s so that her students might learn to listen to narratives and experience creation of their own mental images of a narrative's storyline.

Structural Influences

The principal, who had a sign on a wall in his modest office that reads "Be Nice to People," admitted that discipline was becoming a problem at the school. In his discussion about concern over the recent attacks against the school by certain parents, David pointed to specific structural constraints on educators. He concluded that the root of the problem arose from the struggle to realize egalitarian ideals within the paradox of protecting the specific individual rights of certain students while also serving the needs of the larger community of students.

> I don't agree with the idea that no matter how bad little Johnny is, he needs to be in school. That's a baby sitting concept of school. . . . It's a rights versus duties kind of thing where we've lost sight of the duties which the individual has towards society. But everyone knows about their rights.

Janet also felt that the turning of education into a right versus a privilege had generally harmed the legitimacy of education as a social institution.

Susan, the special education teacher, believed that the social problems, in combination with certain structural factors, further impacted many students' low academic performance.

> I look at the progress notes that teachers are sending out—the number of students failing. The curriculum is getting more difficult and the ability of our students coming in is lower and so more and more students are not passing. . . . There are so many of the drugs and alcohol related problems. So I think many factors enter into it.

Susan perceived that the demands of special education policy created a particular strain on the effectiveness of the educational system. At one point Susan broke down and wept as she related the following:

> As a special education teacher I really hate to think or say this, but I really believe that special education is going to be the downfall of public education [long pause]. This is because the regular education teachers are being forced to take on all these special education kids and there is no way you can, over a long period of time, deal with all these kids.

Satie explained that the labeling of so many children as "at risk" signifies not only the influence of special educational programs but essentially expresses a "social revolution" that ultimately acts to "cripple" students in terms of their ability to withstand adversity.

> To me, some of them don't need to be labeled that way. Now they get a hangnail and they are labeled at-risk. It's like a social revolution or something where we are just crippling these kids. I'm not saying me or other teachers, but by the actions that are thrust upon us by legislators or the federal government. They [students] are not learning that there is supposed to be adversity in life and you are supposed to stand-up to it, look it in the eye, and move on.

Several of the teachers mentioned the problem of raising standards, in terms of making the curriculum program more rigorous, which in turn required the quality of the content to diminish to accommodate the learning ability of the average student. Many cited how such a policy reflected a basic assumption that all children ought to and can successfully achieve a college preparatory program of study when the reality is that not every student can or will desire to attend college. Lisa, for example, perceived that such a policy was not only unrealistic but actually harmed these students by saying to them, "'I'm sorry. You can't be different. You can't have a different goal or expectation." In addition, Lisa's reflection on the frustration and challenges presented by disciplining misbehaving students epitomizes the perception of many of the Shelton Valley informants.

> They've [policy makers and administrators] tied our hands behind our backs as far as discipline. We can't really do much with the kids. When we do, we have parents criticizing us—you are picking on my child! So we are forced to accept this behavior and this kind of student. We are forced by the public to do that and we are expected to perform miracles with the kids that have a very poor attitude about school. They are here to disturb others and keep them from learning and we have to overcome that and still increase all these expectations that have been placed upon us.

Although many of the teachers felt overwhelming frustration because their "hands were tied" in terms of being able to negotiate certain federal and state policies pertaining to special education, the state's curriculum and accountability systems, and the school's unresponsive, site-based management, some related how, within the arena of their school, they actively resisted what they perceived to be spurious and nonproductive imposed changes. For example, Satie consciously resisted what seemed to be thoughtless reforms, whether they be within the realm of school curriculum or district policies. She observed that younger teachers do not seem to understand how to negotiate the continuous "parade of bandwagons" such as cooperative learning. Nor do they know how to stand their ground in terms of demanding that students take responsibility for their learning. Thus, it is the more mature and experienced teachers who are left "holding the line."

Some of the teachers who are my age, or a little bit younger, we say, that somebody has got to hold the line. [laughs] That's exactly what we say. We are holding the line. When we are gone, who's gonna do it? Cause a lot of the younger teachers weren't raised this way. They have not been taught some of these things. And we are whistling in the wind, more or less, because there aren't many of us. I sometimes feel like I am way out of date or just plain old fashioned. And then I think, no. I really believe that's right. If I were still teaching language arts I'd be teaching kids how to diagram sentences because that's how I learned to write and kids can't write today!

Cheryl expressed how she "holds the line" by not giving in to the prevailing forces that seem to involve teachers as accomplices in reducing student responsibility and the lowering of academic standards and expectations.

I won't lower my expectations of my students simply because somebody else expects less of them whether it be their parents, or my administrator or themselves. . . . Unfortunately we don't have the support in the administrative arena and a lot of teachers feel like they have to do this [lower expectations] because they don't want to fight the battle. It's a battle they just don't want to fight. So they protect themselves, and it makes them look good too. I call them the rescuers. They rescue students by throwing them a life preserver instead of teaching them how to swim.

Still, Cheryl's determination to "hold the line" was challenged in a manner she could have never imagined—she received an obscene and threatening phone call from one of her students. She reported the incident to the administration and the local police, not to take anyone to court, but to communicate "loud and clear that I'm not going to tolerate such behavior." Cheryl explained that many teachers and the assistant principal had recently been under attack not only by students but also parents.

Cheryl was the only teacher from either of the sites who mentioned the importance of teachers' unions. A long-standing member of the American Federation of Teachers (AFT), Cheryl reported that she had tried to recruit other teachers and often wrote letters to political representatives on behalf of specific educational issues. Cheryl was totally convinced that teaching, despite public disregard, is a highly professional field. Thus, respect for her work was essential. However, recent incidents had given her serious second thoughts about remaining in the teaching profession. "I've had doubts about remaining in the profession because I won't stay in a profession in which I don't feel any rewards and my rewards have always been that I'm making a difference. When I get to the point in which I don't feel like I'm making a difference, that's when I'll leave." Cheryl predicted that "a lot of the good educators are being driven out due to lack of support" and foresaw a time when she might be driven out as well. "When I can no longer teach and give the kind of quality education I want to give, when it is no longer supported administratively or from the community then I won't teach any longer either."

The divisiveness between the school and certain parents had, according to Susan, led to mistrust and a disrespectful attitude among certain students toward their teachers. Like Cheryl, Susan found the situation demoralizing.

> The truth of the matter is that we really don't get support from the public. We no longer get it from the students. That use to be my main source to keep me going and, with our students—it's almost like it's us versus them. That is their attitude. . . . I don't think that I need to be buddies to all of my students all the time, but it just seems to me like there is a bridge. I think a lot of it is from the home, at least in this community. I mean I cannot tell you how often I hear, 'well, you're just picking on my child.' And its, 'no, your child is just not performing in school and that has nothing to do with my like or dislike.' They don't want that. They want an excuse for it. . . . We get *so* much of that— looking for an easy answer and the responsibility is not on the child. It's *your* responsibility if they don't perform.

The one word that embodies the main issue for most Shelton Valley teachers is "responsibility." This specific word appeared more often in their responses than any other descriptor. However, the antagonism between certain parents and the school's professional staff needs to be considered in light of the fact that no aspect of the school's reform policies directly addressed the need to further engage parents in the decision-making processes at the school. My observations led to the general impression that parents were not highly involved with Shelton Valley; their presence was limited to chauffeuring their children to and from school. Also, the teachers and the principal did not make reference to the Shelton Valley PTA or its activities in any of the interviews.

The frustrations surrounding the social and structural problems at Shelton Valley were also reflected by many of the teachers' visions of education in the 21st century. The final section on Shelton Valley reviews how Shelton Valley teachers imagined the future of education in the 21st century given current social issues and the trajectory of official educational reform policy.

Imagining the Future of Education

Each teacher and the principal were asked as a final question to reflect back on our conversations and consider what they envisioned to be the future of education in the 21st century. The informants were encouraged to express both what they expected to happen as well as what they felt would be an ideal outcome. Thus they were comparing the present situation and its likely trajectory to an idealized perception of what education could offer our society.

The contrast between Mary Jane's and Roger's perspectives on the nature of technology and the dominant discourse of educational reform was also evidenced in their prognosis of education in the 21st century. Mary Jane's technology-driven understanding of reform at Shelton Valley reflected her perspective on education's future in general. She perceived that education would be run more like a business and that the focus of curriculum and instructional reform was securing access to information. Her technology-centered vision of future learning environments included teleconferencing, each teacher having their own workstations, and districts being networked. In her school of the future, pencil and paper would go by the wayside because students would use laptop computers. CD-ROMs and the Internet would replace textbooks; in fact, "books would only be used for leisure." Teachers would still have a role but rather than direct teach, they would focus on guidance through curriculum development and an instructional approach primarily student driven and thematic in structure. Mary Jane believed that "we won't have schools like we have today. They'll be totally computerized interaction. Everything will be done through terminals. They might have terminals available in subdivisions [malls]."

Mary Jane's sense of education's inevitable technology-driven future was also evidenced by Roger. In contrast, however, Roger did not perceive that a technology-driven approach would necessarily address issues that truly change the learning experiences of students and the quality of student's lives. He predicted a growing "new frontier" perception would drive the infusion of technology into education, a perception epitomized by what he described as "teacher in a box" telecommunications-based instruction (distance education). He believed that educators would continue to try new technologies because they are desperate to motivate their students. In turn, education would be overtly driven by high-tech marketing. Roger foresaw widespread use of the Internet as inevitable because "people have bought into it." He glumly concluded, "We will be connected and we'll have more computers but I think we are going to be about where we are now with the kids."

Whereas Mary Jane had only one projection—a technology-driven vision that she predicted would be resisted in vain by some—Roger expressed both a likely outcome and a preferred scenario. Roger's ideal vision involved a greater focus on changing the relationship between the teacher and the student through smaller class size and adoption of a more "Aristotelian model of instruction." In Roger's idealized scenario teachers' professional experiences centered around reflective practice, which included "more training of teachers—not in technology—but in how to teach and *why* they teach. How do other people teach? That ongoing process of life-long learning . . . . We ought to be looking at the mechanics of teaching philosophically, not just technologically, and let this be a constant enrichment of what we do."

Most of the other teachers at Shelton Valley also envisioned a technology-centered educational environment in the 21st century. Lisa wanted students to have access to computers within the classroom (versus computer labs) and the Internet. She also hoped that teachers would have access to "appropriate software." She foresaw curriculum and instruction "shifting into the Information Age philosophy" as a means to develop critical thinking skills.

Janet also focused on the presence of computers and information technologies, stating, "I cannot see a successful educational system ten years down the road without a lot more technology. I think you have to have it." Janet perceived that networked systems and centralization of student information within databases would streamline teachers' paperwork and "keep the bureaucracy to a minimum," a perception that ignored the fact that automation of personal data does not reduce bureaucratic controls but rather acts to make them invisible. She also believed that electronic technologies would make instruction more individualized, a quality that could thwart the labeling of students, although she was uncertain how this outcome might occur.

Cheryl also believed that there would be more computer technology in schools and that the future of public education was uncertain—there was a possibility that vouchers would become acceptable and thus children from more wealthier families would be enrolled in private schools. She also predicted a strengthening of state control over teachers and the curriculum through greater dependence on standardized testing. Cheryl, however, did not believe that a technology-driven reform policy would address social problems arising from the diminution of traditional family values even while the expectation that teachers address such problems would increase.

Susan's and Satie's predictions also focused on the escalation of socially based challenges facing educators. Susan foresaw that schools would be "more technologically oriented" but also envisioned "massive discipline problems" and the placement of "problem kids into more detention-type schools with uniforms and military-type [settings]." Satie also predicted the development of having "more responsibilities thrust on schools until it reaches the point where we'll be more like a pre-prison than a school." Susan believed that policymakers and citizens do not realize the number of students whose lives are devastated by broken homes, drug, alcohol, and emotional and sexual abuse. Satie echoed Susan's concerns and, you may recall, was consciously "holding the line." Thus when asked what characterized her ideal vision of education's future, Satie sighed, and after a long pause, said with quiet determination, "I'd like things to be the way they were 24 years ago."

David predicted that education in the future would continue much as it had in the past but "the form and substance of education will change and the delivery system will dramatically change" while "the need for education will increase." David perceived that the world would see a vast improvement in the quality of education in third world countries, a factor related to the spread of telecommunications and electronic media technologies. He also predicted changes in the form and delivery of education arising from networked systems. David also acknowledged escalating social problems challenging the system of education. He expressed how, "I long for the day when school is a privilege and students do what the teacher says they need to do. If not, they don't belong there." David had spent several years teaching Native American students and expressed great respect for their sense of community and traditions based on sharing. He contrasted these values to the dominant culture's focus on individualism and personal property. He stated that one thing he would like education in the future to reflect and teach future generations is a greater sense of community giving and the ideal that "we have a moral, ethical and societal obligation to assist others."

In conclusion, despite the centrality of Shelton Valley's technology-driven reform program, the energy and imagination fueling this effort was not utilized as a means to invite the surrounding community into the school or create cohesion and a greater sense of community within the school itself. Rather, decisions evolved through a top-down approach whereby the process of adoption became characterized by factionalism and a blind technocentric perspective in spite of the insights offered by the principal and the teachers. Thus Shelton Valley was poised to accommodate a performance-based culture rather than an authentic culture. As a result, the teachers could not "name their world" with a standing of political agency in the sense elucidated by the work of Paulo Freire (1970). Therefore, in relation to the aforementioned social and structural problems, their sense of direction or determination as a community to meet these challenges was that much more weakened. Although the determinants behind the perceived antagonism between the school and its community of parents were complex and systemic, the situation was exacerbated by an obvious lack of means through which the institution of Shelton Valley was accessible by the larger community. Indeed, given these factors it is not surprising that the rationale for acquiring electronic communication technologies was to simply access information and improve the efficiency of testing versus the creation of a broader learning community possibly augmented by electronic networked systems.

In contrast, the next chapter relates the story of Zepeda Elementary and illustrates a school's struggle for reform in terms of how the school functioned as a place that was significant to an economically marginalized community. The school symbolized and embodied the community's struggle to actualize social praxis even while it struggled to negotiate the technique of control technologies. Thus, the story of Zepeda's quest for community solidarity stands in contrast to that of Shelton Valley's journey down the blind alley of technocentrism.

CHAPTER FIVE

The Story of Zepeda Elementary School

In schools like this one, and most of us have been here for a while, we have a lot invested and we want our children to succeed. We realize how vital it is for them to be successful. Our society hinges on whether or not the people that we're standing on, are going to survive or not. In a capitalist society the rich people are standing on the backs of the people down here [in Zepeda Elementary's community]. I am well aware that what I do is crucial to society.

Jane, teacher at Zepeda Elementary

I think schools could become centers of community like they were. But centers of community not in the transmission of the received culture but centers of community in the reformation of communities that have been dispossessed like this one. There is talent in this community. It just has to be developed. There are resources here. They have to be identified. I think schools can become the bulwark against the forces of oppression that come down on communities of poverty. My vision of Zepeda is that it will become a model for urban education.

Antonio, principal at Zepeda Elementary

Zepeda is an urban school residing in a large central Texas metropolitan area. The city is neatly divided economically by a federal highway and Zepeda, located on the poor side of town, serves a large percentage of economically disadvantaged students.[1] The 1930's style of architecture of the main building symbolizes to the generations of Hispanic and African Americans, which it has served over time, the constancy of the community. A low income residential area including two public housing projects and light manufacturing industries surround this small but sturdy school. The neighborhood features modest homes, many of which are thoughtfully cared for with front yards of colorful beds of flowers and statues of the Virgin Mary. However, one block away from the school signs of poverty and neglect are evidenced by abandoned houses and vacant, trash-filled lots.

Behind the main building of the school stand several portable classrooms and a playground area. Within a short walk from this central area of the school grounds one finds the athletic facilities, many of which are marked with graffiti. While inside the main building the observer immediately notices the classroom walls, which feature student's drawings and projects as well as old blackboards and the highly polished hardwood floors. Within this rather traditional school setting, the two computer labs (a networked

PC lab used by all grade levels and an Apple lab used primarily by the lower grades) seemed out of place, an incongruency with the age of the building and the sensibility of a forgotten past, which it tacitly communicated to the observer. There was no attempt to modernize the building. If anything, the 1930's period architecture and interior acted as a constant reminder of the schools long history—both as a place of learning and as a site that symbolizes the heritage of the local community. Many generations of the neighborhood's citizens had passed through its modest front doors and the story which unfolded refers to the reawakening of Zepeda as a place of learning as well as a public space for the community. In fact, Zepeda's story reveals a journey toward the creation of a school as a public space where parents, their children, and neighbors could meet and discuss the needs of their community, the future of their children.

This journey was initiated and supported by the school's affiliation with the Alliance School Project (ASP) and the city's local chapter of the Texas Industrial Areas Foundation (TIAF), a nationally based network of Interfaith Organizations dedicated to building community through raising the political awareness of poor and socially disenfranchised minority citizens. The first section of this chapter recounts how affiliation with ASP and TIAF resulted in Zepeda's truly remarkable passage from one of the lowest performing schools in the district to becoming one of 220 schools to receive the National Blue Ribbon School of Excellence Award. This section of the chapter also examines the experiences and attitudes of administrators, TIAF leaders, teachers, and one parent, the PTA president. The second part of this chapter specifically addresses Zepeda's focus on students' reading skills. This effort not only encompasses curriculum and instructional changes but also the sociocultural and economic challenges that deeply affected the experiences of Zepeda's educators and its surrounding community. The last section of this chapter reviews teachers' responses to the "crisis" in education and their vision of education in the 21st century as well as their perceptions about technology and educational reform policy.

Schools as a Community's Public Space

Unlike Shelton Valley Middle School, the issue of technology infusion was not at the center of Zepeda's reform effort. However, Zepeda offers not only a contrast to the reform efforts of Shelton Valley Middle School, but also raises important issues regarding the priority of technology diffusion in light of the particular needs of a school and its community. For example, a poor urban school may find that its creative energy and financial resources first needs to address deep social problems that arise from poverty and social and economic discrimination—sitting hungry and angry children in front of a computer does not necessarily increase their academic opportunities. On the other hand, the administration and teachers generally acknowledged that it was important for Zepeda children to have computer-based skills. All of the participants seemed painfully aware of the social and economic disadvantages of their students and believed that the exposure to technology was one way to bridge the gap. However, their major concern was to provide students with basic skills in mathematics and reading and instilling in them the confidence to stand up to social prejudice and face their own insecurities. In fact, Zepeda serves some of the poorest minority children in the city where the average family income is approximately $12,000. At the time of this study, Zepeda had been a participant in the ASP for a few years. ASP is a consortium composed of Texas Interfaith Educational Fund, TIAF local chapter, the Texas Industrial Areas Foundation Network, campus staff and parents, school district officials, Texas Education Agency, and Regional Educational Service Centers, and at the time, consisted of 59 schools in 18 various districts within Texas. ASP's goal was to develop schools so as to restructure the relationship among stakeholders and utilize strategies toward the improvement of low-income students' education.

One of the major constituents of ASP, the Industrial Areas Foundation (IAF) founded in 1940 by the late Saul Alinsky, is a nationally-based network of multiethnic, broad-based, interfaith organizations located primarily in poor, and moderate-income communities. When the local chapter of TIAF approached the principal of Zepeda, Antonio, and invited the school to become a member of ASP, Zepeda was the lowest performing school in the district (according to TAAS scores). The teacher turnover rate was very high, fifty percent of the first graders were being retained and the faculty morale was low. Moreover, the school had no relationship with parents and the community. Kathryne, a representative of the local chapter of TIAF, explained that TIAF had been highly successful in organizing parents within schools of poor communities to lead a school and its community toward a common goal such as eradicating a neighborhood's abandoned properties and building affordable housing. In the case of Zepeda, however, the group hoped to accomplish more in terms of improving academic achievement.

The Turning Point: Establishing a Common Goal

Antonio, who had been Zepeda's assistant principal for over five years and a teacher in the community's schools, was very familiar with both the social and academic problems facing the school. Shortly after Antonio became Zepeda's new principal he realized that the school and its community of parents lacked a common goal and were operating under false assumptions. It was time that the teachers and community members faced the reality of Zepeda's low academic performance. Teachers, assuming that parents were unconcerned about their children's achievement, gave students passing grades on their report cards despite the students' actual poor performance. As a result, the parents assumed their children were adequately performing in school. Antonio reported that, with the assistance of the local chapter of TIAF, the parents held the teachers accountable and pointed out that there were two things that TIAF and Zepeda wanted to overcome: the racial stereotype of the intelligence of African American and Hispanics and the racism that is generated by class differences.

Antonio recounted the story of a fateful PTA and community meeting, which became the school's turning point.

> Our first step was a community meeting. That was our cathartic experience. I think change comes through two ways: It comes through coercion or it comes through having some catastrophic experience, a spiritually awakening experience or some cathartic experience. Coercive change usually reverts back to the previous behavior when the agent of coercion is removed. That is what I have observed in life. Change that comes about through come cathartic experience or spiritual experience seems to be lasting. So we needed that experience. And that occurred when I asked a parent to read out student achievement data and make comparisons between this school and other schools at a public meeting with parents and teachers. So of course the teachers were very angry with me and wanted me to defend them. They felt they were being attacked, and the parent did attack. He said things like: 'Where are the good teachers because they are sure not here. This is all you can do—20% and 17% passing. And you call this teaching? What are you doing all day long?' We had to have that experience. We had to have that catharsis so that we would stop waiting year after year for next year. That way we could acknowledge that we have failed institutionally and now, we can change. That enabled us to change everything.

Antonio also explained that although the first step was to change the reading and mathematics curriculum and the instructional approach, the specific instructional system was not the most important element. Rather, its embodiment of a new beginning for the school was paramount.

> One of the first things that we changed was the reading and math system that we used. . . . But the particular system is not critical in and of itself. Those are just books and materials and there are many that are just as good as the one we chose. What was important for us in the psychology of our school culture was to put the old system out. That way, you send the failure with the old system. Psychologically the teachers were able to say it was those old, bad books. We have new, good books and now we can be successful. That way the guilt wasn't so heavy on them. Just like in the scriptures when we send the scapegoat out into the wilderness, all the sins of the community went with the scapegoat.

As a member of ASP, the participating school and its community, under the guidance of the local chapter of TIAF, were committed to guiding the school staff in a specific direction. In terms of staff development, teachers were invited to become a member of a collective that worked to improve their teaching and in turn improve student learning. This goal was especially challenging as traditional classroom practice is centered around the self-contained classroom and the isolation of individual teachers. Parent and community development focused on the pursuit of educational achievement and the larger goal of developing a community that values education.

With such broad social goals in mind, Antonio realized that Zepeda had taken an important step toward reform. Once both parents and teachers reached the consensus that nothing less than high student achievement for Zepeda's students was acceptable, all of them could work together toward realizing this common goal. However, Antonio explained that realizing a common goal was indeed only a first step. The next step was to build a sense of solidarity and community where trust was the foundation of the relationship between teachers and parents. Antonio believed that this opportunity arose when the parents, with assistance from TIAF, demanded that the city council and county commissioners grant their request to have an on-site clinic. This clinic would give Zepeda access to preventative medical care. Certain members of the school board and individuals from outside the community representing the religious right were concerned that the clinic would be used for reproductive services and bitterly fought this request. The process of negotiation took eight months. According to Antonio, fighting and winning this battle built a foundation of trust between the parents and the teachers.

> The health clinic was necessary to coalesce the community and the school staff around a core issue so they would see themselves as one and have a common enemy [religious right opposition] against which to resist and then that would bond the staff and parents together. The event was more important than getting health services. . . . Teachers got to see parents differently—as being advocates, being resilient and being proactive. Parents got to see teachers differently—as being people who were interested in more than being here from eight until three o'clock but willing to put themselves out and to spend time organizing politically for something for the children and the community. That was a cohesive event and we needed that experience to bring us together.

This experience also represented a major breakthrough for the community and parents of Zepeda toward realizing their own sense of empowerment. Kathryne explained how, at the time their request for medical services was under consideration, the school board had just had a fight over sex education with members of the city's religious right constituency. Consequently, some board members feared the religious right's political power, which, in fact, showed its force against Zepeda. At this same time, the city temporarily closed a clinic located a few blocks from the school. Zepeda's parents and community members, with the help of the local chapter of TIAF, demanded the city provide local access to adequate medical services. This situation underscored the battle with the religious right regarding the community's request to have a clinic at Zepeda such that, according to Kathryne, when the final meeting with the school board occurred, one parent, who had never acted in the capacity of a leader or spokesperson for his community, stated, "no one's asked what we want. No one came to talk with us. The people who are telling us not to do this or that we should do it some other way, don't live here." Kathryne explained that this parent's act of speaking out was "a very powerful experience. And I think it really developed a sense of power for the parents." Kathryne further explained that once a deep sense of commitment takes over, "and when people try to speak for you on your behalf or think they can speak better than you, you have a real sense of anger, which we find is really one of the most important qualities of leadership, that people have anger and a passion for something." Antonio explained that the function of the TIAF local chapters is to "develop leaders in the community and the issues will arise from amongst the community. The iron rule of IAF is wonderful: Never do for others what they can do for themselves."[2] IAF accomplishes this by developing circumstances that enable a community to take charge of their own political reality. Antonio stated that one of his duties as a principal is to recognize those within the school community who can act as leaders. "That is what I think a principal is: A principal is a talent scout and spends time looking for talent and then develops that talent." It was apparent at this point that Antonio had adopted the roles of both school administrator and community activist.

Kathryne explained that TIAF local chapters build relationships, first with the principal of a school and then with the teachers, based on people's self-interest, which she noted is not selfishness. Rather, Kathryne explained that "teachers, whether they are burned out or not, have an interest in having their school being successful instead of at the bottom of the list." She also explained how TIAF's role is not only to facilitate but also develop original approaches or solutions to problems such as Zepeda's collaborative partnership-based after-school program, which eventually had expanded to a network of twenty-two schools.

Also, although Zepeda had a permanent full-time health service team, other schools shared a team of health practitioners so that approximately sixteen schools would have health services at the other schools for a month at a time. This arrangement required a three-month commitment from a participating school and parent's commitment to participate. In effect, such opportunities became the means for generating "social capital," which is an effort to build and maintain reciprocal relationships based on mutuality and respect.[3]

Another way of building social capital is through local neighborhood house meetings. Theresa, the school's PTA president, was active in coordinating neighborhood house meetings, where members of the PTA, local TIAF representatives, and Zepeda teachers visit parents and other community members in their homes. In fact, this form of door-to-door interviewing of Zepeda's parents and neighbors of the school community established the initial direction of TIAF and Zepeda's efforts. TIAF responded by directing the community's effort toward acquisition of school clinics and an after-school program. The process of garnering fiscal support through the city, university, state legislature, and local businesses was challenging and characterized by setbacks and disappointments. Building and sustaining a collective vision toward a specific goal is an ongoing endeavor toward overcoming learned complacency as Theresa indicates in the following quotation.

> It is difficult for someone to take responsibility at our level. As a parent, a community member, there is no time to think about what's going on and realize responsibility and accountability. People are just trying to cope with today. What we are trying to do with the neighborhood meetings is provide opportunities to stop for one hour and enjoy coffee or a meal and talk about what is going on. It's creating these little moments to come together that is the backbone of our success. But there is not enough of this going on. If there was, there would be a thread of common ground. We have a good start, but it is only a beginning. We're not used to considering the idea that you are responsible for others. Some people think—'who do you think you are?' But, for the most part, people are helpful and want to get involved. . . . Even though we have a vision, it takes work to realize it.

According to Kathryne, "social capital" was created and maintained through both house meetings and large group "revival-type" meetings held at local churches. She explained, that TIAF members believe people hold many things in common—that people deserve a certain dignity and quality to their life, "and there is some common responsibility for people who live together in society or community to work at that together." Because historically, some people do not have and never had a voice in public life, "decisions are made by people with money. We [IAF and its local chapters] say there are two forms of power: organized people and organized money. And if you think about media, about who *really* holds the power in the community in terms of business or corporations, it's very much tied to money." Kathryne concluded that consequently "we worked on the other form of power, which is organized people." She stated that people can be taught leadership and how to do a "power analysis" by asking who has the authority to make decisions and who allocates funding. Kathryne pointed out that the parents standing up to the religious right to defend their children's right to adequate health care and their ability to go to the principal knowing that the principal will listen to them and act on their requests, is extremely empowering. "For the community members to be able to know what they want, to be able to work hard on it, fight for it and win—energy comes with that and that's power."

Antonio recognized that Zepeda had become a symbol for the community's solidarity and power, a position attributed to its affiliation with the local chapter of TIAF. He also realized that such a redefinition of Zepeda as the political center for the community did not align with policy elites' technocentric vision about the purpose and nature of public schools, although it may express its forgotten historical foundations. However, he emphasized how meeting the state's TAAS standards had given him "political space" to make Zepeda a political center for the community.

> As long as you're successful, you have the political space in which to operate. . . . By successful I mean meeting the measurements of the agent of society [TAAS]. When you stop doing that, you lose control. I think we've pushed enough and stepped outside enough that if we stopped being successful we would probably feel some corrective action brought to us. So every year continues based on the caveat of what will this year's scores be.

Based on his experience, Antonio believed that most reform efforts, such as the recommendations made in *A Nation at Risk*, are not successful because "the reforms are superficial and will therefore be inconsequential because they don't go to the heart—the locus of the problem is about power." He believed that "relational communication" or "building relationships among the people" was central to the process of reform. Antonio's position reflected the local chapter of TIAF's emphasis on building "relational power" by means of reciprocal relationships which can only be established through face-to-face communication.[4] Kathryne explained that face-to-face communication is especially important for establishing relational power and thus "public conversation."

> Does it take a social contact in which to grow, develop and learn? We would say, as an organization, yes. It really takes meeting, having mentors and others you engage with and have conversation with—it is public conversation. This is having discussions, debates and maybe even arguments sometimes; but ultimately, compromise, negotiation and coming to some common agreement. Public conversation is geared toward action: What do we need to do?

Both Kathryne and Antonio explained how they believed in building community through engaging people as citizens through the process of the political, in an Aristotelian sense. Kathryne explained this point as follows and relates it to the issue of power.

What people do when they participate as citizens is to participate in the public life of the community which is, in the Aristotelian sense, politics. Which is also the polis. Politics is about how we make decisions. How we live as a society and power is part of that. Power, from Latin and from Spanish means simply to be able to act. So, what we are talking about is the ability to act. But if you think about churches, the community-at-large, power is one of those words people feel real uncomfortable with, and so is politics.

Kathryne believed that the parent's decision to have a special sixth-grade program at Zepeda was an example of an exercise in relational power. The Young Scientists program, a special sixth-grade class which features an accelerated curriculum of science and mathematics, was offered only to the highest achievers at Zepeda. The program aimed to have these students qualify for and attend the local science magnet school and ultimately attend college. This was the only sixth-grade class at Zepeda. Those students not participating in the Young Scientists program were bussed across town to a middle school. Kathryne explained why the decision to have the Young Scientists program was so significant to the school and to the recognition of the community within Zepeda.

It's a real different way to think about school; the decision to have an accelerated science sixth grade class would fall into the hands of the parents. But we had parent meetings and discussions with parents talking in small groups with each other to find out their hopes and problems. The bottom line question the parents needed to answer was: Do I want this program at my school because it is good for kids and our community even if my child is not accepted?

Kathryne noted that although a science magnet school was only a few blocks away from Zepeda, parents in the community "just do not think to send their kids there." She perceived this situation existed because of the following reasons.

A child's vision of their future is based very much on the level of education and the kind of work their parents and others surrounding them engage in. Otherwise they cannot see it. We see this a lot in our organization. People can't do what they can't imagine. So how do we work on imagination for teachers, parents, for ourselves?

Kathryne also explained that building community and relational communication required that teachers and parents interact. In fact, school policy required that each teacher make a home visit and meet with the parents of each of their students. Also, parents helped with the interviewing and selection process of hiring new teachers. The school/PTA newsletter was published in both English and Spanish and all PTA meetings were bilingual. There were several parent/PTA activities including monthly health advisory committee meetings and other gatherings dedicated to examining issues surrounding student achievement.

The approach to school reform adopted by Zepeda seems radical when compared to typical reform models specifically because most reform efforts, unlike Zepeda's, do not acknowledge or address problems related to power (Sarason, 1995). Clearly the local chapter of TIAF had given Zepeda a new direction and a foundation of community solidarity upon which to build its future. However, the academic success of the school, which had afforded Antonio the political space he needed, would not have been possible without the cooperation of the teachers. Therefore, the following sections examine the programs of change in curriculum and instruction adopted by the teachers in addition to their reactions to the school's allegiance to TIAF and its reform philosophy. Also, the philosophy of TIAF, specifically its emphasis on building community through relational communication, was adopted by Antonio as a model for managing Zepeda, especially regarding how he related to teachers. In this sense the TIAF model of building community acted to restructure the culture of Zepeda, specifically in terms of the power structure and the relationships between the administration and teachers, teachers' collegiality, and the parent's relationships to the school as a community.

Changing the Culture of Zepeda: Building Solidarity

Academically, Zepeda had come a long way. As discussed earlier, before its affiliation with TIAF, Zepeda had been the lowest performing school in the district based on its performance on the state's standardized tests (TAAS). The first curriculum reform effort was to eliminate their Gifted and Talented (GT) program and instead utilize this curriculum for all of their students. However, the curriculum primarily focused on building basic skills in reading and mathematics. In addition, the school also practiced inclusion, and thus did not have a pull-out program for special education students. Student attendance improved dramatically after Zepeda's on-site clinic opened and several incentives were developed, which rewarded those students and their families who worked to achieve perfect attendance. Those who did were honored at PTA and TIAF meetings. In fact, the school also received several state awards honoring their efforts toward maintaining a high level of student attendance. In addition, specific programs targeted the reduction of student retention. In general, Zepeda developed an impressive array of school-related programs ranging from general reforms (i.e., health clinic), youth development programs, and projects devoted to improving literacy skills.

Various committees and incentive programs arose from the collective efforts of teachers, TIAF, and the administration. The committees (i.e., instructional teams, PTA, and campus leadership) especially enabled the teachers to create and maintain collegiality. Majorie, for example, believed these committees, although challenging in terms of demanding more of teachers' time, nevertheless provided opportunities for teachers to reflect and engage in discussion. Sharon reported that, "we all care about each other and can be open with each other about individual problems. It's like family."

One story exemplifies the challenges that the teachers faced in terms of maintaining and building trust and collegiality. For example, the deliberative approach to consensus in one case demanded that certain teachers had to make sacrifices for the benefit of the school's entire community. Sharon explained that the pre-K and K teachers accepted the burden of larger class sizes to accommodate the school's goal of maintaining high reading scores.

> One reason we do have low teacher ratio in first grade is because we decided last year as a Campus Leadership Team, which has a representative for most grade levels, that we wanted to keep the ratio low in first grade because of the importance of reading and so we decided as a whole to do that by cutting funds in other places. . . . That was a hard decision for the people who will not necessarily benefit right away, especially in pre-K and K, so they have real large classes right now. They don't benefit in the future from first grade having small classes like the other grades do, so that was quite a decision for them to make with us.

However, even though the pre-K and K teachers agreed to this arrangement, more budgetary cutbacks and a sense of alienation from the higher grades eventually spurred resentment. Not only had an increase in class size compromised the quality of instruction, according to kindergarten teacher Marjorie, but additional cutbacks for pre-K and K eliminated field trips, which meant that their students would be denied necessary life experiences, not simply enrichment. Teachers of every grade level explained that most students have not been exposed to life outside of their neighborhoods, a factor which they believed negatively affected the quality of their general academic performance. Consequently, Jane decided to take the risk and act as an advocate for her students. She secured the support of each of her pre-K and K colleagues and together they met with their school administration. Jane believed this was risky because it openly challenged the power of the administration.

> At the beginning of this year I felt that our school was ignoring us, pre-K and K. We didn't have any money. We didn't go to special areas. We weren't allowed in the auditorium for programs. . . . I was real angry and advocating for my kids. Nobody else was going to do it. Sometimes you do have to get mad and make a case. I'm real lucky, and one of the reasons I stay here, if you like to teach, is that I like to work for Antonio. He gets mad at me, but he gets over it. Because I was real angry with what was going on with what I thought were injustices.

> There was no equity. It all went to the older kids. . . . I organized all the
> teachers, eight of us, and went to talk to Antonio and the Assistant Principal and
> asked them—what can you do about this? I feel totally isolated from the rest of
> the school and I don't like it. I did not get a lot of what I wanted but I did the
> best I could and what I had to do.

Jane stated that Antonio agreed to provide the pre-K and K budget with $1,000 if they could find a way to raise money to match these funds. Jane was offended by his proposal, but worked with the other pre-K and K teachers to organize a basketball tournament at the school. The event enabled the teachers to meet their monetary goal. It also provided a forum where the teachers, parents, and community members worked together to realize a common goal—the betterment of their school and community.

One could view Antonio's decision to not simply adjust the budget but rather to invite the teachers to find a way to participate in raising extra funding as an example of IAF's Iron Rule. From this perspective, the experience empowered the teachers to act on their own behalf while becoming more directly involved with community activism. However, another interpretation of this scenario might be to underscore how Antonio's decision ultimately furthered the intensification of the preK and K teachers' responsibilites (Hargraves, 1994). In either case, Jane openly appreciated the uniqueness of Zepeda's environment, which supported a teacher's effort to "rattle the cage."

> We were a little confrontive about it but at least I vented what I was feeling. And
> things improved somewhat. I didn't get everything I wanted and had to put out
> to get what I got—hence the basketball tournament. It didn't kill me. But I am
> fortunate to be in an elementary school where I can do that. I would say that
> they're more rare than common. I hate to say that. Not as many schools are as
> safe as this. Advocate for your kids and make waves and make change for the
> better. . . . I wasn't comfortable doing it, but I knew I could do it and not have
> horrible repercussions. . . . So I am real fortunate and I think that we all feel that
> way. We all don't get along with our administrators off and on and they have a
> hard job. But I feel like Zepeda is an environment where I can do that. I can
> rattle the cage and there is not going to be anything horrible that will happen.

Jane, in fact, noted that Antonio was "open-minded in many ways" and that "he respects us and our ideas." Her positive impression and open appreciation for Antonio's particular form of leadership was also expressed by several other informants. Antonio seemed to have secured teachers' respect by granting them autonomy through collective decision-making. In addition, he honored his teachers' professionalism through soliciting and adopting many of their suggestions. For example, unlike the previous principal, Antonio listened to Margarete's suggestion that Zepeda abandon its pull-out GT program and instead adopt the district's GT curriculum for all of their students. The school sought and acquired the district's approval to follow through with Margaret's suggestion.

In the case of another curriculum program designed and initiated by a teacher, Zepeda's Young Scientists sixth-grade accelerated program, Antonio sought and secured the support of the school board while the teacher acquired financial assistance from the local business and university communities. In addition, Zepeda's after school alumni program and computer summer camp were created by fifth-grade teacher Christine. Also, Sally had designed numerous literacy-related incentive programs.

Johanna's statement epitomizes the general impression of many of the informants: "Antonio stays out of our way and lets us do what we need to do. Yet he is very approachable and stern when he needs to be and flexible where he needs to be. He's a good role model as far as leadership and he's willing to take risks." Johanna also explained that before affiliation with TIAF and Antonio's leadership, the culture of Zepeda was stymied by isolation and a lack of accountability, factors which she associated with the previous principal.

> I was a student teacher for a third grade class and three quarters of the children were not reading on grade level. There was not parental involvement. . . . The principal at that time isolated himself, and the faculty was very isolated. [There was a] very low teaching morale. Just so many problems.

Cooperation among teachers and between teachers and their administrators was one level where the culture of Zepeda changed to embrace a deliberative approach to decision-making. Another level of change within Zepeda's culture pertains to the realm of parents and their relationship to the teachers and their changing roles as both educators and social advocates. As mentioned above, parents participated in the selection of new hires. Given this, one important factor is that although the percentage of Hispanic children was high (86%), the ethnicity of the faculty was predominately white. However, the criteria for hiring new teachers did not focus on ethnicity or cultural background but rather on awareness and passion for social justice that would ultimately strengthen the political solidarity of the school's community. According to Antonio, the parents and administration sought candidates "who are not so intent in following rules and regulations." Antonio sought to avoid those teachers who had what he termed "missionary zeal," but rather who possessed "anger about the injustices of society. . . . Missionaries want to save the natives from themselves and make them more like them. People who are angry about injustice want to see poor people get a shot at the good things in life. They don't necessarily want to turn them into middle class people."

Thus, the cultural background and ethnicity of a teacher was not the essential point. Rather, according to Antonio, teachers need to be willing to devote time and energy to organize politically for Zepeda's children and their community. Antonio believed that "if parents never have the opportunity to see teachers in any other role except the teacher role then its hard to see them as anything other than foreign to the community." He did not believe that his teachers needed to actually live within the community to empathize with the poor, "but they do need to go into housing projects and visit the homes of people who live there and have a basis on which to become empathic."

After the "cathartic" meeting with the Zepeda parents, those teachers who chose to stay at Zepeda and their new colleagues launched a professional journey unlike any they had previously encountered. Most of the informants participated in the neighborhood marches in support of the school clinic. They attended PTA and school planning committee meetings as well as TIAF meetings, which usually were held at TIAF-affiliated churches. One teacher described the TIAF meetings as being "revival type." One such meeting, held at a participating TIAF church in the neighborhood surrounding Zepeda, featured a gathering of community members, TIAF leaders, parents and their children. Local politicians competing in an upcoming election were featured guests. Parents asked them to state their position on issues related to the TIAF agenda (i.e., continuance of monetary support for school clinics and after-school programs). The TIAF meeting was also an occasion to generate public support for the passage of a bond issue for public schools. The meeting began with the church minister's introduction and a performance from the church's choir. The atmosphere was festive as each of the participating school's accomplishments were shared and acknowledged by the audience.

The meeting featured a "call and response" format, with the speaker querying the audience and the audience responding with enthusiasm in unison. The meeting's format was indeed revival-like, and generated great enthusiasm among the people. It was a celebration in the fullest sense of the word, or what Antonio called "public dramas." Antonio described how TIAF works to create "public dramas" at their meetings, which are designed to foster "a political process to energize the community around political issues. So we have drama performances such as choirs from local churches" and other forms of community involvement such as neighborhood walks. Many of Zepeda's teachers attended this particular meeting to show their support and a few of them were key speakers at the assembly.

However, such "public dramas" seemed foreign to many of the white, middle-class teachers at Zepeda. In fact, a few of the teachers mentioned that they were initially suspicious of TIAF's motives because of their concern about the issue of separation of church and state. Majorie mentioned that when Zepeda first joined the local TIAF chapter, she was concerned about the religious affiliation of the organization.

> I thought it [TIAF] was strange, I'll be honest. We are so into the separation of church and state and I do believe in that. So I thought that it was strange that these people were going to come in and help us. But still, they were going to do an awful lot. It just seemed odd at first. But then as we got into it, I realized they were not pushing religion. They were trying really to make social changes. I like the fact that it is interfaith, that it is not just one religion.

Another teacher who is Jewish also expressed concern about TIAF's intentions. She related a conversation she had with the principal.

> My first reaction to Antonio was, are they going to preach about Jesus? Because I'm Jewish and all I knew was that it was a religious organization based on churches. I didn't hear any of the words like synagogue or anything, so that was my first question to him: Are they going to be preaching? And he said no and so it was okay. My initial reaction was whatever they can do to help us, let's try. It's worth a try. We weren't doing it, obviously, on our own.

Not all of the teachers mentioned the issue of separation of church and state as a concern. Most felt that TIAF had greatly aided Zepeda to achieve academic success. However, there was some friction in the beginning between the teachers and the local TIAF chapter representatives. Johanna remembered that during their first meetings, TIAF representatives would "roll their eyes if we weren't real committed to participating on Saturdays." Johanna described how they "had a bull session one day with them and we aired our feelings and so they tried to quit rolling their eyes. First they portrayed that if you didn't come on Saturdays and to night meetings that you weren't committed to these children and I was offended by that." Johanna explained that she lives about an hour from the school and has children of her own for whom to care and also attends graduate school. Therefore, for her to give up weekends and several evenings a month was a real sacrifice for her and her family. Attending to her personal responsibilities did not mean that she was not committed to serving her students. Fortunately, over time "we seemed to work out those difficulties and rough edges and it's been real positive since then." However, she also added that "some people have chosen not to be involved with TIAF and not to do anything that they have sponsored. But that's very few. I would say maybe one or two."

Shelly, the librarian, also made reference to how TIAF had initially approached the teachers. She expressed that although it was perhaps proper that TIAF "holds our feet to the fire," she also said that "they have to be very careful or they make us real angry and we don't want to do anything. So they have learned. They don't come in as they did at first—*we're* going to fix the problem. And that was a little uncomfortable. But by-and-large they have backed off and come at it from a different angle."

So before TIAF could establish a framework upon which to build a relationship between teachers and parents, they first had to establish trust between TIAF and the teachers. Subsequent involvement with TIAF did help to establish a sense of solidarity between teachers and parents and the community-at-large. However, the teachers expressed various levels of political awareness regarding the role of parents and the community within schools. Johanna, for example, explained that for her the realization that the parents truly did care about their children's academic performance was an essential turning point. She and several other teachers made the distinction between parents' ignorance versus willful neglect. Johanna, in particular, believed that some parents' inability to be more active in their children's education arose from the traditions of the Hispanic culture, that holds teachers in such high regard that it is unthinkable to question them. In contrast, Jane believed that Zepeda's parents had always been concerned about their children's academic success. During her fifteen years at Zepeda, Jane had become very familiar with "family legacies," and one recurrent theme offered by parents, many of whom are quite young, is that they do not want their children to repeat their mistakes and thus very much want their children to acquire an education. For Shelly, the issue did not reside with the parent's attitudes; rather it was the particular culture and structure of schools themselves that tended to alienate parents and the public in general—a factor exacerbated by the effects of poverty. Shelly believed that many parents were "uneasy" and possessed "a fear that the educational system is not doing what it is supposed to do. A lot of people are scared about what they see happening to their children" and in this regard were highly suspicious of schools and teachers.

In general, affiliation with TIAF's local chapter and the building of "relational power" through several church-based meetings and neighborhood walks helped to open the door of Zepeda to the parents. Marjorie, a kindergarten teacher who has taught at Zepeda for several years, explained that, in comparison to the past, parents now seemed to have a more comfortable relationship with Zepeda. She attributed the change to the support of TIAF.

> I think that more people generally feel better about coming to Zepeda, the parents feel more a part of it. And they feel more welcomed. And they were always welcomed but it was just—they did not think they were welcomed. I really believe they did not. They did not know what to do. They just did not feel like they were part of it [school community]. And I think that today they feel very much a part of it. I think TIAF did that. And I don't know if we could have done it without TIAF. Because they seemed to have the key for opening up these doors that we did not seem to have before.

According to Georges, who had spent part of his childhood in the neighborhood, Zepeda's move toward creating a sense of community solidarity began with the "cathartic experience" between the teachers and parents. "A couple of years ago the community slapped itself in the face to wake itself up. There is a dilemma going on in this community." Making a passing reference to IAF's "Iron Rule," Georges explained that "the only way that dilemma can be solved is by the community itself. It can get as much help as it can from the outside but if it doesn't come from within, it's meaningless." And, according to some informants, many parents simply remained uninvolved with the school or community activism. Despite this, hope arose from the fact that parents and teachers were now working together. Johanna's comment embodies this perspective.

> Not every parent is involved. But I guess you could say that it's getting there. We have a strong PTA leadership and as that happens, they'll be bringing in more people. I guess it is more of a feeling of community in that teachers and parents are finally working together.

However, despite the coordinated efforts of parents and teachers, Georges believed that some of the factors that limited parental involvement arose from broader social issues. His dream to "see the community come full circle and create its own vibrant ideals where everyone is working together," could be achieved only through "connecting with one family at a time." For Georges, who was very active in TIAF, the key to building parental and community support was to continue the creation of "the conversations instead of just communication," a notion he appropriated from TIAF's Southwest regional director. Georges explained this distinction as follows: "Communication is just talking with each other and not bringing forth ideas that are really relevant to our society and doing something about it. Communication is just one-sided. We have TV and radio for communication. But in conversation, it takes individuals to sit down and talk with one another to develop conversation." Thus, Georges referenced the need to build relational knowing through face-to-face conversation.

Georges and other teachers at Zepeda believed that, in general, our culture may be characterized by social and political isolation, factors that are exacerbated by poverty. According to Georges, the situation crosses through all ethnicities. "It's not just white Caucasian, it crosses all colors. I know Hispanic individuals who divorce themselves from their own culture. Even if they grow up in a middle class setting and not in the barrio, they can become responsible for it. They can also give back to that community and develop some type of ownership to enrich it in some way." Georges also perceived that our culture's normative social habits can undermine efforts to create a sense of community solidarity. "If we are isolated, if we don't have the faculties to do that [make social connections], then a lot of time we are truly separated. We have our doors closed and the TV on. . . . People in our society are sheltered. They don't want to step out of their homes. Life revolves around a glowing tube [television]."

The needs for a school like Zepeda, according to Georges, are very different from those located in wealthier, suburban districts. "Things that need to happen in this school don't need to happen in the Northwest areas perhaps. For example, you need to have health services here." Also, in order for the school to support the creation of a political space for the community this meant that the school needed to address factors that are not understood as typically essential to the success of school districts. For example, according to Georges, the creation of time and opportunities to create dialogue with parents was especially important to Zepeda, although this factor may not be recognized by state legislatures and in fact was antithetical to the ultimate goal of efficiency.

> You need to have constant, constant dialogue with parents because if you don't, you lose them very quickly. So there needs to be time set aside when you freely go about the community. Perhaps how we are going to go about things, is to just simply converse as opposed to following the mandates from the school district, like assessment needs. You fill much of the time with such things. So time is taken away and its so precious. You cannot build a community if there is no time to work with it. How can something be supposedly successful, no matter how you measure it, if you don't give it time?

Despite the influence of broad, social issues, the teachers generally acknowledged the central position of power held by parents, especially regarding Zepeda reaching and maintaining its academic achievement. Many informants emphasized that a trusting relationship between the school, parents, and community members was foundational for Zepeda to exist as a symbol of solidarity and the community's quest for social equity. This active and intense involvement with the community demanded two things of teachers: (1) adoption of more responsibilities, a challenging task given teachers' extreme workloads, and (2) the expansion of their roles to include more overt political activism. The next section examines the second point in more detail.

The Politicization of Teachers' Roles

Through the assistance of TIAF, Zepeda was gradually evolving into a viable political center for the community. Thus it is important to understand how teachers constructed their role in relation to this specific aim—whether or not they understood themselves as political agents and how they perceived the school as a political site. On what level were individual informants aware of these elements and how did the politically based goals of TIAF influence their work as educators? For example, Toby's comment that teaching at Zepeda enabled him to serve the community was also expressed by many other informants. Pre-K teacher Jane who had been teaching at Zepeda for fifteen years stated "I like it here. I feel I am making a difference."

Although many teachers commented that Zepeda's association with TIAF had dramatically changed the school for the better, Jane believed that a sense of community existed before Zepeda joined with TIAF, although affiliation with the organization had created more solidarity and thus "political clout."

> I always felt like there was a sense of community even before TIAF. There has always been a hard-core group of families that did a lot for this school. I don't think maybe they were as politically astute and knew how to band together and be the squeaky wheel that gets some grease. But I think they had a good sense of self in wanting good things for their children.

Jane had a very strong commitment to the children at Zepeda and its community. She believed that this deep commitment was necessary for her to remain a teacher at a school like Zepeda. She was also quite aware of the broader social and political meaning that teaching in schools like Zepeda raised for teachers, whether they seemed aware of it or not.

> I feel like every teacher at this school is committed because believe me you'd wash out here. If you're not committed to what you're doing, you're not here for very long because you got to have heart and have a commitment. You have to like your kids. . . . In schools like this one, and most of us have been here for a while, we have a lot invested and we want our children to succeed. We realize how vital it is for them to be successful. Our society hinges on whether or not the people that we're standing on, are going to survive. In a capitalist society the rich people are standing on the backs of people down here. I am well aware that what I do is crucial to our society. Maybe it is as important as what anybody else does. I don't want class wars. I want my child to grow up in a safe environment where she has respect for all people. Hate is not a family value. We may be the exception. I don't mean to be thumping our drum, but I really think most teachers here, want to be here. They are not here because we could not go any other place. I think teachers on the west side [a wealthy school district] think that, but that isn't true. I think we're pretty dedicated.

Jane's political stance was expressed through the story of defending her students and Zepeda against those who held negative stereotypes against the poor in general. This story was also told by several other teachers. For example, Johanna described how she has become "more politicized" through her defense of the school and its community against negative stereotypes. She explained how she "gets into fights with people who say you can't do anything for the east side [of the city]" or who taunt her with questions about whether she's been stabbed or if her students bring guns to class. She quickly pointed out that "I chose to be here. I begged to get a job at Zepeda," a commitment that has caused her to "get real dedicated" to her school and its community. In fact, Johanna was distressed over typical public attitudes toward poor people in general. For example, she expressed outrage by a former district board member's statement, which indicated that the parents are the ones to blame for the neglect and poverty of the east side of town, thus totally ignoring the larger structural forces that create social and economic inequities.

Johanna explained how TIAF's presence helped build community through the generation of solidarity—specifically that large numbers of community members versus the typical involvement of only a principal and a few teachers acts to create political power.

> It [TIAF] has helped because a lot of people think that for the east side, you're not going to get anything, especially when Antonio goes by himself or two or three teachers show up at board meetings. That's what had always happened in the past. It helps for the board and elected officials in the city to know that there is a group, hundreds of people who vote, and if you don't deliver, well, you won't get the position. . . . So I think it's just the power in numbers who are willing to put up a fight for the east side.

However, Johanna was quick to add that although teachers may be deeply committed to the cause of fighting for the rights of the community, "teachers still don't have any regard. We're not held in very high esteem, and just because we say that the kids need computers or books, they [those in positions of political power] don't listen. But a huge number of people, *that's* the difference. They don't listen until there is a revolt."

First-grade teacher Sharon, who had experienced all of her six years of teaching at Zepeda, also had to defend her choice to teach at Zepeda. She was frustrated by negative stereotypes of the community and the students. She also declared that her experience at Zepeda had been very personally rewarding.

> I just think that these kids are very loving and giving, and they only view themselves as being poor, and I think they're just real special and I want to, I bet I can really make a difference in their lives. And I get into all these debates with people that—I don't feel like poverty necessarily makes poor parenting . . . people don't know what it's like. They just have these stereotypical ideas.

Sharon told me that although she had what she needed as a child, her mother, a single parent, struggled financially, "so I guess I can put myself in their situation, have empathy for them, not feeling sorry for them to an extent that I'm not helping them to succeed, but that knowing the importance of them needing to learn and prosper."

Third-grade teacher Margarete explained that she also defended the students and Zepeda against negative stereotypes. In her story, which involved her experiences at another Texas school, she stressed that some of the worst perpetrators of offensive stereotypes were teachers.

> A teacher aid once asked if I had a particular student in my class, which I did and then started talking about the kid's family—they lived in a trailer park and the father works at a car wash and that he gripes about the lunch card in the cafeteria—he goes and pays but there's always some mix-up. I thought I'd like to meet this person—a homeowner, he worked, he's paying his dues and the child's not on free lunch, so he wasn't so bad after all. Some people have different views about things I guess.

Shelly, the school librarian, described the role of TIAF as becoming "a kind of a conscience" for the school in terms of exposing the staff to new ideas about learning and experiencing different roles. In fact, many of the teachers expressed that teaching at Zepeda afforded them a sense of serving the community. A few believed that they had become politicized through their teaching experience at Zepeda, especially as it became affiliated with TIAF. Toby, for example, a non-traditional teacher with an academic background in journalism, expressed that, "TIAF has had a very heavy and positive influence on Zepeda and what has happened here [in the community]. . . . I would say that just from my association with them, one of my plans or one thing I am interested in for future plans is community organizing."

Toby's perceptions about the needs of Zepeda illustrated how he had been influenced by the general philosophy of TIAF. At one point, he made reference to the "Iron Rule."

> Here you have a disenfranchised community that doesn't feel like a part of the larger community. They don't understand that they can take the power that is there to be taken. It may be a struggle, it's not just there to take. But it can be done. The education level in this community is fairly low and that is the kind of thing that cripples a move toward organizing yourself to get what you need, or taking power because people don't know where to begin. They need an organization like TIAF, not to do things *for* them, but to show them *how* to do it. And also to identify and locate those leaders who are out there who will need to be trained and be instilled with the confidence that they *are* leaders and *can* make a large difference in their neighborhoods.

Toby believed that his being politically aware and active within Zepeda's community added "many roles and dimensions to the job as a teacher." This expansion of role did not, however, make his job seem "more real" as such a stance would "denigrate the job that teachers do in other schools and in other areas." However, Toby believed that teaching in a school like Zepeda was highly challenging because academically "the kids are not getting the reinforcement or foundation at home, whereas kids from other areas of town come to you already with basic skills." Also, he added, "we have the role of social worker added to our jobs in these neighborhoods— making sure the kids are clean, getting enough sleep and eating well."

Georges explained that, having spent time as a child in the neighborhood and still having family within the community, that "for myself, I have been able to bring a little bit of my own wanting to be here. I need to be here because I've seen a lot of things that have been barriers to my friends and to myself." Georges perceived that what youths need is an adult who gives them a sense of hope for their future, "and I think teachers that stay here a while develop that sense. . . . So for the most part I think a lot of teachers at this school have that same belief—that there is a reason that they are here. The teachers that are here have a lot of coreson [heart]. They show it by going that extra mile." Georges believed that many of Zepeda's teachers make personal sacrifices and volunteer their time for love of their students and that such a level of dedication is rare in schools.

Many of the teachers commented on the dedication of their colleagues. Georges, for example, was especially grateful to another fifth-grade teacher, Christine. He praised her dedication and passion for the students' welfare. Several of the teachers praised Shelly, the librarian, for her role as the catalyst for the school's reading campaign. Shelly perhaps epitomized the typical Zepeda teacher, who not only wants students to achieve but also to develop an improved sense of personal and cultural pride. "I am concerned about what happens to these kids from now on out. If they don't graduate, if they don't have a good feeling about themselves and being able to cope with society, then what we've done hasn't helped very much." Shelly, who much earlier in her career, had left teaching for a year "because I was worn out," explained why she returned to teaching. "I had a—and this ties in with who I am spiritually in terms of my commitment to society—I tend to need a mission. A mission is important to me. . . . I've always been a person concerned with underdog issues." Marjorie, a kindergarten teacher, stated that she stayed in education because she "wanted to help children. . . . and [it was] the missionary syndrome. I wanted to do something good for society." Jane also wanted to fulfill a need to contribute to society. "I'm needed over here. Low income students need you."

As pointed out above, Antonio had explained that he was actively seeking teachers who were not inspired so much by a "missionary zeal" but rather were "angry about social injustice." However, those teachers who admitted to possessing a "missionary zeal" seemed also to possess anger at social injustices. Even so, only a few teachers were deeply self-reflective and even conflicted about the political implications of the schools' mission. Shelly's misgivings about the political implications of the school's reading campaign is a case-in-point.

Frankly when I look at what we are doing here at Zepeda, forcing kids to become readers, I question, sometimes, the entire idea. I don't know that I want children to buy into my own lifestyle. . . . So the very idea that I am trying to sell children all this myth, that if you get an education and work hard you will have a better life, I am not totally convinced that some of these families out here don't already have a better life, time with their families perhaps. I know that is also romanticizing poverty and that is not true either. But I am just not convinced that what we are trying to sell, the product that we are trying to sell— get this good education, get in the rat race, be a lawyer, have a good job, make money, travel, etcetera—I'm not sure that has *anything* to do with what the good life is all about. So, there is a part of me that questions that whole myth and the way that *I* bought into it. The way I explain that away is that this is the society that our children live in, and it is *not* okay for me to make that choice for them. I need to give them every tool I can give them so at some point they can choose for themselves. But if I *don't* give them the educational tools they need, then they won't have a choice. So I just lay the whole issue aside.

Shelly was one of the few teachers at Zepeda who shared this depth of critical self-reflection. It is clear that the political and social reality of poverty inspired Shelly as a teacher and "defender of the underdog." Although this was similar to Marjorie, a self-described "missionary sort," and other teachers' perceptions, no other teacher expressed a critical awareness of the power of white, middle-class ideology and its possible oppressive effects on those who live outside the dominant culture. Shelly's insight could be interpreted as blasphemy because it questioned education's traditional aim of inculcating the dominate culture's values. Or, her stance could be perceived as naive, a fact she acknowledged (e.g., the romanticizing of poverty) but rejected. Her compromise was to accept that poor, urban children need basic skills so that they have at minimum a chance for personal choice and can live within and between the two worlds—the values of the dominant culture and those arising from their unique cultural framework.

Jane expressed a self-reflective, although pragmatic perspective about her role. "I am real aware of what I do—institutionalize children. But I try to do it in a kind and just way because they have to learn to work in an institutionalized setting to survive in society." Jane, however, remained highly critical of the typical Horatio Algier myth of success.

There's a myth in this country that it's real easy to move from one social class to another, and that's a *big lie* because it's not! It's almost impossible to move into the middle class these days. But that's the myth—that you can pull yourself up by your bootstraps, move easily from one economic strata to another. And you can see it everywhere—on TV. And that's not true! You can still do it, but it's very, very hard. It's *crushing* ! People try, and they work hard but then their kid gets sick or something and it's too much.

It is clear that most of the teachers seemed to be highly committed to serving the needs of poor, urban students. This aim was supported through the introduction of TIAF, which served to raise the general level of political awareness among many of the teachers. However, the effort to build collegiality at the campus level and an extended relationship with the surrounding community are complex endeavors. As Georges expressed, social barriers such as complacency and isolation need constant attention through conversation, a point also raised by the PTA president Theresa. Under the guidance of TIAF, Zepeda's mission was not only to raise standardized test scores and build a sense of solidarity at the school, but also to instill in their students a sense of pride in their culture and hope in their future despite the reality of their poverty. However, one specific means through which the school's academic aims may address social and economic barriers was to ensure that all Zepeda graduates had acquired excellent reading and language skills. The next section examines the school's effort to change the status of reading within the school and the community. This endeavor not only addressed issues related to curriculum and instruction, but also social and cultural barriers.

Changing the Status of Reading at Zepeda

After the "cathartic experience," the teachers were faced with the task of revising the curriculum. Antonio endorsed Margarete's suggestion that Zepeda use the district's official Gifted and Talented (GT) curriculum for all students including resource, for which he received permission from the district. Antonio recalled that, at the time, adoption of the GT curriculum symbolized for the teachers a way to leave the painful past of failure behind. Although adoption of the GT curriculum may have symbolized a psychological turning point and a new beginning for the teachers, it also provided actual structure and direction to the instructional enterprise. The GT curriculum, a "back to basics" approach, was very focused and narrow in scope with an emphasis on reading and basic math skills. While the GT curriculum was used for grades K–3, the upper grades developed a more thematic-based curriculum. Although the school had eventually acquired better TAAS scores, the pre-K and K teachers were concerned about the general intensification and acceleration of the curriculum.

Despite concerns related to scope and sequence, most of the teachers agreed that, for the particular needs of Zepeda students, a highly structured and focused curriculum, centered around the acquisition of basic mathematics and reading skills, was both necessary and highly successful. This was evidenced in the school's teacher-initiated enrichment and support programs. Also, high standardized test scores were ultimately equated to political cache. This political cache of being a high performing school enabled Zepeda to initiate and sustain broader social initiatives for the school and community. Therefore, it was imperative that Zepeda keep its TAAS scores high even if this imposed end stifled the instructional means. Thus, preparation for the TAAS test had now been integrated into the curriculum. For example, in one-fifth grade class I observed, the teacher devoted a certain amount of time each day to TAAS instruction. Shelly, who teaches first grade, reconciled the reality of being required to devote precious instructional time to developing testing skills by equating testing skills to "social skills" that the children are expected to possess.

> I think that any school that does good on the TAAS makes an effort to do good. It's not that they're teaching toward the test, they're just exposing the kids to what has to be on the test and its basic skills. So in my opinion I don't see anything wrong with that because it's not going to hurt a child in life to have these skills that people expect them to have.

Despite the collaborative decision to focus on the TAAS, not all of the informants concurred with Shelly's reasoning. Many were very uncomfortable with a district and campus educational policy that emphasized high stakes standardized testing. Christine regretfully stated, "basically, our curriculum is driven by TAAS, especially reading and math." Pre-K teacher Jane reasoned: "Yeah, we've improved our test scores, but I think we are really focused on score improvement and there is so much more to education than passing the TAAS test! That is real limited and I don't agree with testing." Although Jane recognizes that the "powers that be" are only interested in test results, "I don't agree philosophically that we can look at students in terms of cost versus improvement attained. I don't think it is a business or that individuals are a business. . . . In education we have standardized everything, including people."

Georges, who would "like to see our educational system stop relying so heavily on standardized tests," also believed that the school's Electronic Book Shelf (EBS) reading program (designed for grades third through sixth and requires that each student read a minimum quota of book pages in a given timeframe) focused too much on the quantitative measure versus the innate pleasure of reading in and of itself. A computerized drill and practice-based test, whose content was designed by the teachers and librarian, was used to measure a student's comprehension of each book's content. Data from these tests helped teachers monitor individual student's reading progress, the effectiveness of their teaching strategies on individual students, and also formed the basis of students' grades in reading skills. For Georges, "it [EBS] does help test comprehension. It gives us an easier way to measure that success. But I think in the end it has to be that the students are grasping the book content and enjoying it for the love of what it is and not just because they need to finish those pages. It is important that they read because they *want* to read." Toby concurred, describing the EBS system as simply a "drill and practice routine." However, Christine believed that EBS was structured in terms of its goal but also flexible enough such that each teacher could present curriculum content in his or her own manner, especially in social studies and science. All of the other informants perceived that the EBS system was highly successful and were comfortable with this instructional framework, especially since it seemed to be effective in terms of helping them to meet standards.

Despite the variance in personal philosophies about the policy of high-stakes testing and quantitative performance measures, the teachers and administrators understood that they had to do something about their students' poor reading and language skills. In response, Zepeda had introduced several reading incentive programs and the librarian had purchased three new computers dedicated to CD-ROM–based encyclopedias for the library, which featured various reading levels. However, at the time of this study teachers found that although students seemed excited about using the computer, their poor reading skills became a real barrier to the computer's success as a viable teaching aid.

The highly structured instructional plan and several incentive programs for students eventually helped to raise students' TAAS reading test scores. However, teachers' efforts were constantly challenged by a more elusive element than effective curriculum. The following subsections examine other sociocultural influences, which the teachers believed affected students' attitudes and performance in reading and language skills and academic achievement in general. These concerns were: (1) media, (2) poverty and isolation, (3) peer and cultural influences, and (4) discipline and violent behavior. The following chart outlines the complexity of Zepeda's challenge by indicating the disconnect between Zepeda's literacy educational framework and aspects of a broad sociological framework.

Table 5.1: The Dynamics of Developing Reading and Language Skills

Educational Framework	*Sociological Framework*
(1) Curriculum	
Teachers' collaboration via teams	-popular culture and media
GT materials	-peer and cultural influences
Thematic based units	-poverty and isolation
	-discipline/aggressive behavior

Continued

Table 5.1—Continued

(2) Instructional Strategies	-popular culture and media
TAAS drills	-peer and cultural influences
Reading incentive programs	-poverty and isolation
Structured but flexible design	-disipline/aggressive behavior
(3) Technology	
CD-ROM encyclopedias	-structured curriculum
EBS system	-face-to-face communication
D&P based tests for comprehension	

The Influence of Media, Poverty, and Isolation

A common thread that weaved throughout the informant's perceptions was the desire to foster the potential in each student despite challenges posed by poverty. Indeed, the quest to instill a respect and love for reading, not just the skill of literacy, was the aim behind many of the teachers and the extensive reading incentive programs offered by the school. However, several of the teachers, when referring to the quest to create a "love for reading and learning" not only mentioned the challenges that poverty brought to their endeavors, but also the children's social habit of viewing television and film (videos) rather than engagement with reading or conversation. Many of the teachers found the violent content of much of the media to which the young children of Zepeda were exposed as being very disturbing. Some perceived that the children's limited life experiences (many had not traveled beyond their neighborhood) and social isolation were being exacerbated by the passive process of extended hours of watching TV and videos whose content seemed inappropriate for young children. These social habits seemed to reveal a deeper problem—neglect of children by their caretakers. Many of the teachers, however, did not understand this phenomenon as being particularly special to the students and community of Zepeda; rather they believed that it was systemic and normative within the general culture. The following quote by Johanna exemplifies these perceptions.

> They [her students] watch things that I would never allow my kids to watch—ever! . . . It's cable, and it's parents not being home or not supervising their children and their watching all kinds of garbage. . . . They're just young parents and I think the whole—it's really society. I mean people don't have morals anymore. . . . We've been talking about this at school. We can talk to these kids

about having good character, having good character, having good character, don't do drugs, and they go home and their father is, you know, snorting a rail of coke [cocaine]. It's real difficult for them to hear it at school and then they go home.

Several informants mentioned that children's conversations and imaginative writing directly reflected the content of movies, television programming, and advertising. For example, Margarete noted that in a writing exercise in which students could go anywhere in the world with a famous person, most chose a popular movie or sports celebrity as their companion and having a McDonald's Happy Meal as the destination. Margarete also was concerned about the violent content of the movies the children watched and how it seemed to have become common sense for them. "I'm shocked by what most of them watch. There are some pretty horrible movies and they've seen them—violent, very violent. And they don't think anything of it!"

Toby was adamant about the negative effects of television on learning. "I think TV is one of the single most detrimental uses of technology that we have." Toby explained that the generalized effect of television has been to foster children's dependency on technology and immediate gratification. He also felt that although resources such as The Learning Channel and Public Broadcasting exist, they "seem to be utilized by those who already have a firm educational base." Toby related that he often overheard his students talk about the movies they see which he described as, "Freddie Kruger—a lot of schlock, horror movies that really don't seem to me to be appropriate for children." Toby's perspective on the effects of mainstream media left him in a awkward position for although he was "very much against censorship, I think there's some common sense that needs to be exercised."

Christine, a strong advocate for computer-based instruction, believed that exposure to television, versus computers, specifically had disengaged children from valuing reading. However, because of the growing commercialization of the Internet and the popularity of video games, Christine believed that both TV and computer usage must be monitored carefully by parents. "I know a lot of parents who say 'oh, my kids spend a lot of time on the computer!' And I ask, 'what does your child do on the computer?' Well, you might as well as hook it up to the TV!"

Marjorie, who teaches kindergarten and has a total of 34 years' teaching experience, often compared the present condition of teaching to her earlier years as a teacher. Today, she explained, teachers needed to literally entertain children—"teachers are challenged to make learning exciting and to be 'big bird' all of the time." Other teachers referenced the need to entertain students. However, only Marjorie recognized that this seemed to have occurred while the perception of teachers by the public had shifted—"they [teachers] are not as respected as they once were."

To Marjorie, the most insidious challenge to teachers was the negative effects which media seems to have upon children's general behavior and their ability to think and reason. It is not so much the content, although this is often a problem, but rather the habit of spending so much time in the act of watching media that seemed to have replaced or altered basic familial social interactions. This phenomenon seemed to be further exacerbated by the pressures of poverty. For example, Marjorie explained that lack of conversation with parents or elders in the community had negatively affected children's language skills. She did not attribute the apparent decrease in language skills to the challenges of ESL (English as a Second Language), for she has always taught poor, Hispanic children. Rather the changes in family patterns of social interaction, time once spent in social discourse that is now occupied by passively watching TV, videos and video games, could, she reasoned, be a strong factor in diminishing children's language skills.

Like many of the teachers, Marjorie believed that what she was experiencing at Zepeda was not an isolated phenomenon, but reflected a change in the larger society's values. "I do know that children do not know as much as they did before. . . . Well, the children today have more to cope with than we had. I am thinking of the drugs. The world has changed. And it's not just our country, its worldwide. There's more to deal with. And the parents are struggling to make a living."

Jane concurred with Marjorie's perceptions about the limitation of the children's language skills. She explained that much of her time is devoted to the development of students' language skills. "We work on language because they are very limited in language. Some are not but most are. They know what they want to say but many times they do not have the words to express it." Jane perceived that the problem resided with the effects of poverty. Many of her students "do not have the influencing experiences that children with money and affluence would have had. They have not been everywhere and done everything. They are essentially isolated in their neighborhoods and the projects." Because of their isolation, she believed that her students are especially vulnerable to the negative effects of media. Jane had witnessed this in her students' imaginative play and like other teachers was shocked by how many students were constantly exposed to "slasher movies." Shelly also explained how the isolation of the typical Zepeda student was exacerbated by the media in terms of its negative impact on their imaginative thinking and communication skills.

> Our kids don't have experiences. . . . You can only write so many stories about murderers coming in and slashing you up or ghosts coming in with their heads cut off—Freddie Kruger kind of stuff. That's what their experiences are, by and large. Not all of them. We have a huge group of kids now who are not that way.

But children who don't go anywhere or do anything only have the television as an experience and therefore their experiences are real scary stories.

Georges not only noted the negative influence of certain media such as horror films—"it does become a part of them. It does. Whether good or bad"—but also explained that his students experience everyday realities of violence. "I have students in here who come in and talk about all the movies they've seen and what they see at night—drive-by shootings—and you wonder how it's going to affect them. At the same time this kid will say, 'look what mom bought me, or I need to get home, my mom worries'—so right there, that's the buffer." Thus, Georges believed that if a child does not have "a loving and caring person at home who is able to interject some positiveness into that individual, then of course they are going to take from what they see and get . . . the negative stereotypes in the media."

Toby acknowledged the negative effects of media on learning but also explained that, especially for his children who have limited life experiences, it can enhance the quality of learning within the classroom.

> I think that when you're teaching a lesson on volcanoes that making a clay volcano in class, and boiling an egg to show the three layers of earth are great activities and kids learn from them. But then, if you put on a video tape and show them Mt. St. Helen erupting, I think that will impress them with the actual power more than anything else would.

To counter the influence of media on their students, some teachers, such as Christine, integrated information about propaganda and media advertising into their social studies curriculum. Toby, who taught second grade, believed that a more formalized curriculum addressing media literacy should be adopted for all grades, beginning in pre-K.

The vulnerability of children to the influence of media on their imaginative thinking and values often led the teachers to discuss the importance of critical thinking. However, many lamented the fact that schools inadvertently teach children what to think rather than how to think. Shelly offered the following reflection on this issue.

> We need to do learning instead of talking about learning. . . . To see the thinking process so when they are confronted with media and other information—kids don't have the power and knowledge and awareness that things are not really true or how to make judgments. We don't teach them much of that. We assume they get it at home and I'm not so sure they do.

Shelly had assumed a leadership position in terms of the school's literacy campaign and believed that addressing the issue of literacy was very complex as it was as much a curriculum issue as it was a social issue, a point raised by other informants. Thus, in addition to the influences of the media, poverty, and isolation, the teachers also reported on the negative influences of peer and cultural factors, which is discussed in the following section.

Peer and Other Cultural Influences

From the perspective of Marjorie, her students' poor language skills reflected their parent's limited vocabulary. "It is really sad that [in comparison to suburban children] they walk through the door, I would say at least two years behind in language skills." Marjorie believed that the root of the problem was that parents did not understand the importance of reinforcing or modeling the valuing of scholastic achievement. "My own children were very little when they heard about college. But these children have never heard of college and they have no idea so they don't want to go." Marjorie also pointed out that parents do not understand how simply modifying the valuing of reading can positively affect their children's academic ability. For example, by simply taking time to read to and with them. Other teachers concurred with Marjorie's perceptions and the issue emerged as so important that Zepeda became a participant in a local adult literacy program and created their own program designed specifically to train parents how to read to their children.

For Shelly, the problem with reading was not just the influence of popular culture, media, and poverty but also a specific resistance to reading itself. This resistance to reading, she perceived, seemed to be exacerbated by an anti-intellectual and functionalist approach to the value and purpose of education in general.

> I am not sure that critical thinking and conversation, dialogue and analysis has ever been part of or the moral of public education. I think parents are really afraid of that—the kids are too young. You cannot talk about any topic that anyone can get upset about so that pretty much eliminates most topics of any value. We say we want good education. What we *really* mean is that we want our kids to get the best jobs and get paid the most.

Shelly added that this situation is not just the fault of education, but rather "is part of society and the way society is in this country and we [schools] are simply a part of that society." Thus, according to Shelly, the fact that "research on children's motivation to learn points to peer influence—period, what we have been trying to do over the past five years is to change the status of how kids feel about being a reader." Like Marjorie, Shelly perceived that reading has not been "valued among so many families, kids and society in general, particularly in certain school situations." Shelly also explained that many parents admitted to her that reading was so very hard for them and no one ever pushed them. Thus, she reasoned, as did Marjorie, that parent's own poor reading skills may inhibit them from assisting their children. Shelly also explained that because children are media literate and watch complex narratives, they may find books on their reading level to be uninteresting. Nevertheless, the teachers "have become the extrinsic motivators." Shelly stated that Zepeda children will learn to read "because a child is too young to make a decision at an elementary age that they will not be a reader. It cannot be a choice." Indeed, the array of incentives and support programs made it seem as if Zepeda was literally marketing a positive perception of reading to its students. Therefore, for Shelly, the key to Zepeda's academic success had been the creation of a sense of community involvement and "intentionality." She stated that "there's a lot of group focus and intentionality and a sense of everybody getting into it."

Discipline and Violent Behavior

Zepeda's endeavor to inculcate positive attitudes toward academic achievement and reading had one other barrier to face—discipline problems. Not all informants mentioned this factor as a challenge specific to the complexities surrounding reading. However, most teachers did explain that time spent with behavioral problems diminished the quality of the general instructional experience. Those teachers who referenced discipline problems shared particular stories to communicate the complexity of their experiences and feelings about this issue. The teachers' experiences offered a wide range of impressions. For example, Jane believed that she successfully avoided discipline problems by securing the trust of parents through making home visits.

At the time of the interviews, however, the mandatory home visits policy had been changed. Teachers could choose between having conferences or home visits. Shelly, for example, did not go on home visits, but chose to regularly schedule conferences with parents. Shelly believed that, as a first-grade teacher, she acted in the capacity of a primary caregiver. Thus, socialization plays a significant part in her role. She added that "my children bring a lot of outside issues with them that need to be taken care of before they can learn." Shelly admitted that she had discipline problems with a few students. During one particular observation she fought back tears when she realized that a set of toys, which she had planned to use in a lesson, were missing. The repeated incidents of theft, she explained, betrayed her good-heartedness and left her feeling confused about her deepest commitment to her students and profession. Weeks later, however, she was happy to report that the missing toys had "reappeared" in the storage closet where she had last seen them.

Another teacher, Johanna, believed that one major contribution to discipline problems at Zepeda, and schools in general, was the mandatory inclusion in classrooms of emotionally disturbed children. Marjorie also held this position. Another contributing factor is that many more parents are quite young and immature and have poor parenting skills. In addition, according to Johanna, teachers are forced by societal demands to keep their morals and attitudes out of the classroom. However, Johanna concluded that "if I don't do it, who's going to? I think moral responsibility can be bringing in your homework."

The principal of Zepeda explained that the school's policy is to make a safe environment for learning through behavioral discipline. If a child disrupts a class s/he is put in a time-out situation first in the classroom and later outside the classroom. If their behavior persists, particularly if it becomes violent, they are sent to an off-campus alternative center. Zepeda had a full-time counselor/social worker who was available for private and group counseling sessions for the students. In general, Johanna believed that Antonio supported the teachers when he enforced discipline procedures, but, at one point in the previous year, she had to take discipline matters into her own hands. She described her story about five particularly disobedient students with much emotion and difficulty.

> Last year, [pause] I had a rough class [pause] and I made this big announcement. I said—I'm not teaching you, you, you, you and you. I'm done. As far as I'm concerned, there are only fifteen of you in this class. When the five of you decide you want to learn, let me know, but I'm not going to mess with you anymore.

She stated that she had spent more time disciplining these five students than teaching the other fifteen and that "I just could not do it for myself, mentally. Sometimes you just *have* to. You can't sacrifice fifteen for five who don't give a crab." She explained that, despite requests, the parents did not offer their support. "Parent conferences don't help. Consequences don't help. Kids who are spray painting the walls outside—that's some of the kids I had last year. Pretty hard core. I tried very hard up until early December and then, no more."

Johanna described herself as having high standards for her students and refused to reward those who misbehaved or would not work hard. "And the kids know I'm strict, but they learn. So every year I have some mad parents and they yank their kid out of class" indicating that the problem was with Johanna or some other "bad student," but never acknowledging the misbehavior of their own child.

The problem of losing precious instructional time to discipline problems was also an issue for third-grade teacher, Margarete. For example, she shared one particular story that, for her, epitomized the discipline challenges that many teachers face on a daily basis. The incident involved a moderately emotionally disturbed child. She explained how trying to teach this student was a futile effort, and had a direct negative effect on the quality of the learning environment for the other students. As with Johanna, Margarete's recounting of her story was very difficult and emotionally painful.

> The students that are moderate to severe, it's just really hard. It takes its toll on the class. The class misses out because we're spending so much time taking care of them—calling the office, writing him up, sending him to time-out, getting work for him. It's just a big distraction. And the one I had last year [pause] we just didn't feel *safe* with him in the room and that's not good. These kids, you know, their home environments aren't so good, so stable and safe, and they have to come to *school* and not feel safe? . . . We lost a lot of instructional time when he was in the room. It wasn't like I was teaching. He would make noises, be throwing things, turning over things, dumping out his desk, just really distracting behavior and it lasted the whole first semester.

Margarete also related that most educational policymakers are out of touch with the reality of the everyday classroom because, "they're thinking of the ways schools use to be when kids come and sit down and do their work and say 'yes, mam' and 'no, mam.' But that's not the way it is anymore. They're saying F-U and B-I-T-C-H, all kinds of things. And this is elementary!" When asked how she dealt with such behavior, Margarete explained that its demoralizing effects were compounded by the fact that teachers have very little power.

> It's real hard when a kid tells you to shut-up or F-U bitch. It's not a pleasant thing. Your day just goes downhill from there. [long pause] So, you write them up. That's all you can do. You just focus your attention on someone that wants to be here. That's what I do, right or wrong.

Marjorie believed that many discipline problems arose from the emotional disturbances of certain students. She explained how she felt helpless and unqualified to help these children.

> I feel that the children I am with everyday advance in their year with me. I'm getting them as far as I can take them, as far as they are able to go. And some can't go. Not because of lack of intelligence. But because they are carrying a big emotional load that makes it very difficult for them to think. And then you try to work on that. The trouble is, that we are not qualified to do this. You really feel inadequate dealing with some of these big time problems that really takes a professional, and there's no professional in here so I got to do the best I can.

Marjorie also reported that there was an increase in the number of students who seemed to have moderate to severe emotional problems. Although this may be an artifact of inclusion practices, she also pointed to the fact that the general character of society had altered in subtle but profound ways. For example, Marjorie explained that more than twenty years ago the poverty for Hispanic children was much more extreme. Even so, changes in morals and values had affected the way people raise their children and thus the quality of children's behaviors.

> I think there was greater emphasis on the home and the family and I think they taught values at home more than we do today. Things like sharing and caring for other people than ourselves were really taught and I think that's been lost. I really don't see it anymore. I think in a lot of cases it's religion because this should be a solidly Hispanic Catholic neighborhood, and I don't see that either. They don't seem to go to church anymore, not all of them, but the majority of them say they've gotten away from religion. Which I think is a part of it. And that is part of the family system and value system. . . . The adults have problems coping with their world and don't always have time to deal with the children and so they are left to fend for themselves. Well, it's a different world than when I started teaching.

The complex array of issues related to the school's literacy campaign illustrates how the crisis in education is anchored by deep, systemic issues within society-at-large. This is evidenced, for example, in the fact that the teachers associated the challenges surrounding literacy to broader social issues such as poverty, the colonizing effect which commercial mediated reality has on youth culture and children's imaginative thinking as well as the loss of traditional values. Also, when directly asked whether or not a crisis exists in education, the teachers responded that the foundation of the crisis resided not in education, but rather in society-at-large. This response was similar to that given by the Shelton Valley Middle School informants. With the exception of Christine, who was very much concerned about the issues of chronic underfunding of education and lack of adequate access to new technologies, all other Zepeda informants referred to their common belief that education's "crisis" simply mirrors a crisis or breakdown in the general social order of modern culture. This perception was also reflected in the teachers' visions of education in the 21st century. The next section reviews these perceptions. I begin by examining the problems that Zepeda's students experienced during their transition from elementary to middle school.

Renaming the "Crisis": Toward a New Social Vision

One problem related to the educational "crisis" issue that was mentioned by most of the informants was in reference to how Zepeda's students found it difficult to transition from elementary into middle school. Although students seemed better prepared academically, they struggled with particular aspects of the middle school culture. For instance, the scale of middle school, its large facility and student population, the fact that they had several instructors versus one, and, most insidious, the economic gap between Zepeda's children and more affluent students and its social and emotional effects—the combination of these elements had a negative impact on students' performance. Antonio characterized the transition as such: Students moving from an environment in which they were a majority to a social environment where they are the minority and in which they become immersed within a wealthier middle class social environment, "something which they had only experienced as an imaginary world of TV and now it's real for them."

As with other problems, the Zepeda staff designed programs to address these concerns. For example, Zepeda began to rotate teachers in the fifth grade; integrated more project-based curriculum in the upper grades; instituted the Zepeda Alumni Program which enabled former students to access the library and volunteer tutors; and a clothing drive. Zepeda also received funding, with the help of TIAF, to support the hiring of a liaison person at the middle school, who monitored student's academic and social experiences and then reported the information back to Zepeda's principal and the student's parents. Even with these initiatives, the academic failure of Zepeda's students at the middle school level was high.

The librarian believed that Zepeda's teachers prepared their students via these programs as best as they could, but that there was nothing they could do about the structural reality of their students' economic and social status. Speaking in reference to the transition of Zepeda students from elementary to middle school, Jane related that, for most students, this is the first realization of the extent of their poverty and class status.

> They can't compete materially. That's the heartbreaker. It's sad. They may have been aware that they did not have as much as everyone else, but now its—some people have everything and now I have not very much. But they cannot compete materially. And since our society is so focused on greed and material goods, and that your worth is based on what you have rather than who you are, I really feel like we have [pause] I tell you school doesn't need to be restructured, our society needs to be restructured! We seem to be gluttony, fame and infamy and I'm real troubled by it. I don't think schools are so much in trouble as our society and what we find to be so valuable is really disturbing to me. It teaches children so many things that are so invalid.

Margarete also believed that lack of traditional cultural values was the root cause of the crisis situation. She explained that the gap between the ideal of schools and their reality was directly related to a breakdown in the family and the values that support a family-centered way of life. To some extent Marjorie's observations reflected the rhetoric of the religious right reform efforts, but, as a teacher, Marjorie placed these concerns in the context of how society's system of values and the consequent abandonment of its children is naturally played out in the behavior of its youth within the context of school.

> I think the whole breakdown is the family. I just honestly believe that's what's happening. That's why we have this big gap because of the breakdown of the family unit. . . . Not that we're doing poor jobs. It's just that they [students] have so many problems that teachers can't just come in at eight o'clock and start teaching. That just doesn't happen like it use to. The concerns in the 60s and 70s were, you know, spit balls and food fights. Now its pregnancy and drugs and I think that all just comes back down to the family unit. . . . Parents taking back that basic responsibility.

Marjorie's perception of education in the 21st century also reflected these points especially in reference to the presence of violence in schools and society in general.

> I don't know. I'm scared. I'm scared. If they don't do something about all of the hate. The violence. I see very little learning going on in the future. I think the [economic] gap will widen or else you might have it where certain kids will go to one school and other kids will go to another type of school. . . . That's what I see. I mean that's not a good picture but I mean I just can't imagine everyone coming together and the world being peaceful and everyone learning side-by-side. I just don't know how that's going to happen.

What is significant, I believe, is not only the fact that Marjorie envisioned a bleak future, but that she could not seem to imagine an alternative.

Johanna was also concerned about the negative behavior of students, a factor which she associated to broad social issues. In addition, Johanna and Shelly believed that certain policies, especially those related to discipline within the educational system, were exacerbated by the present social condition. Johanna offered her opinion as follows:

> I think it's management of students and discipline. And where it's also a crisis, because learning can't happen, is because of the gang violence or children not coming to school because they don't have anything to eat or they're not healthy. So I think it's a global type of thing. I don't think it's just because they don't have computers in their classroom. . . . I've seen and heard about classrooms in this city where the discipline is so out-of-hand because no one's making these kids responsible for their choices, in terms of their behavior.

Johanna expressed similar concerns when she related her vision of the future of education. She foresaw, because of budgetary constraints, fewer teachers and larger class size. She also believed that some kind of voucher system would eventually be adopted.

Shelly expressed deep concern about the social problems of poverty and lack of interest in reading. Ironically, she believed these problems were exacerbated by policies created to address equity and the rights of students, which seemed to have inadvertently degraded the overall quality of education. Additionally, those students who were not "college material" also suffered because, according to Shelly, the educational system did not provide an adequate means to meet their needs. Thus, the system still manages to create its own form of "failures" despite its emphasis on equity and student rights. You may recall that the special education teacher from Shelton Valley Middle School made a similar point. Shelly believed this to be a very complex and difficult situation for public education because it drives to the heart of our competitive versus egalitarian-based system of education and its function as a sorting mechanism for social and economic status. Shelly explained what she perceived to be the real crisis in education in the following quotation.

> I think the real crisis is that our children are not learning a whole lot. It's an extremely complicated problem having to do with educating masses. In fact, it is so politically charged that we are not able to track kids at all, and I can argue both sides. . . .If you got children who are college material, gifted kids, and you are trying to deal with kids who don't want any part of it [school]. We have no way in education of dealing with how those kids need to be educated. There are so many problems in education that I don't think the Information Age is the issue. It doesn't even get on the chart for me.

In relating her projection of education's future, Shelly explained that the system of education, even with electronic technologies, would not fundamentally change. Although some schools may be "technology rich," she could not imagine this occurring in inner city schools such as Zepeda because of lack of funding. She also imagined that vouchers would become a reality and this would further exacerbate the economic marginalization of schools like Zepeda. Shelly also reflected on the future of education by comparing the past 30 years to the present condition, specifically regarding teacher training and the concerns of teachers.

> By and large the students coming out of the education programs are a lot like I was 30 years ago. Still just as naive and just as unaware and just as undereducated. I don't see much difference. . . . We are still asking the same questions about kids—why didn't he learn? So, I'm not so sure it is going to be so different thirty years or so down the pike.

What Shelly would like to see in the future for Zepeda is that students and teachers would engage in "*doing* learning instead of talking about learning" and that students "have to become readers and critical thinkers." In general, Shelly would like teachers to teach fewer hours so they have time for reflection. "I don't see things changing very much unless magically people decide that teachers need more time to think." Thus, Shelly believed that "to a great extent, things will be the same. It's a big bureaucracy and it moves slowly. . . . I've done this [teach] for 30 years and have learned that changes come very slowly. The only positive thing that has not changed is that there is still as much love and concern for the kids."

Georges indicated that the top-down approach of policy elites has been painful for teachers, but even more so for students because they are the ones who internalize such educational dictates. Georges stated that "the only crisis in education is not listening to our youth and what they say. We're just dictating to them what needs to happen and what kind of standards need to be kept up." Georges believed that the problems with education reflected a larger and deeper crisis in society. "It's just a reflection of our society. There's so many conflicts out there. We are still grappling with the whole idea of racism and inequity between the rich and poor. The school system is just a microcosm of what we see out there."

Also, Georges was adamant about the fact that the infusion of electronic technologies would not address the real crisis facing both schools and society, because, despite technical skills, children would still be returning to a difficult home environment. This point was also raised by Margarete. George's perception, that we are "not listening to our youth," seemed to indicate that many children, not just the poor, have been abandoned by both parents and society. He explains this point in the following quotation.

> It's [technology] not going to change anything. Kids will still go back to homes where there will not be anybody home and deal with whatever is going on in their surroundings. Those are the real, I guess, 'technologies' that need to be looked at—the human technologies. And if you don't have that, you can surf the Net as much as you want, but you always come back home. I mean, technology, of course you can say, yeah, it will benefit, there is no way I'd hesitate—supply us with laptops, that would be great! But that will not be the key to it all. That will not solve all things that are going on. You will still have your discipline problems and non-parent involvement. It's always going to be there unless you find a way to work with the individual. Find the root of why it's happening. Why there is no communication.

In his forecast of education's future, Georges longed for an educational system that would not be centered around standardized testing and a competitive ideology. George also made frequent references to the theme of "not listening to our youth" and offered an approach to education that addressed this issue.

I would like to see our educational system stop relying so heavily on standardized tests. Instead, look more at what the individual has garnered and how they can relay and convey information and their own insights and realities back to hope, and how they can become a citizen. In other words, their own importance of life as it is. That would be my dream that an educational system would look toward that as the standard in which we have students who are living and giving back to their communities. . . . That needs to be the system that we develop—a system of understanding. An understanding of why things happen. Why things are. We need to stop having an educational system where we give them a sense of 'this is why this happened and that's it!' That's what I hope. The reality is, I don't see that coming in the near future.

Toby acknowledged the reality of the Information Age, specifically the creation of a deluge of information and information anxiety, and believed that schools needed to teach critical thinking skills so that the future generation would not become overwhelmed: "Teach them to filter [information] and make choices and use common sense." Although Toby's perception reflected the concerns of policy elites who also emphasized critical thinking skills, Toby's reason for focusing on such skills ultimately was to create politically astute citizens, not just effective "knowledge workers." Toby believed that allowing young children to watch slasher movies illustrates a general absence of skills in being astute citizens and further indicates that "something has broken down somewhere along the way—our values are lacking."

Toby's projection of education's future painted a picture of a crossroad where education could "just be like it is now. It could be very technology-oriented or run by Dow Chemical or IBM—the IBM school. We are kind of at a juncture now. There are several roads to take and I don't think we are leaning toward one or the other." What Toby would *like* see happen, however, is that education "return to more traditional ways." He reasoned that "traditional education is not working so well now because so many other things are now nontraditional." Toby explained how a more traditional classroom setting would "necessitate a traditional family setting. To see less of a breakdown of the family you would have to see more cohesiveness of the society—not this fragmentation that we have now. That's what I'd like to see, but I don't think it's possible or realistic at all." Toby also explained that although his perspective may be criticized as mere romanticizing of the past, "for the future, I can see a lot of potential harm rather than the benefits that come from a lot of changes that are going on."

Sharon envisioned that education would still struggle with high dropout rates in the future. She perceived that the crisis in education was accurately depicted by policy elites in that education was not able to meet the needs of the developing Information Age. However, Sharon did not feel that schools were at fault. Rather the state of "unpreparedness" was due to lack of adequate funding. Sharon also believed that the infusion of technology was not necessary to reform schools. She stated that a commitment to the creation of a common vision among teachers and administrators, much like what Zepeda had initiated a few years ago, was fundamental to successful reform.

Jane, as did most teachers, related her prediction to her personal practical knowledge (Clandinin & Connelly, 1995) of schools. She wanted the elimination of standardized testing and the categorization of children. Her ideal vision of education in the 21st century centered around schools honoring the importance of early childhood education in low income areas, interage grouping and greater emphasis on the arts. She also wanted children to be taught to be "a force for the good" of society.

Marjorie expressed in her outlook on education's future, much like Margarete and other participants, the presence of social problems.

> I hope that society has improved. I hope that the world has settled down and that we are not killing each other and we are concentrating more on caring for each other. If society is better, education will do well. But we are reflecting all the problems that we have in society today. It's overwhelming! I would not know how to cope with all this. Where do you begin? I hear the politicians saying we need more family values. But how are you going to legislate that? You can't make people have family values if they don't have them. . . . I hope that it finally swings back and we do have more family values or more caring people.

Antonio would not venture into expressing what might unfold for education's future. However, he had a definite ideal vision of what schools could become and how Zepeda embodied that ideal vision.

> I think schools could become again centers of community like they were. But centers of community not in the transmission of the received culture but centers of community in the reformation of communities that have been dispossessed like this one. There is talent in this community. It just has to be developed. There are resources here. They have to be identified. I think schools can become a bulwark against the forces of oppression that come down on communities of poverty. My vision for Zepeda is that it will become a model for urban education.

The only informant who offered a technology-centered response when asked to reflect on the "crisis" in education was Christine.

> *We're* [Zepeda Elementary] in a crisis! [waving toward the interior of her classroom which did not have any computers] Do you see any computers in here? And the problem is that schools aren't prepared because to be able to do this [use new information technologies], you need mega money. . . . And whether or not schools use it to its full extent and take advantage of it, is going to depend on whether or not people are given the time to plan it.

Many of Christine's colleagues referred to her as the school's "computer wiz." She setup the PC lab's network system and was responsible for its maintenance. Having taken several classes in computer programming, trouble-shooting, and networking, Christine was the "trail-blazer" at Zepeda. It is not surprising that she expressed a technology-centered vision for education's future. She envisioned schools having computers functioning like textbooks and that teachers would be "less of an imparter of knowledge because you got something better—you got that computer— the world to find your knowledge." Christine seemed comfortable with imagining that knowledge exists outside of individuals and described how telecommunications technologies would expand curriculum and fundamentally alter instruction to include interactive broadband (visual/audio) media.

Christine admitted that her perception of education's future was technically centered and understood that "some people find this terrifying." When I suggested that teachers may resist adoption of certain technologies because these technologies did not fit into their model of pedagogy, Christine could not imagine such a consideration, so convinced was she that technology could be only a positive force in education. Also, Christine had no misgivings about using technology as a means to reform education because "it's a benefit. It's changed the business world and makes things run much more smoothly." She did not perceive the growing presence of new technologies in our lives as signaling dependence, but rather was the measure of growing improvement in the quality of life, making it "easier." However, at one point when Christine explained the difficulties that educators faced with coordinating the integration of new technologies into education, she realized the contradiction in her thinking—the reality was that the addition of technology actually made teaching more complex, when the illusion is that technological innovations make things easier. Also, Christine was critical of the commercialization of the Internet and World Wide Web and acknowledged with regret that the marketplace influenced the diffusion of technology into education, especially regarding the "targeting" of poor urban schools for ILS. Also, Christine described the Information Age to signify the social challenge of the "bombardment of information" as well as signifying the ease and convenience of access to information; literally having it "at your fingertips in a matter of seconds."

Christine's focus on technology-based issues was unique; she was the only Zepeda participant, including the principal, who fully engaged information technologies as part of Zepeda's reform plan and future. The singularity of Christine's position, I believe, is important. Thus the next and final section on Zepeda examines how the informants perceived computer and information technologies in relation to educational reform. I found that the teachers' perceptions about the nature of the current crisis and their perceptions of education's future was further complicated by their perceptions about the relationship between society and technology.

The Influence of Technological Innovation

As explained above, Zepeda's affiliation with TIAF led them to emphasize the building of "social capital" or the measure of a community's collaborative time toward building reciprocal relationships, an endeavor that emphasizes face-to-face social interaction. Also, because the school focused on addressing difficult socioeconomic issues, many participants downplayed the priority of computer and information technologies in terms of educational reform. At the time of this study, Zepeda had very little computer technology. Only some of the lower grade classrooms had one computer, as did the one-sixth grade class. The upper grades had two labs, one PC and one MAC, both stocked with old equipment. The library had three newer computers with CD-ROM–based encyclopedias, although the library's cataloguing system was not automated or networked. The school was scheduled to be wired to the state's educational WAN at the time of the study and still the only access to the Internet was in the library and was used by very few teachers and the librarian.

Antonio and Margarete explained that the introduction of computer technologies does not guarantee academic achievement, but that the most certain path to successful educational reform is working with personnel. Antonio, who believed that most reforms are superficial because they avoid the issue of power, referenced other schools in his district that had invested in new technologies "and their performance didn't change. . . . Technology is just a tool. It's the relationship between teachers, students, and parents that determine whether or not learning will take place." His position about educational technologies resonated with his personal feelings about computer technology. Antonio had not and did not plan to own a computer. He added "I feel computers are wonderful but they isolate us from being relational with other people." Although Zepeda was soon to be connected to the state system's WAN, Antonio explained that despite his personal feelings. "I don't divorce myself from the need for children to be technologically proficient. They have to be proficient in their use because that's the future."

Magarete also believed that the key to successful educational reform was people, not technology—a realization she based on her experience with Zepeda's reforms.

> It would be with the teachers, parents and the principal—that's where I think you have to start with reform. I don't think you can keep all the same teachers

and just give them new supplies, new desks or computers, and you have reform. It comes from the staff and parents. That's where reform starts. Because that's what we had to do when Antonio started.

Margarete further explained her position on this issue through a story about her past experience at another technology-rich school.

In a lot of districts, like at Tempte for example, because I was there, I know they had spent thousands of dollars on getting new Macs for every kinder, first and second grade class. All of the schools got these brand new Mac computers and they were very nice. But you had the same old staff, the same teachers that had been in the same classroom for fifteen or twenty years. They were expecting 'our scores are just going to shoot through the roof.' They thought they would have improvement. Achievement would go up. But it's been four years and it's still not improved.

Margarete's comment, to some degree, reflects her understanding about the relationship between society and technology, which was not philosophical but rather pragmatic and critical. Margarete defined the relationship between society and technology as being purely monetized. "I think technology is for money, to make money. Make a few people very rich. . . . What I hear mainly in the media would be technology is to make money." Such an attitude also supports her critical understanding of policy elites' technocentric vision and reform policies. Convinced that "computers cannot teach," Margarete was concerned about a common unofficial policy within several local school districts that was to redirect funds allocated for teachers' aids to purchase computer technology. "You know, a lot of places cut their staff and their assistants so they can buy more computers." She then pointed out a pragmatic truth: "You don't have to pay insurance on a computer, you know, all the benefits that come with hiring a person."

Both Kathryne and Antonio perceived that the use of any technology that acted to mediate the communication process (i.e., electronic mail) needed to be used with care, since, through the process of mediation, the experience of face-to-face communication is lost. This factor is especially important if one aims to create purposeful relational interaction toward the goals of building community and relational power. Kathryne explained how, as an example, the technology of polling and surveys can change and delimit social interaction. When the community and TIAF first debated the needs of the community and what particular issues they were to address, most people suggested that they conduct a survey. Kathryne related why this procedure, however, was not applied to their discovery process.

We've become a 'survey culture' and that is really related to technology. But there's no human action in surveys. There may be information, but there is not the building of that kind of relationship [that arises] in discussion and dialogue where people learn to know each other and become vested in a relationship and are willing to work together and take some action together. . . . Surveys could be a good documentation. They have their place. [But] we had to work real hard to keep people from wanting to just put the survey out there as a substitute for meeting and having discussion because it's easier and it's less risky.

Some of the teachers' impressions about computing technologies offered some interesting contradictions. For example, Jane, who had a new Mac computer in her classroom, believed that the computer offered her students another means through which they could practice their reading and language skills. Still, both she and Marjorie preferred "hands-on" activities for their young students because the tactile and socially based experiences seemed most engaging and enriching. This perspective has also been proposed by educational psychologist Jane Healy (1998) and other researchers (Armstrong & Casement, 2000) who have raised critical awareness about the negative effects of computer technology on young children's cognitive and emotional development. Similarly, the librarian was very excited about how students appeared to relate more positively to doing research when they used the CD-ROM–based encyclopedias. Even so, despite the fact that Zepeda had very little money for more experiential learning, such as visiting museums or parks, Shelly preferred these activities to the use of the computer simply because her students' life experiences were so limited. However, Shelly was thoroughly convinced of the computer's ability to motivate students.

Maybe kids would get bored with it [computer based instruction] eventually. They do with other things. But because of its newness, and it is appealing because of its immediacy of reaction to the child and interaction. Kids tend to shut down by fourth and fifth grade. They're bored and don't want to sit in the classroom and listen to the teacher. . . . They tolerate a whole lot more learning on the computer than out of a book. They think they are not reading somehow. Books have gotten such a bad rap that reading on the computer has a different feel and they're willing to tolerate that.

Shelly was quick to point out that computer technology "is not the answer to all of our problems," and she would not just "sit kids in front of a computer all day." Still, she perceived that the interactive feature of good software "offsets the mechanical and technical aspect. There has to be a human element. But you put a poor teacher next to a computer, the computer might win. It would win as far as I'm concerned."

A few of the teachers mentioned that computer and telecommunications technologies could have dehumanizing effects. Johanna thought this was the primary negative effect that characterized the relationship between society and technology. Jane also raised concern about technology's potential dehumanizing effects, especially within educational contexts. Others were concerned that technology was becoming both the means and end of the current educational reform movement. In this context, Jane, for example, worried about the obsolescence of computer technologies and a typical school's ability to spend limited resources on "high fiscal outlays to just keep up." She also noted that, although corporate America complains that public schools do not prepare students for the Information Age, these companies' bottom-line interests prevent them from offering any real assistance to schools to address this concern. Jane also believed that technology had advanced so far that it had outpaced society's ability to adequately negotiate it effects. Specifically she believed that more information may not be what society needs right now. However, Jane's understanding of the Information Age was complex and included reference to having "easy access," creation of a global community, and the danger of sensory overload. At one point, the paradox of the new information technologies became apparent in her attempt to negotiate the issue of isolation. On one hand the experience of isolation could be potentially exacerbated through a transformation and diminution of social interaction by new information technologies. On the other hand, these same technologies had the potential to eradicate the perceived isolation of schools through transcending the limits of time and space while offering a democratization of information, an outcome that she believed would "level the playing field."

> In that way it levels the playing field somewhat so that everybody has more or less but you have to have the technology first. And the technology is expensive. In that aspect it could be limiting but I think it really increases our global involvement and makes things a lot more equal in many respects. . . . I hope it does not become isolating. I still think we need to interact with actual human beings. That is still going to be the way life is.

Jane's perceptions about the relationship between society and technology indicates, I believe, how teachers move between the knowledge spheres of their personal practical knowledge and that of teachers' professional knowledge landscapes (Clandinin & Connelly, 1995). Sometimes this "border crossing" can lead to rather contradictory reasoning. While Jane fought to get new computers for the pre-K and K classes, she also believed that "my priority in school is my children, not computers."

Other teachers, such as Georges, recognized the importance of public school's need to "continue to grow with all the new technological advances. He also believed that "there is a community out there that we need to bring in and educate as well [about computers]. If we don't, we leave too many people behind." Georges was concerned especially about the division between those districts that are technology rich and technology poor or the "digital divide." This situation was an artifact of a general widening of the economic gap between the rich and poor.

> There is a strong push by our government to downsize a lot of the [equity related] programs that have been effective. And this new technology, I think it will develop into another avenue where people will be left out again. It's scary that society is building again the haves and the have-nots.

Georges' perspective on the relationship between society and technology was very philosophical. He explained that "an easy answer would be just to say it makes life a little bit simpler. But we have so many contradictions that it is not going to make life simpler by adding things." Georges believed that technology was essentially a paradox, existing both "as an enhancer and a divider." He understood technology's essential nature as expressing whatever we bring to it as both individuals and as a society. Perhaps it was his fine arts background, but he conceived technology as a plastic and expressive medium that can present "another way of thinking." He also understood that technology can be internalized and signifies change or growth for better or for worse. "Perhaps it [technology] develops within you and as each person encounters it [long pause]. It's a growth and that growth will either be negative or positive." Georges' perceptions seem to point to the idea that society's and individual's relationship to technology is inherently political and perhaps moral. He further eludes to this point in an example he offered, which illustrated how technology can act to express social values, specifically the isolation that arises from class division.

> Technology allows us to create whole cities with huge walls around it. A subdivision with huge walls. That in itself becomes an isolation. How was that isolation created but with the technology to be able to create your own surroundings? Your own hobblaire. A division was created because technology was there to create an electric gate and electric surveillance cameras. You are isolated. You have separation. I don't know [pause]. If that division, that technology was not there, there would be communication. It is like that.

Georges' picture of wealthy citizens isolated in walled and gated communities under the watchful eye of electronic surveillance systems seems interesting to contemplate in terms of his reference to the loss of communication. The paradox is evident. With the advent of the Information Age and its networked systems, on the one hand there exists a greater potential for global communication within an aspatial and atemporal cyberspace "reality" through connectivity. On the other hand, we have developed, by means of such technologies, more sophisticated means of delineating physical isolation and social stratification. This paradox was exacerbated by Georges' prediction that the gap between the "technology haves and have-nots" would become a serious social problem in the future: "Life will be unpleasant for those left out of the computer Information Age." Georges defined the Information Age as "having access to many ways of receiving information," such as radio, television, newspapers and the

Internet. Georges, however, stressed that access was not the point. Rather, students need to be taught to go beneath the "surface content" and "start to explore other avenues of seeing" to develop a critical perspective. These other avenues included the act of dialogue and building a sense of identity and solidarity with their own community.

The librarian Shelly also expressed a complex understanding about technology. For example, she stated, "I'd like to think technology is an outgrowth of society's ability and knowledge. It's just a tool. Technology is a tool that we use to improve our lives. That is what I hope it is." However, Shelly pointed out how such a perspective was naive and inadequate. "To me, when I think in terms of how technology is becoming so powerful in our lives, that *we* become the tool. That's scary! That's science fiction— computers taking over kind of thing. I don't know." Shelly stated that she was uncomfortable thinking about the question. But she felt this attitude was not atypical. "I am typical of society to a degree. It is one of those things that you really need to think about [technology and society] but I just don't want to think about it, and I don't think that's uncommon. It's just too 1984ish and I don't have any control over it."

Shelly further reasoned that, in general, people do not question the current policy to infuse schools with technology because "people *do* buy into the idea that if getting information and education and learning is going to get you a job . . . and get it faster . . . we think it's good!" She believed that it was not culturally acceptable to raise questions about technology's relationship to society although "it is probably the most important question" facing society today. Shelly, a sensitive and caring person, related that she had stopped reading newspapers "because there are things I just don't want to read about." Although she could perceive the paradox of technology, she struggled to maintain the "hope that technology remains just one of many tools to help us create a healthier and happier—and a more compassionate—society." Then she quickly added, "But somehow, technology and compassion just doesn't match."

Toby also expressed a very complex understanding about the relationship between society and technology. He believed that, in general, society was too dependent on technology, especially media, and the negative outcome of this was the expectation of "instant gratification." He predicted that "someday in the not too distant future a lot of the technology we lean on is going to break down." Toby further explained that "our society has a strong fascination with technology right now. You see it in entertainment— all plots that are wrapped up in the changes technology will bring. Futuristic movies set in the future right now are heavily involved in predicting." Toby was uneasy about the current rate of technological change.

To me it seems that the whole pace of society is speeding up. The tempo is increasing more and more and that is not good, as it seems the crescendo, it almost seems like an explosion is imminent. I think that the way society is running now, violence, a lot of that, and I'm not sure what is causing that effect. But it seems to be a symbiotic relationship with technology and how fast technology is changing. I think people have such a hard time keeping up with that. It leaves a sense of impotence with people. It keeps people confused and ill at ease. I'm not sure what words I'm looking for here [long pause]. A disorientation. That's what I was searching for—a sense of nonimportance. [It's] unimportance that people are feeling.

Despite certain teachers' misgivings about technology in schools and their complex understanding about the relationship between society and technology, most of the Zepeda teachers believed that students needed to secure computer technology proficiency to be successful in middle school and later in the job market. This understanding reflected the discourse of policy elites. Both Marjorie's and Sharon's perceptions were typical of such responses. In fact, Sharon made reference to policy elites' influence to further legitimate her own stated position, a position that also reflects a naive understanding about the adoption of new technologies.

[Marjorie] I really do believe we should do it [infuse schools with computer and information technologies]. Because this is the future of the world and this is where we are headed and if you don't know it you are going to be left out. And I want our children to compete. And they won't be able to without technology. They have got to have it. That could mean good jobs later.

[Sharon] Having technology in education is a benefit because, it's just like they're saying, it's changed the business world and it makes things run much more smoothly. . . . I just view it as our quality of life improving. That it makes things easier.

However, in later conversation, Marjorie expressed skepticism about the assumption that a technology-driven policy would solve the social problems challenging education today. She believed that it is erroneous to assume that "it [computer technologies] is going to take care of our problems." She perceived that as a society we tell ourselves that "all these wonderful things we have will solve our problems, but of course, they're not going to." She then predicted that "and the more we depend on it [technology], the worse trouble we are going to get in if we don't watch very closely."

Georges, who expressed a very complex understanding about technology was also pragmatic about children needing to acquire computer skills. However, he took exception to how typical top-down technology infusion policies were used to control teachers' work and direct the learning experience. He stated, "I don't want it dictated or shoved down my throat. . . . Don't let this tool be another facet in which we say 'we're going to standardize your ability to complete this test by using technology. You need to be able to do this. If not, you fail.'"

Georges' demand that electronic technologies not be used to further control teachers' work raises another important question related to technology infusion into schools—the nature of teachers' resistance to technology adoption. Although the issue of fear was mentioned as a barrier by some of the participants, most of the teachers qualified this factor by pointing out contextual and structural constraints. For example, the most frequent reason suggested by the participants regarding teachers' resistance to electronic technologies was lack of time to learn how to feel confident about using them in an instructional situation. Johanna believed that teachers would resist if the technology was being forced on them, a condition she perceived to be exacerbated by the fact that most top-down reforms incorporate very little teacher training and support. Marjorie, who thought that a major barrier was "old teaching habits," also explained that the drill and practice learning theory embedded in much of computer-based instruction is unappealing to many teachers. Toby related that resistance was mostly a generation-related condition because older, more experienced teachers were not required to learn about computers until recently. Also, Jane explained that a mystic surrounds computers—"either you're a nerd or not"—and most teachers do not see themselves as a "computer nerd." Shelly perceived that lack of technical support was a major barrier to technology adoption and was the reason why she was taking computer training classes. Only Christine believed that a teacher's willingness to learn about technology reflected their level of teaching ability. She explained that teachers who attended technology oriented meetings and workshops were generally those teachers who were not threatened by technology because "they were also secure in their teaching ability."

The teachers at Zepeda were not required to have any additional training in technology other than that required by the state or district. According to Christine, even though the teachers seemed to understand the value of students' acquiring computer experience, training in keyboarding was lax. This factor was openly admitted by Toby. Christine complained that, in general, the teachers were not interested in using technology in their instructional practices, they did not attend her computer training classes, and seemed only capable of conceiving of computers as simply a drill and practice application. The laxity in giving students adequate time with keyboarding instruction, according to Christine, was having real negative effects—Zepeda students were far behind their suburban counterparts in middle school in such skills, a factor that, she believed, only exacerbated other academic, social and economic disadvantages.

However, there were a few teachers, such as Johanna, who taught her students to use word processing and required that her students use it for all of their research papers. Johanna would also have preferred to have four to six computers in her classroom with CD-ROM encyclopedias. She envisioned herself training her students to use the research software and preferred the idea of having computers in the classroom rather than having to work out an elaborate class management scheme to get them down to the library, a factor she felt wasted precious instructional time.

In addition, Christine regularly scheduled her students to work with Marjorie's kindergartners in the lab. The fifth graders taught the kindergartners how to use the computer and assist them with completion of their computer-based tasks. Also, first-grade teacher, Sharon, took her students to the MAC lab every day for 40 minutes where they used a drill and practice program in reading and mathematics skills, which, she felt, was very effective.

In general, most of the informants at Zepeda, given the school's lack of access to computers and telecommunications, found it very difficult to imagine what they would do with Internet access and more computers or how the technology would change their instructional practices. Georges' perceptions about electronic technologies were similar to Jane's who recognized telecommunications' potential to eradicate the isolation of schools. Georges also believed that the use of telecommunications could help bring the outside world to the children of Zepeda, remedying some of their physical and social isolation.

However, because Zepeda's reform strategy revolved around the goal of making Zepeda a center for building and sustaining a solidarity within its surrounding community primarily through the process of face-to-face communication, connectivity's supposed potential to eradicate social and economic isolation was looked upon with healthy skepticism. Also, the reality was that for most families in the community, access to a computer, much less the Internet, was nonexistent, and would likely remain so for some time. Georges asked rhetorically, "How do we remedy this right now?" His remedy was simple, yet profound, and, I believe, reflects Zepeda's general position, under the guidance of TIAF philosophy, on the use of technology to reform education.

> I think there is a plausible remedy now and that is as long as we are able to communicate to these individuals here [students] that who they are is very important and they do have the abilities right now to go out and discover new things and ideas. Perhaps now we may not have access to the world but your world is here. And you can access that and you can discover your world here and we can communicate with that. Maybe they can take that with them and when they get to the next level, from here, if they have their world with them, they can add to it for the rest of their life.

As you can see, the story of Zepeda offers a very different educational reform narrative because, through its affiliation with TIAF, the school had focused its vision on recreating Zepeda as a civic space for the local community. Zepeda's reform program emphasized securing "social capital" and "political space," and thus is quite unique when compared to more typical technocentric reform efforts. One is thus compelled to compare the two narratives—Shelton Valley Middle School and Zepeda Elementary— and note how each school is very different in terms of their particular needs, and how they addressed those needs via their reform efforts. As pointed out in the following chapter's comparative analysis of the two case studies, technology stood in a different place for each school. At Shelton Valley, technology was at the center, whereas for Zepeda it waited at the margin.

Notes

[1] At the time this study was conducted Zepeda Elementary enrolled 460 students and approximately 86% were Hispanic, 13% African American, and 1% white. Ninety-three percent of the students were classified as "economically disadvantage," which was very high because the district and state level was at 50%. However, the mobility rate was average (21%). The number of students classified as Limited English Proficiency (LEP) was very high (29%) in comparison to the district (13.8%) and the state (12.8%).

[2] Ernesto Cortes, Jr. (1995, p. 300), Southwest regional director of IAF, stated that the Iron Rule is the "centerpiece of IAF's organizational and educational philosophy." Cortes explained that "the most valuable and important aspect of intellectual development is self-development, which is critical to the accountable utilization of power. The Iron Rule recognizes the preciousness of self-discovery." Ultimately the Iron Rule leads to the practice of leadership and self-determination, a process dependent upon participation in political deliberation and development of reciprocal relationships through collaborative action.

[3] Ernesto Cortes, Jr. (1995, p. 305) defines "social capital" as a term that identifies "the value of a community's relationships." In contrast to "human capital," which are individual skills, "social capital is a measure of how much collaborative time and energy people have for each other." Cortes admits that although an unfamiliar term to many, social capital "is crucial to the resolution of crises and the alleviation of poverty" as are more familiar forms of capital, such as financial capital. In terms of educational settings, Cortes referenced the work of James Coleman (Essential Schools), who defines social capital within the context of education as "attention from responsible adults" that students experience within traditional institutions such as churches, schools, families, and neighborhoods (Cortes, 1995, p. 306). His central point is that social capital focuses on building and maintaining reciprocal relationships based on mutuality and respect.

[4] Ernesto Cortes, Jr. (1995, p. 299), Southwest regional director of IAF, explained the importance of "relational power," in terms of building community, as follows. "Relational power is complicated because it involves a personal relationship, subject to subject, developing the relational self." He further explained that the IAF and its affiliated programs, such as local city chapters, teaches people to develop "the kind of power that is imbedded in relationships, involving not only the capacity to act, but the reciprocal capacity to allow oneself to be acted upon. In this context, relational power involves becoming calculatingly vulnerable. . . . In a word, empathy" (Cortes, 1995, p. 299).

CHAPTER SIX

Embracing the Lifeworld:
Understanding the Technopessimism
of Educators

> . . . *at what cost have we come to accept as our lifeworld, this world which is moulded by the instruments of our civilization. To what extent have we, by adapting to it, become maladapted to our own selves? Does our civilization produce a lifeworld to which we belong through* our culture of living, *or does it leave the entire domain of sensory values adrift, in a state of barbarism? The inability of our dominant culture to think reality as it is lived is in itself a reply to these questions.* Technical culture is lack of culture in all things non-technical.
>
> Andre Gorz, 1989, author's italics

Through this study I have sought to understand how current reform discourse as political texts function as a sociopolitical framing device and ultimately create a specific technocentric social vision. A framing device acts as a means of constructing a world via language and narrative form (Bruner, 1990). Thus, the general aim of this research project was to better understand this process by means of gazing at the narrative framework of technocentrism through the eyes of educational practitioners. Also, because current reform efforts emphasize a technology-driven reform policy, this study also placed emphasis on issues germane to technology infusion, including the examination of how the dominant social narratives about technology influence educational reform policy (e.g., constructing technology as a tool and/or social process).

An analysis of the actual reform discourse revealed a dialectical play, or as described by Kleibard (1992, p. 186), "a dramatization of ritualistic myths about America and its values played out on the proscenium of the public school." However, as previously discussed in Chapters One and Two, the two perspectives—the dominant technocentric position of policy elites and an alternative perspective, which represents a traditional humanistic framework that emphasizes social justice—are exceedingly out of balance. The technocentric discourse has achieved dominance through the rhetoric of "inevitability" and also by way of the continuity of its historical influence. The narrowing of social discourse is of great concern because educational reform discourse exists as a "narrative space," where social discourse acts to construct a broad social framework or social vision. Therefore, this study set out to compare the basic assumptions of policy elites, in terms of educational reform policy, to that of teachers to discover to what degree, if any, the dominant social vision of policy elites had become normative or commonsense to educational practitioners, and to what depth performance culture had penetrated the lifeworld of schools. Thus, one outcome of this study was to revisit the legitimacy of the underlying assumptions that guide policy elites.

This study also compared the discourse of policy elites, which represents a distinct aspect of teachers' professional knowledge landscape, to the contextualized experiences and tacit knowledge of teachers' personal practical knowledge which, through its inherent emphasis on the realm of relational knowing, has traditionally represented the spirit of a humanistic perspective on education. To further elucidate the negotiation points between educators' professional knowledge landscapes and their personal practical knowledge, I offer the reader a comparative analysis of Zepeda's and Shelton Valley's stories of reform, which explores the differences and commonalities between the two sites.

The comparative analysis of the two school sites is guided by an analytic framework that features four distinct levels. The first level relates to the informants' experiences and the context of their school's reform efforts. This section is presented as a general overview of each site's narrative plot and subplots. In the second section I discuss the informants' perceptions about the sociopolitical aspect of educational reform policy—specifically the "crisis" in education and its relationship to the Information Age rationale proposed by policy elites. In the third level of analysis, we will examine the informants' perceptions regarding questions about the sociotechnological aspects of educational reform policy, such as their misgivings about technology infusion, why teachers may choose not to use electronic technologies, and how the informants understand the relationship between society and technology. In the fourth level of analysis, we explore the informants' projections of education's future given current official reform policy.

These various levels of analyses reflect the dialectic tension between the two major philosophical frameworks that characterize the educational reform debate—the technocentric perspective of policy elites and an alternative perspective, which is represented by their critics. In addition, the analysis captures how teachers attempted to negotiate their personal practical knowledge with factors arising from the broader dimension of their professional knowledge landscape. Also, the aggregate of the data delineates a general perspective on the informants' social visions. As indicated in the previous two chapters, although the reform efforts of Shelton Valley and

Zepeda Elementary were very different, the informants shared very similar social visions. In addition, the interpretation of the informants' social visions draws upon the work of historians Leo Marx (1994) and Howard Segal (1996). I conclude this final chapter with a discussion about the meaning of the findings within the context of a postmodern technological society.

A Comparison of Zepeda's and Shelton Valley's Stories

The story of Zepeda Elementary is about an urban school serving poor Hispanic students which, through a difficult "cathartic experience," gained an identity and consciousness. The "cathartic experience" occurred when the parents confronted the teachers about the schools' low test scores. Antonio, the school's principal, invited the parents to take a stand against the teachers and assert their rights. As a result, many teachers left, but for those who stayed, many experienced an exciting transition and professional awakening.

Through its affiliation with TIAF, Zepeda's community of teachers, parents, and administrators rescued their school from the effects of complacency toward their lack of community solidarity, political engagement, and academic success. TIAF's philosophy, reflected in the aims of building "social capital" and "relational power," acted as a framework through which Zepeda could build community solidarity. These practices laid the foundation for trust between teachers and parents and teachers and administrators. TIAF's Iron Rule, "never do for another what they can do for themselves," allowed the organization to scaffold the school's transition into a greater sense of community solidarity and to exercise the will to secure political power. The academic success afforded Antonio the "political space" to continue in pursuing community-based social reforms. Thus, Zepeda acquired board permission to utilize the state's official gifted and talented curriculum for all of their students and the school fought the board and local religious right opposition to their having an on-site medical clinic, a program that grew to include several other schools serving poor, minority children. In addition, Zepeda developed an accelerated sixth-grade class designed to ready its students for admittance into a local science magnet school, and initiated an extensive literacy program that included a structured curriculum and instructional strategy and several incentives and support programs such as tutoring in reading for students and their parents. Also, many of Zepeda's several programs were conceived and designed by teachers. The informants deeply appreciated how the administration acknowledged their professionalism and granted them autonomy. In addition, the teachers experienced a great sense of collegiality.

The story of Zepeda relates the birth of a new vision of community spirit, a vision that expresses the creation of a school culture, which Nel Noddings (1992) described as one reflecting the value of caring, or perhaps what Thomas Sergiovanni (1994) meant by schools as "communities of learners," which emphasizes intrinsic moral, relational, and cultural connections and where teaching is a practice of stewardship. Therefore, the transition of the school's community also meant that the teachers were invited to not only fully experience the ethic of caring but also become more politically active because the framework of TIAF demanded the politicization and expression of the individual agency of teachers, parents, and administrators. The teachers responded to this in varying degrees. Some deeply internalized it, whereas others participated on a more superficial level. But, in general, the informants acknowledged and appreciated the inspiration and guidance that TIAF had brought to Zepeda and its community.

In general, the story of Zepeda may be characterized by the creation of community solidarity and transitions from failure to success as well as from denial to self-awareness. Zepeda achieved a change in their school's culture through adopting TIAF's community-based framework, which sought to express humanistic and democratic ideals such as the struggle against injustice and the belief in human equality. The school's vision of educational reform, therefore, was not inspired by the technocentric discourse of policy elites. TIAF's focus on building "social capital" and "relational power" through face-to-face interaction eschewed processes that mediated the communication act; therefore, Zepeda's reform endeavors did not emphasize a technology-driven agenda. Thus, Zepeda's story supports and reflects the values inherent in those who oppose the technocentric educational reforms of policy elites. This is apparent in how the school's reform strategy reflected the progressive tradition where schools as institutions exist as political spaces and thus not apart from but within and integral to its surrounding community.

However, Zepeda's curricular reforms embodied a traditional and highly structured approach, especially in the lower grades in the subject areas of reading and mathematics. This compromise was rationalized so that the school would continue to meet the state's academic standards. Therefore, the school's administration adopted a conservative approach to curriculum and instructional elements to meet state academic standards so that Zepeda may serve the broader progressive goal of building solidarity within the surrounding community. Although the teachers had developed many supportive programs, one is left to wonder what possible progressive reforms specific to the core curriculum and instructional practices that the Zepeda teachers might have developed, given their sense of collegiality, professionalism, and administrative support, if the school had not been so positioned by the structural factors imposed by state standards and the school's political necessity to constantly meet them.

In addition, while Zepeda's emphasis on community building initiated academic achievement and social reform programs, the philosophy that guided their efforts, which placed great emphasis on face-to-face communication, affected how the school approached the use of electronic technologies. Their philosophical framework, in conjunction with a highly structured curriculum, resulted in the fact that little attention was given to the development of more innovative applications of what technology the school possessed. Zepeda used their computer technology primarily for drill and practice instruction, which seemed to fit their curricular framework.

In contrast, the narrative of Shelton Valley is a story about a small rural school that, however, was beginning to experience changes brought about by rapid growth and the influx of urban values and lifestyles. Although Shelton Valley's story is also about a school's struggle to find its identity rather than turning to its community, Shelton Valley looked outside itself and adopted the technocentric framework developed by policy elites. As a middle school faced with pressures related to rapid changes in demographics, this once quiet, isolated, and rural environment was rapidly becoming a bedroom community of a nearby metropolitan area. Ironically, although many of the teachers were apprehensive about equating this transition to progress, the school's official reform efforts focused on the use of information technologies and its inherent property of connectivity to overcome their perceived geographic and sociocultural isolation. For those who had taken a leadership position at the school and district level, in terms of its reform agenda, access to information became the paragon of educational progress. Indeed, although most teachers were very concerned about problems within the school's milieu, they did not perceive how the introduction of electronic technologies and its potential to invite another level of change could potentially act to further challenge their conservative cultural framework.

The technology adoption narrative of Shelton Valley weaves a plot around two key characters—Mary Jane, the librarian and Shelton Valley's "technology trailblazer," and Roger, a teacher who taught computer literacy courses. Each of these informants possessed oppositional and distinct philosophies about the purpose of electronic technologies in schools and the nature of technology in general.

Mary Jane's enthusiasm for technology-based educational reform was complemented by an apolitical tool-based perception about the nature of technology. She believed in the power of information, a perception grounded in her experience as a librarian and her battles with conservative-inspired censorship. However, her naive conceptualization about technology constructed the purpose of information infrastructures as simply a conduit for the transportation of data—literally the sending and receiving of information. This conceptualization of connectivity, in terms of emphasizing only its transportation feature, reflects the underlying assumptions that guide "mythinformation" (Winner, 1986) and supports a "cult of information" (Rozak, 1986). Thus, Mary Jane's naive perceptions about the nature of technology, especially connectivity, denied how technology acts as both tool and social process. Therefore, it is no surprise that Mary Jane brushed aside questions and issues germane to curriculum and instructional practices within the context of technology integration at Shelton Valley. She spoke of teachers acting in the capacity of "guides on the side," but lacked a clear perception of how this transformation may come about other than the fact that simply forcing teachers to use the technology would automatically bring about changes in familiar and traditional teaching styles.

In addition, the schools' technology adoption plan had no pedagogically based framework. The purpose of technology-based reform was not, for example, formally guided by constructivist approaches to learning or a project-based, thematic approach to curriculum development. Also, Mary Jane's mythinformation-based perspective was mirrored in many who participated in the district's technology planning committees that were dedicated to building a system of local and wide area networks (LAN/WAN). At one district meeting with an IBM salesperson, it was pointed out that the network would be designed as an efficient "delivery system" for TAAS-based remedial support. Mary Jane and others present did not seem concerned about the fact that this very complex and expensive infrastructure would likely be used simply as an elaborate ILS. There was no discussion of pedagogy, curriculum, or instructional strategy. The purpose guiding the adoption effort was simply to have possession of the technology itself. However, since educational policy over the past 18 years has largely focused on the acquisition of electronic technology, this nonpedagogical approach by educators to technology adoption is, unfortunately, very common. In addition, Mary Jane's vision of education, inspired by policy elites' technocentric framework, included the dominance of information systems that would eventually enable the replacement of teachers.

The philosophical differences between Mary Jane and Roger led to a personal antagonism and, to some degree, a factionalism within the school's community. Roger, a nontraditional teacher with only two years of experience, had a professional background as a creative artist in marketing and advertising. Roger's background and experience gave him a critical edge in terms of interpreting the technocentric discourse of policy elites. Unlike Mary Jane, he eschewed mythinformation and possessed a complex understanding about the nature of technology and acknowledged its function as both a tool and a social process. He also perceived that children were often mesmerized by computer technology's "eye candy" feature and that adults were as easily seduced by a "technological fix" approach to eternal problems rooted in human complexity. Roger, therefore, was against Mary Jane's, the principal's and the district technology committee's technocentric approach to technology adoption. He opposed the administration's decision to purchase a new ILS system because he disliked its behaviorist-based instructional strategy. Roger also questioned the rationale and the manner in which Mary Jane planned the installation of the school's LAN, which, in fact, was characterized by delays and irresolvable technical problems. In each instance of technology adoption, decisions were made without a needs assessment, open discussion, or planning. This fact was confirmed by several other informants who were frustrated by lack of access to the computer labs and rejection of the school's technology committee's decisions by the administration (which, in this case, involved the principal and Mary Jane).

The story of Shelton Valley's struggle to find its identity through the framework of policy elites' technocentic discourse, I believe, would ultimately fail them in terms of truly meeting the needs of the school's community and its students' academic success. It is true that the policy elites' framework offered the vision of connectivity and this spoke to some of the perceived needs of the school's community, especially its sense of physical isolation. But the isolation that Shelton Valley experienced was not only geographic. It was deeply embedded in the social practices and organizational structure of the school. The lack of communication between teachers and administrators, for example, was epitomized in the failure of the school's site-based management program, which led to the teacher's distrust of the administration and their general disillusionment. There was a serious distrust and lack of communication between teachers and parents, which many teachers specifically described as "us versus them." Parents, however, were not invited to participate in the school's decision-making process. In addition, some teachers believed that many students were not taking responsibility for their education, a situation that teachers believed arose from parents' lack of engagement in their children's education. Teachers also sensed that students had a general disrespect for them and the values that they represented as teachers. This created a grave sense of alienation between certain teachers and students. All of these breakdowns in the community of the school were exacerbated by Shelton Valley's attempt to negotiate the effects of the community's growth and changing demographics, which resulted in classroom overcrowding, a high teacher-student ratio, and an increase in discipline-related problems. However, little energy and resources were applied to addressing the root of many of the school's problems, which were essentially related to a disintegration of the school's culture and a lack of means to express and develop an authentic community identity in the face of compelling social and structural changes.

In addition, although Shelton Valley sought change and reform through electronic technologies, it failed to utilize the adoption process as an occasion to discuss and deliberate how these new technologies would impact not only the curriculum and teaching practices, but also the culture of their school and the integrity of the values of their rural community. Further, what is ironic is that without a deeper level of engagement with the adoption process by teachers, administrators, and community members, it is likely that the introduction of the information infrastructure would only act to reinforce the existing hierarchical structure (Morrison & Goldberg), thus initiating a typical technical-based "change without difference" scenario (Goodman, 1995).

Thus, the story of Shelton Valley's search for identity is one characterized by a shifting socioeconomic landscape, rapid change, and the loss of a rural lifestyle and values. Those teachers, who sought to "hold the line" against what they perceived to be thoughtless changes, sensed that the problems in their school were related to this larger dynamic, and quietly mourned the loss of a time and place that would never return.

Shelton Valley's situation raises an important issue in terms of how schools exist as places and the challenges that new electronic technologies invite regarding this element. For example, in contrast to Shelton Valley, Zepeda's approach to technology adoption was cautionary and deliberate in that it was understood how the introduction of electronic technologies would necessitate loss as well as gain. In other words, in the adoption process, Zepeda asked what it was they were *not* willing to lose, or what in their school community was important to preserve. This was especially evident in the school's emphasis on face-to-face communication as a basis for building community solidarity. The influence of TIAF's philosophy perhaps enabled Zepeda's members to perceive how the nature of technological change is that certain expressions of the lifeworld become irrevocably altered or lost. Ironically, Zepeda truly exercised choice by questioning technology because by doing so they evaded the seduction of policy elites' techno-utopian discourse of inevitability. Their questioning stance also staved off the specter of technological determinism.

The stories of Shelton Valley and Zepeda also raise questions about the access to information rationale regarding technology infusion into schools. For example, both sites struggled with the issue of isolation. Despite the fact that both of the schools' experiences surrounding isolation were characterized by economic and geographic factors, only Shelton Valley adopted the information access rationale as a means to address this problem. In both cases, geographic isolation was related to the political reality of economic containment of the poor. Given this material circumstance, what is the significance of the virtual space and "experience" of the Internet without a political presence grounded within real local community activism? The essentializing of access to information via the Internet effectively signifies the absence of lived political expression and power. This factor was recognized by Zepeda's leadership and TIAF members; thus, they avoided essentializing Internet access and, more generally, access to information. Rather, Zepeda's teachers favored field trips to sites within the local community. Because Shelton Valley adopted a more typical technocentric approach to reform, they did not avoid this pitfall. Despite elaborate telecommunications systems, the teachers were alienated from parents and students and there was an absence of effective communication between teachers and the administration. Consequently, focusing the school's vision on technology/information access acted, not as a heuristic that could incite institutional examination, but rather as a form of denial that enabled avoidance of their internal problems related to a troubled school culture. It seemed, therefore, that what Shelton Valley truly needed was not a WAN but rather a cathartic experience.

The Sociopolitical Context

The Crisis in Education

As explained in the previous chapters, the basic rationale for the crisis in education and educational reform, as perceived by policy elites, was that schools needed to be changed to meet the needs of an Information Age and the demands of an information-based global economy. However, the teachers' responses, with only a few exceptions, reflected a very different idea about what might be the nature of the current "crisis" in education. Most informants grounded their responses within the context of socio-economic challenges, which influenced their school and students and related these specific circumstances to broader social issues. In general, most informants cited a deterioration in what they deemed as "family values," a term often used by conservative politicians and the Christian Right. However, unlike the conservative agenda, the teachers did not attack the poor nor express racist fear or blame with respect to "violent and wanton" youth. Rather, many cited the general violence within our actual everyday experiences and the glorification of violence inculcated by the social mediated reality of popular culture (i.e., television, video games, film, etc.). Some teachers cited our culture's focus on instant gratification and that crass materiality and a peculiar selfish individualism that had replaced, for many people, the value of service and civic duty. They understood that children were positioned to cope and adapt to the values of our culture and that, in general, adults were not taking responsibility for the choices they had made as a society and were in denial about how these choices were negatively affecting its youth.

Some teachers from Zepeda pointed to adversarial politics and a general conservative political agenda, or what has been described as the "cultural politics" of educational reform (Apple, 1996), as particularly troublesome. Teachers from both Zepeda and Shelton Valley also cited an increase in poverty for many children and their families, a widening gap between the wealthy and the poor, as well as the breakdown of the family unit, latchkey children, the high divorce rate, and the poverty this brought for many single parents, especially women. Teachers from Zepeda also mentioned the fact that many parents were very young themselves and have poor parenting skills, although this factor seems to affect all socioeconomic levels due to working parents' lifestyles. All of these factors combined to create great stress and challenges for students and their families, and teachers believed that they witnessed the cumulative negative results of these problems everyday in their classrooms.

Teachers from both sites also mentioned that if schools were unprepared to meet the needs of the Information Age, it was not because schools inherently lacked the ability or willingness to make the necessary accommodations. Many acknowledged that schools as institutions tend to resist change but not all believed that this was necessarily a flaw. A few of the teachers were rather politically savvy about their reasoning, and reflected many points raised by critics of the dominant technocentric discourse. For example, several mentioned that there is very little monetary support for public education. A few explained that corporations, expecting education to serve their needs in terms of preparing students to be more sophisticated in their use of technology, were driven by their bottom-line ends, and thus were unwilling to significantly contribute to education's economic plight. Some teachers and both of the schools' administrators believed that to a great extent the market was driving the infusion of electronic technologies into schools and that education was simply being positioned as yet another market for the latest electronic gadget. For example, Roger, referencing a book published by Clifford Stoll (1995), which questions technology infusion into schools, used the book's title, *Silicone Snake Oil*, to emphasize the overt marketing aim of a presentation given by an IBM salesman to the Shelton Valley technology team. Most of the teachers, however, did not take their critical perspective to a broader political level in terms of relating technocentric educational reform policy to the needs of a global market economy or "enterprise culture" (Peters, 1996).

As with other political issues examined in this study, teachers from both sites often anchored their perceptions about political issues, such as the "crisis" in education, within the context of their personal, practical knowledge. For example, the story of Shelton Valley recounts a narrative of a school that not only sought reform through new information technologies but also negotiated socioeconomic-based changes within the culture of their school and the surrounding community. What was most interesting about Shelton Valley's teachers' responses is that, despite the school's official technology-based reform efforts, the teachers eschewed the technocentric assumptions of policy elites in terms of the rationale for educational reform. In fact, their emphasis on social issues more closely reflected the concerns of a traditional humanistic-based perspective that emphasizes social justice. The teachers' reflections on the social implications of the dominant reform discourse, through the lens of their personal practical knowledge, also expressed aspects of their social vision.

Problems Related to Literacy

A related aspect to the question of the "crisis" in education is that of literacy. This was especially evident at Zepeda, which had developed an elaborate set of programs designed to address this issue. The teachers at Zepeda understood literacy as both a curriculum issue and a social problem in that it was contextualized by the student's cultural and economic realities. Many teachers believed that the "culture of literacy" was not as common sense within the poor Hispanic culture as it was within the context of the dominate white middle class social milieu. According to many teachers, this was due to the effects of poverty, parents' past negative experiences with reading and schools in general, and differences in perceptions about the value of literacy. Therefore, part of the school's extensive literacy program was aimed to address these systemic socio-cultural issues. However, broader social forces acted as barriers to the teachers' efforts. Many of Zepeda's teachers cited the negative influences of our media-saturated society, where the power of the image had eclipsed the power of the word in terms of its ability to entertain and communicate social codes. Thus, it was not just poor Hispanic children who found reading a difficult and uninteresting endeavor, it was systemic—a symptom of postmodernity that crossed all ethnic and economic categories. The teachers pointed out that the act of spending so many hours watching television was another form of isolation that only added to the social and economic isolation of the poor. Time once spent in conversation with family members and neighbors was spent in the passive act of media consumption. Georges believed this particular outcome, exacerbated by the radical individualism that consumer culture inculcates, had a direct impact on the local citizen's lack of willingness to engage in political endeavors. Given this factor, Zepeda's efforts to build solidarity with its community and "relational power" by means of face-to-face conversation takes on another level of significance.

The teachers also expressed concern about the content of the media that their students consumed. Zepeda teachers explained that many of their pre-K–fifth-grade students watched adult movies, especially those from the horror genre. According to the teachers, the content of the media that the children often watched was mirrored in their play, conversations and creative writing. The librarian and other teachers believed that exposure to media, in terms of both its content and amount of time spent in viewing, negatively affected their students' imaginative thinking, verbal and language skills, and their interest in reading. Some believed it inculcated a restless boredom so that, as one teacher commented, "students want you to be Big Bird all of the time." The teachers did not mention the effects of video games, perhaps because few children's families could afford to buy them. In addition, some teachers couched factors related to media within the context of the many stresses their students faced due to the effects of poverty. Georges, however, while not denying the possible negative effects of violent media, believed that a caring parent could be a positive intervening force whether violence arose from a real drive-by shooting or one depicted in a movie.

Teachers from both sites responded to the negative aspects that media had on students' reading skills and imaginative thinking by including more visuals in their instruction. Still, teachers complained that many students could only sustain a ten or fifteen-minute attention span. At Shelton Valley, Cheryl suspected that years of extended exposure to media, especially television, was one of the related causal elements that precipitated Attention Deficit Disorder. Possible evidence that supports this thesis is, in fact, presented in Jane Healy's (1990) book *Endangered Minds*. As explained in Chapter Two, Healy (1990), an educational psychologist, relates the social habit of viewing hours and hours of television, in combination with other media such as video games and on-line activities (Healy, 1998), to both a decrease in, and alteration of, the actual centers of the brain associated with the development of language processing and verbal and reading skills. Based on her most recent research, Healy believes that children's minds today are, in fact, different due to their hours of exposure to electronic media, including computer-based media.

Healy (1990) also mentioned the fact that, across the nation, schools are labeling more and more children as "learning disabled," which she believes is also a symptom of systemic changes in children's cognitive processes, and, in turn, signals a fundamental disconnect between the traditional literacy-based curriculum and the way today's children think. In fact, at Shelton Valley some teachers referred to how so many students are being labeled "at risk" or "learning disabled" for academic failure. One Shelton Valley teacher observed that, in terms of the school culture, labeling students as such, in combination with their pull-out program, acted to "cripple" students in terms of their academic ability and sense of personal achievement. No teacher at Zepeda, however, addressed this particular issue because they did not have a pull-out program and, in fact, taught all students, including their special education students, the state's gifted and talented curriculum.

The systemic aspect of the effects of media was further exemplified by the teachers', especially at Shelton Valley, referencing of peer pressure and students' negative attitudes about school in general. For example, some teachers believed that the media inculcated an anti-intellectualism. Thus, in terms of the peer pressure, students did not want to be perceived as a "school boy or girl," so they deliberately chose behaviors that alienated them from the value of achievement. This perception is corroborated by some research, which indicates that peer-group influences and parental support have the greatest impact on student achievement (Steinberg, 1996).

In general, the teachers' perceptions about the social nature of the crisis in education is reflected in the work and concerns of many other educators and social scientists. For example, in his book titled *Social Intelligence*, Daniel Goleman (1995a) describes how the statistics for violent crimes by teens and teen suicides have sharply increased, adding that in the United States, Canada, New Zealand, and Puerto Rico, one in five children have psychological problems which impair their lives, with anxiety being the most common problem. Goleman attributes these problems of "emotional malaise" to "a universal price of modern life for children," problems witnessed in both poor and wealthy children worldwide (pp. 232–233). He notes that in highly industrialized cultures, the decline in emotional intelligence can be attributed, in part, to the rapid increase in "screen time" children spend before television and computers versus face-to-face interaction since it is the latter that foster social intelligence (Goleman, 1995b).

In addition, in one national report on high school, it was found that anonymity and apathy are two main impediments to academic development (*National Association of Secondary School Principals*, 1996). Clearly the structure of large high schools adds to these problems, yet the authors also pointed to some specific broad, cultural characteristics, such as a society characterized by cynicism about authority, government, and most civic institutional dimensions of life such that the young learn not to value intellectual engagement and social responsibility. Also, as mentioned in Chapter Two, the social sphere is saturated by images of youth-based popular culture, which displaces the meaning of traditional values and established authority. This conflict undermines the validity of the achievement ethic and those institutions (such as education) that embody this norm (Shapiro, 1990; de Alba et al., 2000). This situation, in combination with other factors, has led, in the view of some educators, to what may generally be described as a "crisis in motivation" (Arowintz & Giroux, 1991; Steinberg, 1996; Shapiro, 1990). The crisis in motivation arises from a fundamental incongruency between capitalist interests and democratic ideals, which education has traditionally embraced and is symptomatic of postmodern society. Daniel Bell (1976) perceived this incongruency in terms of a shift from a production culture, which values work and discipline, to that of a consumption culture which emphasizes immediate gratification. Schools are places that reproduce production-oriented values while the media creates an overwhelming culture of consumption. Shapiro (1990) believes that "school and popular culture face each other in a relationship of increasing confrontation and dissonance, each being the focus of values, beliefs and behaviors that are the very antithesis of the other" (p. 53). The "crisis in motivation" also needs to be understood within the context of present economic inequities and the reality of labor within a globalized market in that most newly created jobs are projected to be in the unskilled service sector. Such factors likely influence how students perceive the value of education.

Economic Disparity

The teachers from both sites believed that the social and economic disparity of students negatively affected their school culture and students' academic performance. In the case of Zepeda, the entire population of students was economically marginalized in comparison to suburban schools within their district. The effects that a socioeconomic gap can have on academic achievement was evidenced by Zepeda's students' difficulty in making a successful transition into middle school. Despite the academic gains that Zepeda had achieved over the years, many of their students failed to academically achieve in middle school. The transition from the economically homogeneous and familiar environment of Zepeda, according to many informants and the principal, cast students into the economically heterogeneous culture of middle school. Thus, Zepeda's students were faced with the harsh reality of their poverty during a critical developmental stage in terms of their adolescence and need for establishing peer identity and acceptance. Many teachers explained that their students lacked the enrichment of experiences that their suburban counterparts enjoyed and perhaps took for granted. This factor, they believed, made them more vulnerable to the negative effects of media, especially if they came from a family background characterized by abuse and neglect. In general, the issue of the students' economic marginalization was central to many of the teachers' concerns about their students' academic performance and sense of self-efficacy.

The demographic changes at Shelton Valley brought about by a shift from homogeneity to a more heterogeneous population, including disparity in socioeconomic status, was a profound turning point in the school's culture. This shift within Shelton Valley reflected larger socioeconomic changes within the surrounding community and was a significant dynamic affecting the school in terms of an increase in discipline problems.

Negotiating Discipline Problems

The informants at both sites believed that the structural aspects of the educational system exacerbated the many challenges that teachers faced within the classroom. Informants from each school reported that discipline problems, especially from certain emotionally disturbed children, were highly distracting and effectively arrested the learning opportunities for other students. (You may recall, Zepeda discontinued its pull-out program and all students were taught a gifted and talented-based curriculum.)

Both Margarete and Johanna, teachers from Zepeda Elementary, shared their stories about how they negotiated extremely disruptive and disrespectful students and its demoralizing effects. These teachers believed that the laws governing special education programs in public education needed to be changed to address the reality of this issue. Several teachers from Shelton Valley also held this viewpoint. At Zepeda, Marjorie believed that she was not qualified to teach what seemed to be an increasing number of children, which she perceived required professional psychological counseling. However, the teachers did have some support. Zepeda had a full-time counselor who held several group and private sessions for children who were having problems coping with the challenges in their lives. Also, according to the teachers, their principal Antonio was supportive of them and adhered to very strict rules regarding disciplining disruptive students.

Shelton Valley, which also had a full-time counselor, decided to use a peer-mediation program to assuage their discipline problems, and had some success with this approach. Satie told the story of one student who, although she had broken the school's rules against drinking alcohol on school grounds and had been sent to an alternative school, was readmitted to Shelton Valley because she was classified as a special education student and her parents hired an attorney to have her reinstated based on federal laws guiding special education. The readmittance of this student, however, countered the will of the staff and administration. Satie believed that this incident made a travesty of the school's institutional authority and taught children that there are no real consequences for destructive behavior and breaking the rules. Also, an "us versus them" attitude by certain parents and their children toward teachers exacerbated the discipline problems facing teachers who claimed to feel helpless to defend their authority because, in terms of disciplining students, their "hands were tied." This sense arose from their fear of being sued by disgruntled parents and, in one case, actual verbal threats from a student. In terms of comparing the two sites, parents at Shelton Valley were isolated from the school whereas parents at Zepeda were active participants in the school reform process. Zepeda's teachers also engaged in authentic decision-making, whereas at Shelton Valley, site-based management was an empty gesture of mere performity. However, even with these stark contrasts in school culture and leadership, informants from both sites had issues about discipline and lack of respect for teachers by some parents and society in general.

Informants from both sites associated increasing discipline-related problems to the general social problems of our society; specifically those related to the breakdown of the family and lack of parental discipline and support, especially in terms of inculcating the ethic of caring and related social skills. Some suspected that steady exposure to violence in media may contribute to negative behavior patterns. Although the discipline problems that the informants negotiated were not of the scale or severity of those who teach in some poor inner city schools located in large metropolitan areas such as Washington, D.C. or New York City, the perception that more children were emotionally imbalanced due to poverty and related family and social problems, as well as a general breakdown in traditional social institutions, which in turn contributed to aggressive and disruptive behavior and poor academic performance, was very real for many of the teachers.

The teachers' perceptions, in fact, reflect a general trend. The problem of school violence has become a signifier for the decade of the nineties and the 21st century, such that it has evolved into a significant public health concern (Elliott et al., 1998). In 1993, for example, the National Education Association recommended that a formal coordinated effort by national, state, and local governments be organized to address the problem of school violence. There are paradoxes that characterize the complexity of the issue. For example, a "culture of violence" is glorified in media and has seized great influence due to our culture's ambivalence about firearms, alcohol, and violence in media. Although the destructive power of these elements is acknowledged, their prevalence has a normative effect whereas their use is often associated with highly valued qualities of American culture. Such contradictions create serious confusion for youth and undermine their ability to make health-promoting life choices (Elliot et al., 1998). In addition, many studies suggest that the normative element and repeated exposure to violent media can be correlated to aggressive behavior in children and youth; a desensitization of children to real-life violence; a development of unrealistic attitudes about the efficacy of aggressive behavior; and can predict the likelihood of childhood crime and violent behavior (cited in Elliott et al., 1998, p. 47).

Also, three features characterize acts of violence since the 1990s—increased lethality, which is related to the use of handguns, random violence, and fewer safe places—and are the basis for the general level of fear experienced by both adults and children (Elliott, 1994). In addition, an "ecological" perspective on human development (Bronfenbrenner, 1979, 1989) understands that the various forces that contribute to the problem of violence in schools reflect problems arising from both the micro (individual and family) and macro (sociocultural and economic) spheres. Therefore, the greatest predictors of school violence are related to community disorganization, which reflects the direct interaction of these two spheres (Elliott et al., 1998). Thus, schools do not exist as isolated islands outside the complexities of broader sociocultural reality, but in fact act as powerful "social barometers" (Sarason, 1995). As one informant stated, "if society is better, then schools will be better. We are reflecting all the problems we have in society today." Even so, it appears that demonizing poor youth of color has become a typical reactionary stance to the increasing presence of violence in schools (Giroux, 1997). This position, fully articulated by an increase in youth incarceration, indicates an amazing lack of imagination and disallows as much as it disempowers the social responsibility of adults to children. One needs to ask what values does a culture, which condones pandering to its children, possess? And if youth reflect the values taught by the milieu of a commodity culture, how is it that we, in turn, can judge and condemn those who have adopted what we have essentially created either directly or through willful complacency? As discussed earlier, part of the postmodern condition is the dissolution of traditional values and the emergence of a sensibility of uncertainty and disconnectedness. Many of the informants expressed such a sensibility of unease. Indeed, if a condition of crisis exists, it does not arise as much from the demands of the Information Age as from a general crisis in meaning itself.

Negotiating Standardized Testing

The politics of educational reform had also influenced the realm of teachers' work in terms of the areas of curriculum development and instruction, specifically regarding *technique* expressed as standardized testing and accountability procedures. These procedures of monitoring embody the values of efficiency and thus relate to the control of teachers' work and the general instantiation of performance culture. The teachers' views on the reality of the social policy embodied in educational reforms such as standardized "high-stakes" testing, raises many questions with regard to policy elites' dependence on standardized testing as the means to guarantee curricular standards and accountability. Standardized testing is a form of technology, which, as with all technologies, embodies certain biases. Many educators and social critics have written about the instrumental rationalist perspective that standardized testing constitutes and how these techniques actualize a functionalist perspective on education. The findings in this study indicate that not only do teachers' perceptions about the nature of the crisis in education strongly differ from those of policy elites', their experiences and insights also seem to indicate that the *technique* of standardized testing has eclipsed the position of expressing means to that of an end in itself. Also, it is ironic that although policy elites' vision of educational reform emphasizes critical thinking skills, the usage of standardized testing is counter productive to this end. Such paradoxes, however, generally characterize postmodern education (Hargraves, 1994).

In addition, although it has been recognized that teachers' sense of efficacy and professionalism are essential to successful reforms (Hargraves, 1994, 1995; Sarason, 1995), the overt emphasis on standardized testing, at least for several of the teachers, incited within them frustration and a diminution in their sense of professionalism. Teachers' compromises, in terms of negotiating the TAAS test, were clearly exemplified in the case of Zepeda. As mentioned above, Zepeda, so that it may continue its community-based social reforms, sought to maintain their high TAAS scores, which in turn meant that their curriculum was highly structured and unprogressive to some degree despite the high level of teacher autonomy and inventiveness. In the case of Shelton Valley, creative opportunities were also lost. Although Roger wanted to mentor teachers in terms of assisting them with the successful integration of technology, many teachers' TAAS-driven orientation prevented this from becoming a reality. There was simply not enough time and the pressure on teachers to secure high scores was so great that alternative curricular endeavors were simply too risky. This, of course, was counterproductive in terms of the school's technology-based reform efforts.

The Sociotechnological Context

Questions pertinent to the sociotechnological context raised many issues for the informants. As with their reflections on the "crisis" in education, the teachers related their responses to sociotechnologically based questions to the realm of their personal practical knowledge.

Defining the Information Age

As explained in the first few chapters, a turning point in educational reform policy arose with the 1983 publication of *A Nation at Risk* and the declaration by its authors that education was in a state of crisis due to the fact that schools were not prepared to meet the needs of a developing Information Age. Based on this assumption, the tendency to negotiate a functionalist or technocentric perspective against a more social democratic reform framework was arrested due to the dominance of technocentric reform discourse and its expression of "inevitability." Indeed, in Chapter Two we examined the nature of the Information Age in terms of economic changes brought about by electronic telecommunications and computer technologies. The shift from an industrial-based economy to that of an information-based economy reflected a growing influence of a globalized market economy, where the logic of the market acts to displace the political. This shift to a postmodern era also signaled a change in the fundamental purpose of knowledge itself, where its intrinsic values are displaced by the process of exchange (Lyotard, 1984). Thus, with a market economy dependent upon the production and consumption of information, science, technology, and education naturally become the major "knowledge industries" within an "information state" (Peters, 1996). This "enterprise culture" is further characterized by a "techno-rationalist business world view," which constructs and legitimates a technocentric political framework (Peters, 1996). Thus, the values of a neoliberal market-based Information Age are "protean flexibility, restless entrepreneurism and the willingness to abandon social bonds for material gain" (Winner, 1996, p. 69). Mythinformation, (Winner, 1986), you may recall, is the almost religious conviction that access to information and the dependency on computer technology will produce a better world and expresses the underlying mythos guiding the techno-utopian vision of the Information Age. What makes the discourse of this techno-utopian vision troublesome is the reality of downsizing and the replacement of highly skilled and technically trained occupational groups with service jobs through computerization, automation, and "real time globalism" production processes (Lankshear, 1997). It also signifies the further colonization of the lifeworld by instrumental rationalism. Therefore, the meaning behind the term "Information Age" equates to much more than the production of and easy access to information.

However, many informants initially described the meaning of the term in a rather obvious manner, such as the rapid flow and easy access to information, thus equating connectivity with a mere transportation function, and as explained in Chapter Two, expresses an apolitical perspective (Carey, 1989). In addition, at Shelton Valley, Lisa and Mary Jane, both proponents of a technology-based reform policy, specifically associated the term to the transportation of information and necessary changes, which such information technologies would demand of education. Specifically they used descriptors such as developing "critical thinking skills" to "access information" as central to schools becoming aligned with the Information Age.

Upon greater reflection, however, some of the Shelton Valley teachers perceived another possible level of outcomes that the Information Age may have for schools. For example, Satie and Cheryl wondered about the effects that increased access to information might have on students who were already suffering from *too much* media stimulation. Cheryl believed that ADD/ADHD (attention deficit disorder and attention deficit hyperactive disorder) was a means through which students defended themselves against additional sensory overload. Roger, although concerned about the possible negative effects of "information overload," described the term Information Age as "terrific marketing" and the principal cited that it was "meaningless hype invented to sell computers."

More teachers at Zepeda associated the term with its possible negative social effects. Toby, for example, associated the rapid rate of change that characterizes the Information Age to increased violence and people's sense of impotence and unimportance. Teachers experience students being numbed by sensory overload, because such a condition inculcates a tendency toward superficiality as a result of the trivializing effects of too much data. Other teachers associated the increased production and distribution of information, most of which is text based, with our media-saturated culture, thus exacerbating the distracting effects of existing electronic media. Ironically, this was predicted to be especially so in terms of declining reading skills.

Georges and Jane related the issue to the "technology haves and have nots," emphasizing that a poor community like Zepeda would most likely remain without access to connectivity. Even so, reflecting the rhetoric of policy elites, Jane believed that access to information could possibly help to breakdown the isolation of poverty-stricken schools and "level the playing field" between schools serving wealthy versus poor students. As discussed in Chapter One, although this is a common theme offered by certain policy elites, the retraction of the "Opportunity to Learn Standards" from the *Goals 2000: Educate America Act* (National Educational Goals Panel, 1994) indicates how the playing field is intended to remain status quo.

The informants did not relate the term or the phenomenon, Information Age, to the broader concerns of policy elites' critics. For example, there was no mention of an economic shift from an industrial to an information-based economy. Their ignorance about the economic background led them to assume that the infusion of electronic technology into schools was necessary so that students may acquire technical skills that may lead to "good jobs" in the future. This rationalization, which, as pointed out in Chapter Two, is based on false assumptions especially problematic for the urban poor, but exists nevertheless as common sense to most educators. This situation reflects the power of the functionalist framework, which has guided education since the turn of last century, as well as the rhetorical power of policy elites' discourse to reinforce this framework.

In addition, the informants did not mention associated political ramifications, such as the rise of a neoliberal globalized market economy, and thus did not recognize how education had been repositioned as a major "knowledge industry" for an "information state," a position that serves the increased instrumental rationalization and control of teachers' labor. Many teachers, however, expressed awareness of how schools were being positioned as "viable markets" for new technologies. They also recognized the alarming increase in controls over their work by state and federal regulations. Most of the informants, however, did not seem to understand, or were unable to explain, how the meaning of knowledge had shifted from a position of intrinsic value to that of a commodity—in fact, many conflated the terms information and knowledge. Even so, with a few exceptions, the informants did not essentialize information. Rather, they questioned the wisdom in assuming that more information was good or necessary, especially in the context of how systemic social and economic problems were affecting schools. However, they did not extend their concerns about the effects of media and information saturation on students' academic social experiences toward possible solutions, such as the development of curriculum designed to teach media and technology literacies.

In conclusion, most of the informants did *not* adopt the ethos of mythinformation. However, a few teachers at Zepeda, recognizing the reality of the "technology rich and technology poor," understood that access to information was essentially a power issue. In contrast, there were a few informants who lacked the background and language with which to express any interpretation other than the term's (Information Age) obvious self-descriptive attributes (i.e., "a time of a lot of information"). But these teachers were in the minority. It seems that, for most of the informants, the term Information Age did not signify the techno-utopian futuristic vision offered by policy elites. Nor did their impressions conjure ideas about the rise of an information state as an expression of a neoliberal globalized market economy. Nevertheless, their critical perspective, grounded in their personal practical knowledge, did reflect the concerns that many critics of policy elites have raised and therefore largely supports a traditional democratic perspective.

The Inevitability Factor

All of the informants from both sites believed that the infusion of electronic technology into education was inevitable. As explained above, this outcome was likely inculcated not only by the discourse of policy elites but also was related to the power of a commonsense functionalist-based framework, which has dominated educational policy since the turn of last century. The teachers at Shelton Valley, however, seemed more willing to accept this factor without question or resistance and associated the infusion of technology with students acquiring necessary skills for jobs. One exception, however, was Roger, who possessed a critical if not cynical attitude toward what he perceived to be a market-based impetus driving the infusion process. He also did not believe a technology-based reform effort would fundamentally change schools in terms of the quality of the learning environment. In addition, Lisa, another Shelton Valley teacher, believed in the power of technology to change schools, but she consciously resisted the marketing efforts that measured teachers' dedication and professionalism by the level of their technology proficiency.

Although the teachers at Zepeda recognized the inevitability of technology's infusion into schools, most questioned a key premise of current reform policy—that the infusion of electronic technology would fundamentally change schools. Marjorie, Georges, Margarete, and the principal, for example, believed that technology was not essential to educational reform, but rather it is changes in the *relationship* among teachers, parents, administrators, and the community that creates reform in schools. Also, several informants at Zepeda referenced the issue of equity, in terms of the "technology haves and have nots," and most perceived that although the diffusion of electronic technology was inevitable, urban schools serving poor minority students would most likely be left behind. But as Georges pointed out, the school's sense of community and cultural solidarity, unlike computer skills, are foundational to overcoming poverty's impediments to self-efficacy.

Even though most of the teachers from both sites accepted the infusion of electronic technology into schools as an inevitable factor, the experiences that the Zepeda teachers encountered, in terms of their schools' affiliation with TIAF and reforms centered around building community solidarity, seemed to have made them open to more skepticism regarding policy elites' assumption that schools *need* technology to experience reform. In fact, Antonio stated that he did not believe in the rhetoric of official reform policy. Rather, he thought that Semore Sarason's (1995) work on school reform, which emphasizes the element of power and relationships, reflected the actuality of what effects true reform versus superficial change. Whereas, the teachers at Shelton Valley, which as an organization adopted a technology-driven reform policy, were less able to step outside the rhetoric of technocentric reform policy even while their own school suffered from internal factionalism and mistrust by its community.

Resistance to Technology Adoption

The informants at both sites believed that lack of adequate time was a huge barrier to teachers in terms of acquiring effective training, overcoming the characteristic steep learning curve when working with electronic technologies, and finding ways to integrate their new skills into their practice. This perception reflects research findings related to change and technology adoption where, in one report, teachers were described as "prisoners of time" (National Education Commission on Time and Learning, 1994).

Fear was also mentioned as a barrier; specifically fear of change or a general "fear of machinery" and "the technical." A few teachers at Zepeda declared that they had experienced such an attitude themselves, which they related to their lack of training and experience working with computers. While teachers at Shelton Valley also cited age as a factor, with younger teachers more willing to learn because they are more familiar with computer technology, this was not the case at Zepeda, despite the fact that both sites offered a wide range of teachers in terms of age and years of teaching experience.

Many teachers at Zepeda suggested that technology was a low priority for them because they were negotiating other pressing needs germane to teaching basic academic skills, social skills, and handling behavior problems. This factor was not mentioned by any Shelton Valley teacher. Some Zepeda teachers emphasized that their first priority was serving the needs of their children, not learning the latest technology. However, the schools' reading and mathematics curriculum in the lower grades required the use of a computerized drill and practice program, and the teachers seemed comfortable with using these teaching aids, perhaps because the students' test scores had improved with their use, in combination with several other curriculum strategies. Such factors reflect Larry Cuban's (1986, 2001) conclusion that technology adoption is inherently contextual. He believes that within the context of technology adoption, teachers make "situationally constrained choices," which ere on the conservative side because teachers are positioned by structural and sociocultural factors specific to the cultural environment of their school. Therefore, the issue of teachers' resistance to technological innovation is much more complex than perhaps acknowledged by those who control the policy of technology infusion.

Even so, the technology "trailblazers" at each of the schools (Christine at Zepeda and Mary Jane at Shelton Valley) believed that teachers overtly resisted technology and implied that only those who are secure in their teaching do not resist the adoption of technology. Christine, for example, who believed that the district needed to test teachers for competency in computer literacy, suggested that teachers are not, generally, innovative people and thus "technology threatens their role." Although Christine was admired by her peers for her technical expertise, she was not looked upon as a role model to emulate. Also, few teachers attended her in-service training sessions. The technology-savvy image of a teacher, perhaps, did not fit in at Zepeda, for the teachers were indeed focused on other salient matters such as teaching basic skills, TAAS, discipline, and participating in TIAF's activities. In addition, as pointed out in a later section of this chapter, many of the teachers at Zepeda expressed a cautious and questioning approach to understanding the nature of technology. They also had certain misgivings about the rapid infusion of electronic technologies into education that were related to possible negative social outcomes such as technology's perceived dehumanizing effects. This factor, which was also evidenced in many of the Shelton Valley teachers, I believe, further problemitizes the nature of computer anxiety or the possibility of teachers' general fear of technological innovation.

This disconnect, however, did not seem as obvious at Shelton Valley, where more of the informants expressed an interest in utilizing technology in their teaching practices and were frustrated by the schools' technology-related problems. Even so, Mary Jane generally perceived that teachers were resistant to change, especially technology-based reforms, and therefore, the only way to overcome their resistance was to adopt a top-down approach and use authority to force teachers to comply. The principal generally supported this approach because he also perceived teachers as inherently resistant to change, especially technology-related changes. These general attitudes, however, potentially invite a divisive, inside-outside situation built on mistrust. Those teachers who readily embrace technology are perceived to be inside the "technology circle" and are assumed to be confident, good teachers. Others, who remain outside the circle, are suspected of computer phobia or perhaps resistant to innovation and thus need to be "cured" or "fixed."

The development of such suspicious perceptions about teachers, I believe, arises from a complex set of influences related to historical and structural factors within education, which concerns the feminization of education and the control and instrumental rationalization of teachers' labor. Another related factor is that our cultural bias about the nature of technology as an apolitical tool leads one to believe that questioning technology or to have fearful perceptions is irrational especially since technology is equated to the myth of progress. It is also related to the social construction of the image of the "good teacher" through the lens of expertism (Welker, 1991), a stance especially favored by policy elites. Therefore, in the case of Shelton Valley, many teachers who expressed eagerness to use technology in their teaching practices, unlike Lisa who resisted the technology-savvy image, confessed guilt over the fact that they were not up-to-par with technology. No teacher at Zepeda apologized for their lack of ability or interest in electronic technology. However, this may be an artifact of Zepeda's lack of access to connectivity and its reluctance to secure it in the future. Also, Zepeda's teachers seemed content with using what little technology they had in a rather limited fashion. Even so, it may also be that the general reform framework, which focused on building community solidarity, allowed Zepeda teachers to remain confident in their traditional professional image, which emphasizes the moral craft of teaching versus expertism, especially technological expertism (Tom, 1984).

Misgivings About Electronic Technology in Education

The psychology of teachers' resistance to technology came into greater relief when they responded to the question about possible misgivings related to the policy to infuse technology into schools. For many of the informants, their answer often began as such: "No, but . . . ." It seemed as if it would have been blasphemy to be totally against the use of technology in schools. However, for many it also seemed that they had been waiting for years for someone to ask this question. The most curious mix of contradictions came from Shelton Valley teachers. Because the schools' official reform program embraced a technocentric aim, the concerns of certain teachers seemed rather incongruent with this aim. For example, David, the school's principal, worried specifically about computer technology's possible dehumanizing effects and the inculcation of superficial and passive learning. Unfortunately, these general misgivings did not deter David from pursuing the decision to purchase a new ILS for the school, a point that is discussed later in this section.

Other teachers voiced fears about dehumanization, increased isolation, and potential loss of socialization skills. Cheryl, for example, wondered if it was wise to assume that students really needed more access to information, as she suspected that ADD/ADHD was related to the effects of too much stimulation from an information and media-saturated culture. However, these fears were assuaged by the assumption that electronic technology would, somehow, generally improve the quality of education. This same type of contradiction was found in Lisa's responses. On the one hand, she had no misgivings and saw technology's benefits. However, she also worried that education would become too dependent on its usage, such as one school she visited that had adopted a computer-driven science lab and had completely abandoned its hands-on activities. She believed that this was a huge pedagogical error and that such practices raised serious moral questions for teachers. This point, in the context of the use of simulation-based software versus hands-on instruction, is also raised by Clifford Stoll (1999), Jane Healy (1998), Armstrong and Casement (2000), and Sherry Turkle (1997). In addition, Janet also worried about possible over-reliance on technology by educators. But this perception was dismissed by the pragmatic reality that students need the exposure and technical skills to be competitive in school and the job market.

Some of the teachers offered responses that read like an advertisement for computers, such as "technology is where the future is." Mary Jane and Roger were the only two informants at Shelton Valley who were adamant about their position and did not indicate a contradiction or ambivalence in opinion. Mary Jane, a proponent of technology-based reform, gave a response that reflected policy elites' discourse: "computers only enhance learning." Whereas Roger expressed cynicism about the market-driven reality of technology-inspired policy and described how technology in education can often function as "eye candy" and "a wonderful carrot" that inculcates engagement with the technical artifact versus the instructional content. He also believed that the use of technology in education can make teaching and learning unnecessarily complex and that the mediating or "layering effect" that technology brings to the social interaction between the teacher and student can dilute or act to distract rather than enhance the learning process.

Zepeda's informants also shared contradicting perceptions. For example, only three teachers expressed a positive viewpoint, but their perceptions were also contradictory in that their positive perceptions were tempered by certain misgivings. For example, Christine, Zepeda's technology "trail-blazer," stated that she had no misgivings but then expressed concern about the commercialization of the Internet and the misuse of ILS technology in education. She believed that the predominance of ILS usage in poor, urban schools reflected a prejudice that poor children cannot think, when the only thing they truly lack is background experience. Christine also acknowledged that although it is assumed that technology makes things easier and simpler, in reality, for educators to use distance education and the Internet effectively, it would require a great deal of planning and coordination, thus making the instructional experience more complex rather than simplified.

Shelly, the librarian, had no misgivings except that educators needed to face the reality that technology cannot solve all of education's problems and that they would need to consciously create "the right balance between the human and the mechanical." The principal, Antonio, a self-described Luddite, admitted that Zepeda's children need to be proficient in using electronic technology because "it is the future." However, perhaps due to the influence of TIAF, Antonio preferred face-to-face interaction and eschewed any technique or process that mediated the communication process. Also, Antonio, Margarete, and Sharon pointed out that schools, which had invested in technology, had not experienced academic improvement. Margarete was also very bitter about the practice of schools eliminating enrichment classes and teachers' aids to purchase computer technology.

Many of the teachers at Zepeda, who said they had no misgivings, then qualified their responses by stating that technology would not solve the many problems in schools because they are fundamentally social in nature. Marjorie went as far as to predict that the more educators rely on technology "the worse things will get." Georges, for example, was against administration dictating the use of electronic technology only to control teachers' work or the curriculum. He was especially against its usage to further standardized testing in education. Also, a few of the Zepeda informants mentioned the possible dehumanizing effects of technology, but not as often as Shelton Valley informants, which is ironic given Shelton Valley's technology-based reform program.

Informants from both sites who expressed any misgivings couched their concerns within the context of socially related issues. At Shelton Valley, half of the informants alluded to the potential dehumanizing effect that electronic technology could have on the quality of social interaction within schools. This factor is significant given the school's technology-based reforms. Unfortunately, Shelton Valley's site-based management system was so ineffectual that its teachers had no forum within which they could discuss their misgivings. In addition, because those who are supporters of the status quo or policy elites' technocentric vision are often in positions of authority and power, as was the case with Mary Jane at Shelton Valley, misgivings are generally not given voice, or if they are heard, they are censored. This was exactly the circumstances surrounding Roger's attempts to question the districts' and Shelton Valley's technology-related decisions.

The contradictions expressed by the two school administrators were also very interesting. David, for example, worried about the possible dehumanizing and trivializing effects that electronic technologies could have on the learning environment, yet did not reference these concerns when he made the decision to purchase an ILS for Shelton Valley. An ILS is based on behaviorist learning theory and features an individualized drill and practice format designed to completely control the learning environment with preprogrammed instruction and assessment. Therefore, as discussed in Chapter Two, unlike other electronic technologies that can be used to scaffold thematic-based collaborative learning, an ILS has the potential to effect alienation of the teacher from the instructional process and thus dehumanize the learning experience for students. During our interviews, David avoided discussion about the school's ILS situation. Therefore I can offer only certain possibilities as explanations.

Perhaps David was unaware of how an ILS works or perhaps he believed this was an effective teaching strategy for "learning disabled" and certain special education students, a common assumption given the fact that most ILS are underwritten by federal Chapter One funding. (Compare this assumption to Christine at Zepeda as discussed above.) And since there had been a rapid increase in the number of these students, the administration was desperate to address their academic needs. However, the teachers offered mixed reports about the students' reactions to using the school's present ILS. Eventually, perhaps after an initial Hawthorn Effect, most students experienced the automated drill and practice format to be tediously boring; thus its potential to exact achievement waned over time. But since the teachers' input was not part of the decision-making process, this information was most likely unavailable to David.

It may also be that David's own misgivings were not permitted to cross the border into the professional realm; rather they could remain within the context of abstract, esoteric thinking where they were safe from interfering with "normative" values and purposeful actions. In other words, I suspect that for many of the informants, especially those at Shelton Valley, their misgivings reflected real and sincere concerns that arose from their intuitive and tacit perceptions anchored in their personal practical knowledge as educators. However, when these perceptions countered the status quo, their potential to lead to praxis or action was arrested. This was especially the case at Shelton Valley because the teachers were demoralized by an adversarial relationship with parents and certain students and the fact that they distrusted the administration. In such a situation the vacuum created by mistrust and lack of communication is conveniently filled with the received discourse of policy elites and their supporters. In addition, because the school's technology committee had dissolved due to the administration's repeated rejections of their proposals, the librarian, who demonstrated a technocentric perspective, was the only staff person making technology-related decisions.

In contrast, at Zepeda, where teachers had a strong sense of collegiality, a trusting relationship with the administration and parents, and also a viable system of site-based decision-making, the teachers seemed more comfortable with voicing and acting on their beliefs and tacit knowledge. Thus, with a focus on community and solidarity as well as academic achievement as the school's primary goals, the teachers could decide, based on their misgivings, to reject the use of electronic technologies or at least the possibility of utilizing them in a more convivial manner, an approach to technology adoption that consciously accommodates the building and maintenance of community and democratic-based decision-making (Illich, 1973). Therefore, even though Zepeda's usage of its technology was limited because the school's rather formal and restricted curriculum framework which accommodated a conservative (drill and practice) approach to the use of technology, it nevertheless possessed the *potential* for deliberative conversation about the purpose of electronic technology within the context of concerns related to pedagogy. Dialogue pertaining to technology adoption would underscore the importance of maintaining quality social interaction, the centrality of decisions pertaining to curriculum and instruction, and the integrity of the school's sense of community. It is clearly evident that this was not the case at Shelton Valley.

However, it is very important to point out that teachers from both sites were voicing opposition to the discourse of policy elites. Therefore, their concerns signal an opening up of the space that encompasses teachers' professional knowledge landscape; a political space that is so often dominated by what Schwab (1962) described as "a rhetoric of conclusions" given by policy elites and administrators. In addition, many of the informants' concerns reflected those who question a technology-based reform policy, such as technology becoming an end in itself as well as its possible dehumanizing effects. Indeed, there are factors that educational researchers can learn from the insights of these informants, such as Roger's suggestion about the "layering effect" of electronic technologies and how this phenomenon can possibly have negative or unexpected effects on the quality of social interaction in the learning process. Also, what is most interesting is what was *not* discussed by the informants. For example, a particular quality often used to justify electronic technology in education is that it engenders motivation. This potential outcome, however, was only mentioned by one teacher in defense of using electronic technology in schools. In fact, some teachers at Shelton Valley witnessed the opposite effect in their students, and many informants at Zepeda cited that other schools that had invested in technology did not have improvement in their students' academic achievement.

In conclusion, the informants' misgivings about the infusion of electronic technology stand in opposition to the discourse of policy elites. The general contradictory presentation of their perceptions, I believe, reflects the complexity of technology-based reform policy as well as the adoption process itself. Their contradictory perceptions also illustrate a struggle with the dialectic of educational reform policy. On the one hand, the normative discourse of equating technology-based reform to necessity and progress makes perfect sense. On the other hand, the informants' personal practical knowledge invited questions and issues related to the practical—the creation of a caring pedagogy, curriculum and instructional issues, concern about the socioeconomic reality of their students, and the inculcation of democratic values. In most cases the latter seemed to have greater efficacy.

The Relationship Between Society and Technology

One main thesis of this study is that dominant educational reform discourse is inherently technocentric. As a discourse, technocentrism assumes an apolitical tool-based definition of technology. This understanding about technology is normative and common sense (Winner, 1996; Ellul, 1964; Kerr, 1996). In addition, this perspective presents technology in a nonproblematic manner and rarely considers the possibility of nonfocal or unintended negative effects of technology adoption (Sclove, 1995).

However, critics of this commonsense perspective believe that technology is not "just a tool." Rather, it is a complex social process that can have nonfocal effects. Many technologies, such as freeways or the "information superhighway," operate at a structural level through the control of time and space (Innis, 1951, 1952; Carey, 1989). Therefore the crucial time to debate about a new innovation is *before* adoption takes place, for once infrastructures are in place and become constituting processes within economic and sociocultural spheres, they are next to impossible to change or remove (Winner, 1986). However, the politics of technology diffusion are such that the adoption process is not democratic and thus public deliberation seldom occurs. This is partly an artifact of our apolitical bias and is also partly due to the power structures that control decision-making. Generally, the existing power structure creates a rhetoric of inevitability related to economic necessity and the promise of efficiency and convenience, which effectively narrows the deliberative space for public discourse (Winner, 1986). This is such the case with the discourse of policy elites and their technocentric policy of educational reform. Generally, this is a very serious situation because adoption without deliberation equates to the creation of autonomous technology, whereby a technology's interactions with social and economic structures exist without the benefit of human direction and critical guidance (Winner, 1986). In effect, the outcome is the further penetration of instrumental rationalism and its absolute valuation of efficiency into the realm of the lifeworld (Gorz, 1989; Habermas, 1989;

Ellul, 1964). This, of course, would include the everyday experiences of teachers and students within the lifeworld of a school's social space.

The narrowing of educational reform discourse therefore necessitates an exploration of the beliefs and attitudes that educators hold about the nature of technology. The discussion given above regarding other technology-related issues indicates that the informants possess a complex understanding about technology's place in education. But how do they perceive the relationship between society and technology? Do educators possess a commonsense perspective whereby technology is simply a tool that improves society—a perception that characterizes policy elites' discourse? Or, is their perception more complex and how does it relate to their social vision?

As with the previous question regarding the informants' misgivings about a technology-based reform policy, the teachers' responses to the question about the relationship between society and technology revealed a complex understanding that reflected not so much a contradiction but rather a dialectic. However, there were also those teachers who had a decidedly negative view about the nature of technology and a few who had a highly positive perception.

For those teachers who possessed a positive perspective, their assumptions were related to the notion that technology was "inevitable" in the sense that it is pointless to question it. This rather pragmatic stance, however, did not actually characterize the relationship between society and technology outside the typical apolitical tool-based understanding. For example, Mary Jane, who was a strong proponent of technology-driven reform, believed that technology was "a force" in which all will be involved "whether you want to or not." She believed that technology was a tool that brought about "progress toward more refinement" in society. Thus, technology is an inescapable yet progressive "force." Given Mary Jane's belief that teachers will necessarily have to be replaced by technology, one can only wonder about what the term "refinement" can signify. Also, Mary Jane's perception does not include human intervention or guidance. Rather, her view of technology's relationship to society indicates that much power is given over to technology's ability to exist as a positive, objective "force."

Janet, who also believed in a technology-based reform policy, explained that technology "will be bonded to society until the bitter end." Again, there is no escape. The relationship is inevitable, like it or not. But this perception hardly explains anything. Therefore, to a great degree both informants' inevitability-based explanations represent a tautological understanding and thus illustrate how they were not able to break through the mystification engendered by policy elites' and our culture's commonsense apolitical understanding about technology.

For those teachers who possessed a critical or questioning viewpoint about technology, their concerns revolved around social issues. Cheryl, for example, stated that although "computers are tools of the 21st century," she also imagined them to possess very real isolating effects. For Cheryl, it was the threat of anonymous control over personal data, not just by government bureaucracy, but by the technical systems themselves. She worried about how structural, economic, and communication systems (i.e., telecommunications, stock market, Internet) depended on the use of electronic technologies and thus how vulnerable these systems were to error and sabotage. Satie had similar concerns and characterized the relationship between technology and society as fostering greater alienation. Satie included media in her definition of technology and believed that our media-saturated society had diminished students' ability to think imaginatively and reduced their capacity for acquiring language and reading skills. Jane, another teacher at Shelton Valley, described the relationship between society and technology as possibly dehumanizing and alienating, effects due to the fact that technological advancements had surpassed the social sphere's ability to cope with the ethical and moral issues that many new innovations raised. The principal, David, expressed the same concerns.

At Zepeda, Margarete believed that the relationship was solely governed by a profit motive, to make a few rich. This was especially evident in the case of technology-driven reforms in education. For Toby, the relationship between technology and society was disturbing in that our popular culture reflected a fascination with futurism such that, he believed, society was willing a high-technology future through its fabula. Toby believed that television, in its present profit-driven form, was a "destructive technology."

Although Antonio described technology as "only a tool," he perceived that as a society we were "becoming slaves to our technologies." Similarly, Shelly stated that technology is "just a tool," but also questioned whether or not "*we* had become the tool." She hoped that technology would simply remain a tool to create a "compassionate and healthier society," but added, "somehow, compassion and technology just don't match." Shelly noted that although considering the relationship between society and technology is a highly important question, it is also quite disturbing or "too 1984ish." Thus, most people choose to remain unconscious about their deeper concerns and continue to associate technology with progress and goodness.

The principal at Shelton Valley has a Ph.D. in the sciences and also a strong interest in Native American's ecologically based cultural perspective. As mentioned above, David believed that technology's progress had exceeded the social sphere's capacity to negotiate the moral and ethical questions that these innovations raised. David made reference to a fundamental paradox of technology—that you can use science and technology to solve one problem but in doing so, create one hundred more.

Like Shelley, David wondered if the toolmakers had become blind to the fact that the toolmakers had become beholden to their own creations. In fact, David believed that technology is not just a tool but operates on a constituting level and expresses economic and social systems. He explained how, for example, the effects of the McCormick Reaper on farming facilitated the transformation of family-owned agrarian farming into a mechanized industrial agribusiness enterprise. David also believed that our relationship to technology was related to our ecological problems. Although he stated that he does not like to engage in "pessimistic thinking," he nevertheless predicted, as a scientist, that if humanity does not soon learn from the imbalances that have been created through thoughtless and anthropocentric means and ends, that massive disorder of global ecosystems was immanent. David's perceptions in fact reflect some concerns raised by educational researcher, C. A. Bowers (1995, 2000), whose critical perspective on technocentric reform policy arises from an ecojustice framework.

At Zepeda, Georges explained that the relationship between technology and society was a two-edged sword. Technology, in the context of community, can be "an enhancer or a divider." For example, the current practice of building walled communities policed by electronic security cameras and protected by an electronic gate, he suggested, signify social division, fear, and isolation, and not the spirit of community. Thus, technology will evolve by what we bring to it. Therefore, technology is inherently reflexive because it mirrors and embodies human intentions and values.

Roger offered a similarly rich interpretation. He asked rhetorically: "Do civilizations shape tools or do tools shape civilizations?" He explained that automobiles have changed the way we live and computers have changed the way we think. Also, electronic technologies have essentially reconfigured our perceptions of time and history. He compared cave paintings of past civilizations to the nanosecond response that characterizes the virtual reality created by computers. Roger believed that "the sociological instances" of the cave paintings would nevertheless "endure longer than ClarisWorks." To Roger, it was apparent that technology shapes human reality. How we affect technology, however, is not apparent to us, for it seems, according to Roger, that we easily become "blinded by the machine." Because we fail to take responsibility as co-creators through our inventions, technology remains autonomous.

Roger, skeptical about policy elites' technocentric reform discourse, had struggled against the technology-driven philosophy of certain colleagues within his school and district. Like Cassandra, he perceived the folly in their actions and where it would most likely lead them, but no one would listen to him. Thus, he was labeled as a naysayer and obstructionist when his intention was to engage the possibility for open discussion and give expression to teachers' personal practical knowledge. Another metaphor related by Roger captures this situation. He explained that the Native Americans, by using flint to make arrowheads, risked being blinded by the flint. Thus, he implied that educators are now blinded by the very technologies they seek to acquire and control.

It appears that many of the informants expressed very sophisticated ideas about technology and society. Some believed that the interaction between society and technology could be characterized by a reflexive relationship. Many sensed that technology was acting in an autonomous manner and one related the quest of progress to the breakdown in the natural environment. Also, many of the teachers related their explanations to what they observed in their lives as both teachers and citizens. Thus, the theme of ennui is related to students' restless inattention and boredom and their need to fill the void with endless entertainment. The students' lack of imaginative thinking is related to the pervasiveness of commodity culture's mediated spectacle and the violence that some students demonstrate in their behavior signifies a breakdown in social responsibility evidenced by the fact that young children are schooled on a cultural curriculum of violence, both in media and in real life.

In addition, given Shelton Valley's focus on technology-based reform, one might expect that its teachers and administration would resemble the perceptions of their colleagues who adopted a more technocentric perception. But this was not the case. Many teachers related very complex and critical understandings about the relationship between technology and society. Also, while Roger was the only teacher who overtly attempted to act on his convictions, other teachers' resistance worked on a more diffused and subtle level of expression. For example, Satie, who had no misgivings about using an ILS in schools and, in fact, was the technology committee coordinator when the school purchased its first ILS, was nevertheless very concerned about students' apparent lack of engagement and imaginative thinking and associated these symptoms to an overly stimulated and information, and media-saturated society. Satie also had a rather glum view about the relationship between society and technology. Therefore, despite her indifference to the possible negative consequences of the school's policy to use an ILS (perhaps because she was a key stakeholder in the decision-making process), Satie actively resisted or was "holding the line" against the slippage in the school's authority and rural traditions—the underlying causes of which she suspected were related to our increasingly complex technological, and media-saturated society.

Such contradictions and complexities characterize many of the informants. The most consistent perspectives offered throughout the sociopolitical and sociotechnological issues were, however, given by those who held a very strong conviction about the technocentric vision constructed by policy elites. In this sense, the discourse of policy elites seemed to have created a dogmatic perspective within certain individuals. But this outcome was clearly in the minority. Thus, it appears that most of the informants do not possess optimism and enthusiasm about the techno-utopian vision offered by policy elites. If anything, one might imagine that most of the informants would say that support of a technology-driven reform policy at this time is akin to fiddling while Rome is burning. Therefore, the technocentric framework of policy elites did not seem to fit with the practical-based framework of these educators. In addition, their views on both sociopolitical and technopolitical issues, in general, reflected the concerns of the critics of policy elites and thus are anchored by a social justice-based perspective on education. In fact, the political and philosophical insights of many of the informants acts to expand and problemitize the contained discursive landscape of technocentric reform policy. But given such insights, what do the teachers believe will be the outcome of the current reform movement? What do they envision education to be like in the 21st century given the current trajectory of educational reform policy?

The Projection of Education's Future in the 21st Century

Many of the informants cast their predictions within the context of their personal practical knowledge against the background of the larger political sphere of their professional knowledge landscape. For example, some teachers explained the probability of changes in curriculum and instruction in terms of structural and political realities. Some offered particularly negative visions. Others seemed resigned to the fact that little would change for the better given current political and economic realities. Most of the teachers from Shelton Valley believed that technology would be a major aspect of 21st century schools. Only one teacher at Zepeda mentioned this factor. The majority of the informants couched their vision within the context of issues related to curriculum and instruction and the politics of controlling teachers' work.

The principal at Shelton Valley, for example, believed that technology "would change the form and substance" and "the delivery" of education even while social problems would "still plague education." His ideal vision, however, was that education would reflect values of a greater sense of community and the "moral and ethical and societal obligation to assist others." Roger believed that a "new frontier perception" would continue to drive the infusion of technology into education, but that little would change in terms of the relationship with students. Roger's ideal vision was that teachers would engage in reflective practice and adoption of an Aristotelian model of teaching. Many other teachers at Shelton Valley believed that technology would be a dominant force. A few foresaw more controls on teachers' work through standards and stricter accountability systems. Even so, social problems would continue to be a spur in the heel of education. Although Mary Jane's vision was dominated by technology (teleconferencing, networked systems, computers), she was, however, the only teacher at Shelton Valley, except for Lisa, who referenced the dominance of thematic curriculum and student-centered instructional practices.

At Zepeda, the principal made no prediction other than that he wanted schools to become the centers of their communities, such as what Zepeda was struggling to accomplish. The dominant elements, which characterized the teachers' visions of schools in the future, were related to developing reading and language skills, early childhood education, and a return to "traditional values." For Toby, the idea of "traditional values" meant an experience of community and a cohesiveness in society versus the present condition of fragmentation and alienation. This was also a point raised by Georges. Both teachers, however, did not foresee this shift in society as likely to occur. Also, several of Zepeda's teachers believed that some form of privatized-based system of school management (e.g., voucher system) would be adopted and this would further the economic gap between the rich and poor.

Christine, a teacher at Zepeda, had a highly technocentric vision including the use of computers, distance education, and the Internet. But she also referenced thematic-based curriculum, student-directed learning, and the use of telecommunications for collaborative projects, which she believed would aid in diminishing teachers' isolation. As mentioned above, Shelton Valley's librarian, Mary Jane, and teacher, Lisa, also made reference to such changes in instructional practices along with a highly technology-driven reform program. Thus, only the staunch supporters of technology-driven reform advocated what Lisa described as an "Information Age philosophy," which also employed critical thinking skills and certain progressive approaches to curriculum and instruction. This may be due to the fact that teachers who believed in technology-driven reforms are more familiar with such descriptors as "Internet-based collaborative learning." But perhaps even more important is the fact that these teachers believed that technology was necessary to create such fundamental changes in instructional practices and curriculum. In addition, their technology-based visions were not clouded by issues related to equity, power, chronic behavioral problems, or the ominous signals of a social breakdown. They simply saw the potential of education's future as running smoothly within the context of an idealized imagined state created and maintained by means of electronic technologies. In this sense, their visions reflected the rhetoric of mythinformation. On the other hand, although technology-centered, their visions not only acknowledge the reality of the current reform policy, but also reflected a positive perspective based on progressive constructivist-based practices.

Such a projection of education's future was very different from those informants who imagined a particularly dark unfolding. At Shelton Valley, Margorie and Margarete focused on how the social problems challenging schools today would likely escalate. Margarete was frightened by a future filled with hatred and violence. She envisioned the separation of the privileged from the poor, with the latter attending violent and ineffective schools. At Shelton Valley, Susan and Satie's visions were very similar. Satie saw public schools operating as "preprisons more than a school" whereas Susan believed that the outcome of "massive discipline problems" would lead to "detention-type" or military-based public schools. Unfortunately, Satie and Susan's predictions reflect, to some degree, the reality of our present set of circumstances surrounding the issue of youth violence. Public policy has met the rise in youth crime by building more prisons to accommodate an increasing rate of youth incarceration, which includes the creation of "shock incarceration" or boot camp facilities for juveniles (Elliott et al., 1998).

In general, the impressions that the informants shared about their visions of education in the 21st century paint a pragmatic picture where educational reform is envisioned to continue in the present technocentric trajectory established by official reform policy. Despite this sobering reality, many informants held on to alternative visions of education. Some were grounded in pedagogy, such as a greater emphasis on early childhood education, whereas others emphasized general humanistic ideals, such as a return to "traditional values" and the fostering of community. However, few believed in the likelihood that their ideal visions would manifest. In addition, the greatest contrast arose between those few teachers who projected a technocentric utopian vision and those who foresaw a probable future within the context of an escalating social malaise characterized by violence and economic disparity.

The depiction of the informants' specific projections of education's future in the 21st century reflects certain major threads of concern that weave throughout the other levels of analysis, such as a focus on social issues and an unease about the future of society and technology. In the following section we examine the aggregate of the data in terms of the social visions of the informants.

The Meaning of Teachers' Social Visions

It is clear that those informants who closely identified with the general vision of policy elites were in the minority. One possible reason why is that teachers as practitioners live within the borderland between their personal practical knowledge and that of the professional knowledge landscape of official policies and performity. The realm of their personal practical knowledge is rich and deep, reflecting not only experiences in the classroom but also those extending into the broad social and cultural realities of their students' lives. Therefore, because most teachers have at least one finger on the pulse of the lifeworld, their reactions to the assumptions of policy elites were complex, contradictory, pragmatic, and generally critical. Thus, we have a small group of teachers and administrators from two very different schools with very different reform agendas that nevertheless shared similar perspectives in terms of certain assumptions about current educational reform policy. For example, the majority of informants from both sites emphasized that the crisis was not in schools but within society itself and was related to systemic economic and sociocultural problems, some of which were fueled by the nature of a technological society. Also, most informants offered misgivings about the uses of technology in schools, and their misgivings were underscored when they were asked to explain the relationship between society and technology. In general, these teachers offered a rather dystopian picture of the future within a technological society, a perspective which in fact reflects a general postmodern sensibility that historians Leo Marx (1994) and Howard Segal (1996) describe as "technological pessimism." The thesis of technological pessimism is rooted in historical and sociological circumstances and thus requires some further explanation.

Technological Pessimism and the Act of Questioning Technology

Marx (1994) describes the undermining of "technology representing the actualization of the Enlightenment quest" as "technological pessimism." The power of the Enlightenment was the belief in the expansion of knowledge and control over nature toward the end of attaining a cumulative improvement of life's conditions. As the practical arts of science and technology were appointed as the primary agents of progress, the notion of progress became a metanarrative or organizing framework through which history and social vision were constructed and understood. The basis of foundationalism—an epistemological faith in human capacity to secure access to a timeless foundation for certainty, objective, context-free, incontrovertible knowledge—was confirmed through advances in Western science and thus invited "an historical romance called Progress" (Marx, 1994, p. 21). Progress not only signified material wealth through the subjugation of nature, but technological artifacts also signified a means of realizing a more just and republican society based on the consent of the governed.

Marx (1994) also explains how the practical character of technological artifacts, such as the steam engine, "matched the central role accorded to instrumental rationality and its equipment as chief agents of progress" (p. 15). Thus, by the 19th century the discrete mechanical artifacts were transfigured to reify more complex technological systems, which not only encompassed technological artifacts but also bureaucratic management of corporations, large capital investments, and a cadre of highly trained experts. The simple republican means of ensuring progress through directing technical means toward societal ends "was imperceptibly transformed into a quite different technocratic commitment to improving 'technology' as the basis and the measure of—as all but constituting—the progress of society" (p. 20). Indeed, this technocratic idea of progress can be understood as the epitome of optimistic expression of Enlightenment rationalism. However, according to Marx (1994), it tacitly replaced "political aspirations with technical innovation as a primary agent of change, thereby preparing the way for an increasingly pessimistic sense of the technological determination of history" (p. 20). In addition, historian Howard Segal (1996) explains that "technological improvements offer no lasting escape from politics . . . because of its inherent contradictions and elusiveness, the public interest can never be defined technologically" (p. 42). Indeed, I believe that the contradictory and paradoxical explanations offered by the informants supports Segal's thesis.

Marx (1994) adds that this "technocratic spirit" has been manifested via instrumental rationality, order, control, and efficiency as set forth in the theories of Taylorism and Fordism. Indeed, this "technocratic spirit" was criticized by Lewis Mumford (1962), especially because it bypassed the moral and political goals by assigning technological means as ends in themselves. (This perspective was first offered by Henry Thoreau (1869) who commented in *Walden* that modernity's efforts signify "but improved means to an unimproved end.") Today, the threat of nuclear holocaust, pollution, and degradation of environmental ecosystems reflect the paradox inherent in a technocentric idealism. Moreover, particular to the advent of electronic technologies, technological pessimism, as understood by Marx (1994), reflects a determinative power of technology specifically as a life dominated by large technological systems characterized by electronic communication technologies and the emergence of knowledge-based economies. Unlike a modernistic expression of entrenched power that can be identified, removed, and replaced, electronic media and Information Age technologies possess a distinct technological expression of power. An electronic-based economy is ephemeral and has no central, fixed controllable locus.   Thus, power expressed within the context of Information Age is "everywhere but concentrated nowhere" (Marx, 1994, p. 24).[1]

In addition, according to Marx (1994), if we entertain a vision of postmodern society characterized by "immense, overlapping, quasi-autonomous technological systems," where society must necessarily integrate the operationalization of these systems "becoming in the process a metasystem of systems upon whose continuing ability to function our lives depend, then the source of postmodern technological pessimism seems evident" (p. 25).[2]   This sensibility was evidenced in certain informants' concerns over the development of what they perceived to be autonomous technology and the possible dehumanizing effects of electronic media and information technologies.

Indeed, Segal (1996) perceives that the development of greater awareness of negative outcomes of technology, especially in the environmental movement, has tempered technological utopianism. Despite great numbers of scientific and technological breakthroughs, "there emerged in recent decades a declining trust in the social and political applications of knowledge and more broadly, in technical expertise itself " (p. 39). Segal (1994), as does Marx (1994), understands that technological pessimism has a postmodern edge, as the prospect of autonomous technology—technology absent of human control—"has become a paramount public concern regardless of any statistical and other quantitative evidence to the contrary" (p. 39). Indeed, this factor was evidenced in the responses given by several of the informants.

Also, political scientist Yaron Ezrahi (1994) believes that the growing public distrust of science and technology "is more a symptom of a transformation of the conception of politics than of changes in science and technology" (p. 29). Segal concurs, noting that along with environmental consciousness "renewed political consciousness is a hallmark of techno-logical pessimism" (p. 42). Segal (1996) adds that changes in political processes produced by the demands of women and minorities "may ultimately have been more significant for growth of technological pessimism (or technological ambivalence) than any writing on technological pessimism" (p. 44). He concludes that "technology problems are rarely the real issue," which he believes is "the ultimate irony of the failure of Enlightenment dreams and the profoundest difference between traditional technological optimism" and current technological pessimism. Therefore. the real issue centers around "invariably flawed human nature" (p. 42), for American society and culture shapes its technology "precisely as American values and expectations evolve" (Segal, 1996, p. 35). This reflexive characteristic was also pointed out by certain informants. Indeed, the relationship between technology and society, for many of the informants, was understood to be a complex social process.

Even so, according to Segal (1996), the growing presence of technological ambivalence or pessimism has not seemed to have influenced educators (or policy elites for that matter). Segal (1996) states, "it is distressing—and revealing—to see traditional technological utopianism persisting in countless educational circles" (p. 44). Segal (1996) reports how over twenty years ago it was predicted that "learning machines" were to revolutionize and transform the educational process. The same has been said about the information superhighway and, in both instances, the underlying assumption is the reduction in the number of teachers and the emphasis on individualized computer-mediated instruction. Segal (1996) concludes that such qualities of technology-based instruction arise from the following rationale.

> The replacement of teachers by structures and machines both in the classroom and at home, just like the replacement of (other) workers by robots and advanced assembly lines, is part of the appeal of this ideology [technological utopianism] to those in government and business who seek simplistic—but always financially profitable—solutions to complex problems (p. 44).[3]

Thus, it is ironic that educators seem to blindly accept policy elites' technocentric vision because such a vision, in the name of efficiency, normalizes the need to automate the instructional process and thus reduces the need for teachers. Even so, the public and educators continue to support technology-driven official policy. However, the evidence offered in this study does seem to muddy the waters. Some educators, when given the opportunity to fully express their concerns, harbor deep ambivalence about a technocentric reform policy. Indeed, such complexities, which influence the intersection of technology, society, and education, were examined in 1978 by Maxine Greene. A decade after the 1960's women's, civil rights and anti-Vietnam War movements, Greene wrote that a growing cynicism about the myth of progress was evidenced by concern over economic and environmental problems where, "even for the uninformed, there is a lived experience of what Jacques Ellul calls 'encirclement' by impersonal technique" (p. 9). Greene further explains how these invisible and impersonal forces are "experienced as red dyes in food, asbestos in the workplace . . . behavior modification in the school" which are constantly being disclosed ex post facto" (p. 10). Greene (1978) believes that the overall sense that this situation creates is what Hannah Arendt describes as "rule by Nobody," where, as an effect of efficiency and bureaucracy, no one takes responsibility even while people experience their liberties and rights as threatened. And, Greene continues, "in a mysterious way, all this seems to be linked to science as much as to ubiquitous technique," where the scientific endeavor "appears subsumed under technical activity, engineering and manipulative controls. More seriously, the outcomes of all this seem abruptly to have taken on a life of their own" (p. 9).

In concert with Segal's (1994) and Ezrahi's (1994) perspectives, Greene (1978) believes that the awakening of different voices by people endeavoring to "recapture themes of their lived lives . . . and express their original intuitions of reality" arises as a form of resistance against people's sense of being positioned by "too many official schemata, by others' naming and demarcators," a factor that leads one to feel both restive and mystified. Although it is not the scientific method or scientism that is identified by most people as oppressive "without being clearly aware of it, they are affected by some of the consequences of scientism and positivism, most particularly the subject-object split and the links to technological controls" (p. 12). Thus, Greene is suggesting that for many people in postmodern society "there is a feeling of being dominated and that feelings of powerlessness are almost inescapable" (p. 43). Such sensibilities were evidenced in some of the informants' reported perceptions about both sociopolitical and sociotechnological issues as well as their specific vision of education in the 21st century.

However, Greene (1978) also suggests that such feelings can be overcome through a conscious endeavor to be reflective and critically aware, "for only then can they develop the sense of agency required for living a moral life" (p. 44), a point also raised by Ellul (1964). According to Greene (1978), in order to build a "moral directness, of oughtness," one must cultivate "imaginativeness, an awareness and a sense of possibility" (p. 51). The informants, with a few exceptions, evidenced a foundation for the creation of a "sense of possibility" by their rejection of policy elites' technocentric framework. Thus, the technological pessimism, which many of the informants expressed, can signify possibility, an opening up in the landscape whereupon educators as citizens can begin to build on the foundation of democratic ideals and experience an enlightened social vision. Therefore, if one understands disruption of the given as an aesthetic process, a change in one's way of knowing, although sometimes painful, the process invites an awakening of the imagination (Greene, 1978, 1995). Thus, educators' reflections on current reform discourse and official policy act as a means to manifest their imaginative thinking and social vision. It is also a courageous act as it demands that one gain a "self-conscious distance" from the political dynamic and spectacle and its comfortable mystification (Eldeman, 1985, p. 213).

Therefore, the informants' technological pessimism may be interpreted as a positive indicator that the dialectic between the technocentric perspective and that of the more traditional democratic perspective is still alive, albeit silent. And this is the most important point—the silence, the lack of a forum within which teachers and citizens can deliberate and thus engage the possibility of praxis. The factor that impedes this possibility arises from the characteristic "inevitability" of the dominant technocentric discourse. Therefore, without an active forum for expression, the potential for one's technological pessimism or sensibility to question technology as a means to balance the dominant technocentric discourse of policy elites is lost. Thus, under current conditions, where many teachers lack voice in policy decision-making, such questioning retreats into acquiescence and silence, or, if articulated, it is labeled as the voice of the irrational "technophobic other" and dismissed. The story of Roger at Shelton Valley illustrates how those who do take a stand against technology-driven reform policy are marginalized and ultimately silenced.

These factors need to be considered in light of how our society is at a crossroads—the dawn of a new phase in the development of a technological society—the globalized and marketized socioeconomic reality of "enterprise culture" (Peters, 1996). Therefore, the infusion of electronic technologies into schools and throughout other social and economic spheres is indeed "inevitable." Given this reality, the informant's social visions need to be taken seriously. I believe that what this study reveals is not only the underlying concerns and fears of certain educators within an emerging information and postmodern societal context. What is also portrayed is the possibility for a synthesis between the two dialectic perspectives on education—the dominant pragmatic ties to functionalism as characterized in and through current educational reform policy, and the deep historical ties to a vision of social justice.

In order for this possibility to become actualized and thus expand and open the "social space" of educational reform discourse, educators need to consciously work at creating a more democratic means through which the conversations can begin and be sustained. Also, a critically based and more conscientious approach to technology adoption would ward off the specter of autonomous technology. For, as explained in Chapter Two, the most significant moment in the process of technology adoption is the point *before* adoption takes place, because once technological innovations are in place and become embedded into economic, bureaucratic, and sociocultural practices, they are next to impossible to alter because they evolve to constitute the very systems which they were designed to simply support (Winner, 1986). Therefore, specific to the realm of education, an open and democratic approach to the planning of policy and the adoption of new technologies is imperative.

However, it is important that we give consideration to another possible reading of the informants' technological pessimism; the story of a surrender to the silence and educator's acquiescence to the "inevitability" of policymaker's technocentric utopian dream.   Perhaps, given the complexity of technology adoption in educational settings, there would not so much exist an acquiescence to electronic technology itself but rather to a more generalized rationalization of teachers' work via the *technique* of standards and accountability procedures, elements which inculcate performity culture. Researchers, however, have found that both administrators and teachers ensconced within performity culture can engage in "strategic non-compliance" and thus demonstrate "professional courage" to eschew the "sterile visioning and intimacy-inducing processes" which characterize performance culture (Gleeson & Gunter, 2001, p. 152).   The nature of educators' resistance is such that their pedagogy remains "connected to broader issues of equity and justice rather than just the technical delivery of an externally required curriculum."   Indeed, teachers, in particular, can resist the dictates of performance culture because "they observe and live within deep contradictions between the rhetoric of 'good practice' and the reality of working with children and the community" (Gleeson & Gunter, 2001, p. 152).

What is at stake here is possibility itself. But the discourse of possibility, a specific discourse that serves to reanimate the lost narrative of social justice, can emerge as an articulation of an alternative narrative to the received technocentric narrative of policy elites only through the process of discourse. For it is through our engagement with language and the "dramaturgy in politics" (Eldeman, 1985) that we construct who we are to ourselves. Thus, it is imperative that, through discourse and deliberation, educators awaken to the power of their personal practical knowledge and also engage the shadow of technological pessimism as a means towards interrogating the social vision of technocentrism.   It is clear that the technological pessimism of teachers indicates a potential, a possibility. Nevertheless, if this possibility is to express "professional courage" and thus resistance to the "inevitability" of the dominate discourse versus a silent acquiescence or enthusiastic mystification, it needs thoughtful support. In the next section of this chapter I review means by which such thoughtful support may come to pass.

Questioning Technology Through Deliberation

Based on the findings, I offer one major recommendation that acts as an overarching one for any related suggestions. Basically, educators need to utilize a more reflective approach to the adoption of electronic technologies, which can be realized by means of a democratic process of discussion and deliberation. As the story of Shelton Valley indicates, adoption of the policy elites' technocentric reform framework, without first establishing a basis for community within one's school, may simply act as an unfortunate red herring, in terms of inculcating actual reform. The reality of this factor is illustrated by the success of Zepeda's community-based framework and their ability to achieve most of their reform efforts. In addition, because the framework guiding the reform effort at Zepeda was overtly political, in that its main purpose was to build community solidarity and address inequality, the teachers' roles were politicized such that their personal practical knowledge could express praxis versus an acquiescence to a culture of mere performity. In effect, Zepeda's teachers were invited to become social change agents. This expanded role was supported by a democratic decision-making process, which included not only teachers and administrators, but in many cases, parents and other members of the community. And, as suggested above, although Zepeda had a very restricted understanding about the uses of technology, the school's decision-making process, in addition to the overarching influence of TIAF's philosophy, would have likely enabled the development of a more critical approach to technology adoption— perhaps one that endeavors to express and support the community's as well as acknowledge teachers' social visions. Therefore, I suggest that models of adoption and reform emphasize a democratic and deliberative framework for guiding educator's adoption of electronic technologies.

Also, models of educational reform based on a deliberative approach to technology adoption address the contextuality and uniqueness of an individual site and thus support a community-based approach to technology adoption, which has been recommended by many scholars who study the sociology of technology (i.e., Carey, 1989, 1990; Winner, 1986, 1996; Street, 1992; Sclove, 1995; Illich, 1973). For example, educational historian, Jesse Goodman (1995) offers an alternative approach to typical top-down and technocentric models of school reform. His model is based on the idea of creating a "knowledge-making activity," whereby the reform effort reflects the concerns and visions of community members as well as those that arise from the personal practical knowledge of teachers. Goodman (1995) further explains that a "knowledge-making activity" approach to the development of reform involves both the process of envisioning as well as the means of actualizing a particular vision of reform.

> A departure from current reform initiatives would be a movement that brings teachers, administrators, parents and other interested individuals into the knowledge-making activity of the restructuring effort. It would be a movement that validates the academic, experiential, and tacit knowledge of these people, and then generates a vision of schooling based upon this rich knowledge base. It would also be a movement in which the participants not only envision the type of schooling to be developed, but also the process by which this vision emerges.
> . . . Throughout this century, school change efforts have been initiated and directed by people who do not have this direct relationship to the education of

children, and it seems that this latest school restructuring effort continues, rather than challenges, this legacy (p. 22).

Goodman's approach to decision-making as a "knowledge-making activity" compliments Robert Young's (1990) understanding of the current crisis in education as being developmental—specifically, a crisis in the process of knowledge-making. Basing his theories on the writings of Jurgen Habermas, who privileges deliberative speech as a means of realizing democratic ideals, Young (1990) proposes that a deliberative approach to institutional rational problem-solving in education be adopted to create a "culture of reconstruction."

Goodman (1995) and Young's (1990) understanding of educational reform not only addresses how educators, parents, and other interested citizens would envision the type of schooling they wanted, but also would determine the process by which they determine their vision of reform. Thus, reconfiguring the process of technology adoption within the context of a knowledge-making activity would enable a more critical approach but also avail greater opportunities for a "convivial" (Illich, 1973) use of technology, which acknowledges that the needs of the lifeworld must preclude all other technicist-based desires. Therefore, if educators include concerns, which arise from the broader framework of their social visions when giving consideration to the adoption of a technical innovation, such an approach would invite the possibility of balancing the dominant technocentric framework with democratic ideals. Thus, the adoption process evolves into a knowledge-building and community-building opportunity, which offers the social space for educational reform discourse to act as *social* reform discourse. Thus, the adoption of technological innovation needs to reflect an ecological model which acknowledges technology adoption as situated and contextual (Christal et al., 1997).

In addition, J. J. Schwab's (1983) proposal for curriculum development as a community effort (shared by students, teachers, parents, the school principal, community members, social scientists and professional academics) could also be used as a model for the adoption of technology into schools. Schwab (1983) explains how this community effort needs to be characterized as a deliberative process. Therefore, the introduction of technological innovations would not be assumed as "inevitable." Rather, the goals that these technologies are envisioned to enliven would be fully discussed, questioned, and debated through an "eclectic" approach, which gives equal consideration to a variety of contending perspectives and theories. Schwab's (1983) model utilizes a formative analysis approach; thus, technology integration, for example, would be characterized as a process of trial and error, emphasizing flexibility and open-endedness.

Also, Schwab's approach privileges the teacher. Noting that "teachers practice an art," Schwab (1983) believes that the process of active involvement in deliberative decision-making "constitutes the only language in which knowledge adequate to an art can arise" (p. 245). William Reid (1979) explains that by privileging the role of the teacher, Schwab is underscoring the moral reality of teachers and curriculum development and how teachers' practices are the manifestation of the public interest. Indeed, if teachers are denied this institutional role, they are left to engage the constricted role of technicians within the context of preformity culture. However, the application of a deliberative model could help to address the depoliticalization of teachers and enliven their civic leadership, thus enabling them to "reclaim their moral and intellectual responsibilities to students," which Bowers (1988) believes to have been usurped by a pedagogical framework guided by technocentric values and aims. A deliberative framework also allows teachers and other members of the school community to "name their world" in the political sense proposed by Paulo Freire (1970) and provides a space for the development of a shared world of discourse, which can then relate a purposive mission, such as the integration of electronic technologies, to a common civic interest of creating citizens and acting in the public interest (Reid, 1979).

Schwab's approach also encompasses all of the commonplaces of education—teachers, students, subject matter, and the cultural-social milieu. His model weighs the relative importance of each of the commonplaces. This factor supports an approach that addresses the contextuality of technology adoption, including the recognition of political forces, such as the discourse of policy elites. Also, such a framework for adoption raises the question of whether or not technology would be placed within the context of curriculum as a subject matter or as an expression of the cultural-social milieu. For example, although electronic technologies are studied in specific courses, as technological artifacts and processes they also operate on the level of a "hidden curriculum" and thus act to inculcate certain biases and ways of knowing (Bowers, 1988, 1995; Streibel, 1986; Turkle, 1997). And, as discussed in Chapter Two, in terms of operating within the context of a school's milieu, a technological infrastructure acts to shape and control our relationship to time and space, thus affecting a subtle but profound presence of influence especially in terms of altering the quality of social interaction.

In any case, a deliberative and critical approach would enable educators to consider the focal and nonfocal effects of technological innovations. Also, a deliberative approach to adoption would help to reveal how our commonsense understanding about technology is socially constructed. Through this self-reflective process of inquiry, assumptions such as mythinformation would not be as likely to function in an axiomatic fashion. In addition, because Schwab's model is based on an eclectic approach and therefore gives all perspectives equal consideration, those educators who question technology and a technocentric framework of educational reform, or who fundamentally stand counter to the status quo, would have a forum within which they could freely express their concerns without fear of censor or overt rejection. Ideally, a deliberative-based adoption process would enable educators to not only discuss and debate questions germane to technological innovation and pedagogy, but also address how such questions relate to their social vision, thus exercising their power as both educators and as citizens of their communities. Also, a deliberative approach to technology adoption would help to unpack the constructs of teachers' resistance and computer anxiety, as recognition of the complexity of both of these issues would necessarily become evident.

In addition to suggesting recommendations for a general deliberative-based approach to technology adoption, other supporting issues need to be addressed. Specifically, teachers need to be trained to be aware of the nonfocal effects of technology. This goal could be realized by inviting both teachers and students to be critical users of electronic technologies via participation in research efforts, which directly involve participants in the process of data gathering or in the design of computer-based instructional systems and instructional software. In addition, technology adoption needs to be guided by social constructivist-based learning theory, which ultimately serves as a framework for technology integration and teachers' instructional strategies. Another point is to acknowledge and foster teachers' imaginative thinking and their social visions through encouraging and supporting reflective practice. This factor is related to teachers' authentic participation in decision-making. Each of these suggestions requires that teachers become more actively engaged in the process of technology adoption. However, this engagement requires that they develop a language with which to question technology.

The Language of Questioning Technology

One particular informant, Roger, made reference to understanding computer technology as a media in that it can generate a "layering effect," whereby the use of technology mediates the process of communication and therefore alters and possibly diminishes the quality of interaction between teacher and student. Other teachers mentioned the possible relationships between ADD/ADHD and the effects of over-stimulation from too much media and information. Such insights need to be acknowledged, researched, and brought into conversation about technology adoption. It is proposed, therefore, that teachers need to be trained to be more aware of technology's possible nonfocal effects. This would also allow teachers' usage of technology to be grounded in pedagogy and their personal practical knowledge versus the given rationalization of technocentric policymakers. Such a critical approach to adoption would diminish the possible deskilling of teachers and instead further opportunities for the development of more appropriate and creative uses of technology by teachers. Indeed, Kenway (1998) proposes "a new sociology for education," which addresses the centrality of electronic technologies and media within a commercialized and commodified technological society. A broader context of sociotechnological literacy would demand a curriculum that addresses how the complexities of a postmodern technological society dominated by a globalized market economy may address issues germane to social justice and the ecological crisis. This rationale, also developed by C. A. Bowers (1988, 1995, 2000) and de Alba et al. (2000), is well stated by James B. Macdonald (1995) in the following quotation.

> It appears that any sane attempt to educate the young must deal substantively with the impact of man and technology on his own living environment and there appears to be little hope that we can simply solve our ecological problems with the next generation of technological developments. Ecological problem solutions call for the same value search and commitment growing from the inner knowledge of what we are and what we can be. This is a need to transcend the linear and technical problem-solving approaches of the past if we are to survive our ecological crisis (p. 90).

In addition, many informants sensed the possible dehumanizing effects of electronic technologies. This signals a sense of a loss of control with regard to technology-based learning environments. Training teachers to be aware of nonfocal effects can give them the knowledge to reject or adjust technology accordingly, and thus possess actual versus simulated control over the adoption process. The practice of understanding technology's possible nonfocal effects is also related to understanding how individuals and society construct technology as a tool and/or social process. Therefore, a more critical approach to technology adoption would require a constant fine-tuning of the adoption process itself and thus invite teachers to become researchers about how technology changes the learning environment. Thus, teachers are not simply consumers of a technology-based tool but rather active producers of an innovative and effective learning environment founded on their personal practical knowledge.

I believe that teachers and administrators need to discover and engage a language for questioning technology. This is not as difficult as it may seem, for this language is already present in their personal practical knowledge as evidenced by this study. However, there are barriers. For example, many of the informants mentioned a lack of time to negotiate the many demands and stresses that characterize their daily work. Some reported, in their ideal vision of educational reform, a picture of education which included the acknowledgment and support for teachers' need for reflective thinking, time to imagine and to discuss their deepest impressions with colleagues. For these teachers, this particular ideal of educational reform symbolized a fundamental turning point in the understanding of change regarding the nature of teaching and the culture of schools.

Maxine Greene (1978) has written extensively about the importance that reflective and imaginative thinking has within the lives of teachers and educators in general. The process of imaginative thinking or envisioning is reflexive as it demands that we "be in touch with our landscape," which is to be "conscious of our evolving experiences" (p. 3). The purpose of this approach to educational practice is to "awaken educators to a realization that transformations are conceivable, that learning is stimulated by a sense of future possibility and by a sense of what might be." Thus engagement in the process of imaginative thinking encompasses "social praxis" and "critical consciousness about equality and equity as well as about personal liberation" (p. 3).

This perspective on educators' interior and exterior landscapes arises from democratic theory—that humans can acquire autonomy and efficacy through inquiry and communication (Greene, 1978). Thus, according to Greene (1978, p. 17), "as conscious beings, we constitute the world we inhabit through the interpretations we adopt or to make for ourselves. To take the world for granted as predefined or objectively there is to be uncritical, submissive and submerged." Both Eldeman (1985) and Greene (1978) make reference to the power of mystification. Greene (1978) proposes that the objectivism that supports mystification and positivism be exposed and that educators need to remain in touch with "our perceptual background and thus remaining present to ourselves, we may be better able to ward off the depredations of technique" (p. 17). Indeed, what this study illustrated is that many of the informants remained present to themselves and those values that express their professional commitments, and thus were able to eschew a technocentric social vision by grounding their reflections on policy elites' discourse within the context of their personal practical knowledge. Moreover, the evidence set forth in this study indicates that teachers' "knowledge context" (Clandinin & Connelly, 1995) includes matters related to sociopolitical and sociotechnological issues. In addition, this study confirms the conclusion offered by Clandidin and Connelly (1995) in terms of how there exists few links between the discourse of abstract policy and the phenomenological world of teachers' practical knowledge and lived experiences as educators. Such findings are important because they inform the incongruencies that characterize the interaction between teachers' personal practical knowledge and their professional knowledge landscapes.

Indeed, Greene (1978), making reference to the work of Paulo Freire, advises that all learning must be in some manner emancipatory, and, as educators, we should understand the history of knowledge structures, scientific paradigms and history, such that "it should be possible to understand the dangers of instrumental controls through confrontations with some centers of technology, even with bureaucracies." This enables individuals to pose "searching and significant questions" regarding "how to recognize mystification whatever the source" (p. 19). Thus, if people can be taught to recognize lacks or deficiencies in their lived experiences, "they may learn how to repair or transcend." However, this process of overcoming passivity and withdrawal and remaining in touch with one's perceptual landscape depends on how individuals come to understand and reflect upon their lives. Greene (1978) cautions that "given the complexity of our technetronic society," its hierarchies and distances, "we cannot invest all our hopes in education, certainly not what happens in schools. But we can try— in whatever educative role we find ourselves" (p. 19). This is especially important given the current demands for accountability, standards and discipline, and general functionalist aims, where "teachers (artlessly, wearily) become accomplices in mystification. They lack time and energy to further their students' critical reflection: they themselves have suppressed the questions and avoided backward looks" (Greene, 1978, p. 38). Greene (1978) proposes, therefore, that one of the responsibilities of teacher educators is to work for "more authentic speaking" and thus combat mystification.

This study in fact indicates that some teachers are indeed what Purpel (1996) describes as "unwitting and naive accomplices" to the technocentric vision of policy elites and thus operate under the spell of mystification. However, many other teachers seemed poised to choose themselves as "public intellectuals" (Aronowitz & Giroux, 1991) because their opposition to the given dominant social vision was rooted in a "social utopian" perspective (Goodman, 1995) based on humanistic and democratic ideals. Generally, the informants' concerns reflected those of policy elite critic Siv Shapiro (1990), who believes that the failure to speak to democratic values in the context of educational reform, represents—

> . . . a larger failure to address a sense of critical issues in American public life— the pervasive and largely uncontrolled influence of television and the media, the alienation from the instruments of political democracy, and the absence of just about any form of economic democracy. . . . [and] the erosion of those traditions concerned with community empowerment (p. 15).

However, what remains to occur is that teachers' technological pessimism be channeled into what Michael Apple (1986) calls "contradictory resistance," where teachers' voices become actualized as politically transformative power and praxis so that they may engage in the act of becoming an "articulate public" (Greene, 1986/1996). To this end, teachers need to recognize the value of their social visions and be recognized for their social visions. It would be a mistake to interpret their dystopian perspective as mere pessimistic reflections of "burnt-out" educators. Rather, as mentioned above, their critical stance generally arises from their personal practical knowledge, a love and concern for children, and a belief in the ideal of social justice.

Also, Seymore Sarason (1996) concluded in his book *Revisiting the Culture of School and the Problem of Change* that schools, because they are so closely enmeshed within the community and social structure, are "very sensitive barometers of diverse changes in the larger society" (p. 376). This situation, I believe, makes those teachers who struggle against mystification our (post) modern day Cassandras. Therefore, it is imperative that teachers' critical and imaginative thinking be supported and that teacher education programs reflect not only sociocultural issues but also those germane to sociotechnological concerns.

Traditionally, according to Greene (1978), teacher education has presented an "unexamined surface reality as 'natural,' fundamentally unquestionable." This essentially leads to overlooking "the *constructed* character of social reality" (p. 54, author's italics). However, Hargraves (1994) envisions teachers' roles within the context of a technocratic post-modern society as requiring that they be 'both competent users and innovators with technology and moral guardians against its most trivializing effects" (p. 76). Thus, a basis for a more critical perspective in teacher education, according to Maxine Greene (1978), that would "ward off the depredations of technique" would be to "start with a conception of a technocratic society armed with awesome power, both technical and communicative" (p. 56). It is hopeful that this study is a step toward realizing this recommendation.

Concluding Remarks

I believe that the characteristic technological pessimism of the informants' social visions problemitizes the entire technocentric campaign of policy elites, especially considering the lack of deliberation regarding official reform policy. The meaning I make of teachers' social visions conjures to the postmodern condition, a condition characterized by a crisis in meaning, reflecting the "cultural contradictions" of capitalism (Bell, 1976). There-fore, a new frontier in curriculum research and praxis must consider seriously the nature of teachers' social visions and their vision-making. In addition, the nature of social visions may be used to inform teacher agency, reflective practice, and the development of educational reform policy.

Also, the story of Zepeda's community-based approach to school reform is unfortunately unique. Most approaches to reform reflect the typical technocentric framework as depicted by Shelton Valley. Therefore, popular business approaches to school management (e.g., TQM), along with a general functionalist perspective, frames the current landscape of school reform and restricts, and ultimately denies, many teachers the legitimacy of their voice and imagination. Indeed, popular models of school reform teach that only administrators as leaders are imbued with the need or ability to envision or express their social vision. Also, the need for considering social visions within a broader sociopolitical or technopolitical context—in relief against the background of policy "inevitabilities" and a technocentric vision of education that is being created, infused, and financed without serious public debate—is generally not acknowledged.

Although the technological pessimism of the informants indicates that it is possible for educators to not engage in blindly adopting policy elites' technocentric framework, unless they are supported by a community-based reform framework, such as that experienced by teachers at Zepeda, such political and social insights remain without praxis. Also, in terms of policy, the current imbalance created by the hegemony of particular political and economic discourses has generally left progressive social democratic concerns with little meaning and relevancy. Moreover, the technological and functionalist-driven educational reform discourse is further complicated by the "cultural wars," which characterize educational reform policy, especially the social vision constructed by the conservative Right's and conservative Christian's discourses. Recall that many of the informants couched their concerns within the realm of the sociocultural. The reality is that the fears and unease expressed by many of the informants reflects a general underlying perception that the uncertainty that characterizes postmodern society signifies a loss in society's moral center and thus an immanent social breakdown. Such perceptions are related to the sensibility of technological pessimism. Therefore, the conservative's call to return to cultural and educational foundationalism has great appeal because it is fulfilling a perceived need—reconstructing a familiar social vision. In fact, the power of the conservative Right's discourse arises from the fact that it offers a specific vision of the future, albeit one that is nostalgic in that it refers to the revival of a past time of social and moral certainty and stability as evidenced in the writings of E. D. Hirsh, Jr. (1987) and Allen Bloom (1987). Therefore, their language of certainty and assurance displaces systemic, economic, and structural elements, from which the many problems facing society today arise, and instead projects them into the realms of the personal, symbolic, and moral (Shapiro, 1990, p. 34). This general conservative stance legitimates the control over teachers' work and students' academic performance and has thus led to an increased emphasis within official reform policy on overt control through standards and accountability schemes and has laid the foundation for the development of performance culture within schools. Even so, unlike postmodern discourse, conservative discourse "offers more than a language of critique: it paints a powerfully resonant image of the future" (Shapiro, 1990, p. 23). Critical postmodern discourse has been unable to do this because that which constitutes moral visions and a language of possibility are undermined by the nature of the critical endeavor itself (Shapiro, 1990, p. 89). Shapiro (1990) therefore recommends that critical scholars consider the writing of the religious Left, such as David Purpel (1991/1996) who offers a discourse that affirms a vision of possibility in a world constituted around values of social justice, love, community, peace, joy, and awe. Shapiro (1990) believes that nothing short of this is capable of meeting and confronting "the obfuscating moral discourse of the Right, or of resisting and exposing the social purpose of the pervasive educational language of technique and instrumental rationality" (p. 34). I believe that he may be correct in this assumption.

In fact, other critical scholars such as Michael Apple (1995, 1996), Peter McLaren (1995), and Maxine Greene (1986/1996), have cited a need for building a shared vision of possibility—in effect, creating alternative visions to the "inevitable" one constructed through the discourse of policy elites. In the words of Peter McLaren (1995, pp. 50–54), educators can work together to build a "theology of hope" and a "language of critique and possibility"—to dare to envision beyond the given and act upon our social visions of possibility. I believe that the crisis in meaning expressed by the informants' social visions begs for a means to name and build a "theology of hope," a vision of possibility. Thus, ultimately, the issues surrounding current educational reform policy—the discourse of inevitability fashioned by policy elites and the narrowing of public discourse, a dominant technocentric and functionalist political framework, mythinformation and the rapid infusion of electronic technologies, the alternative political framework guided by the democratic tradition of social justice and teacher's resistance—together reflect a search for meaning within a story about power and social justice.

Indeed, it is this search for meaning toward the realization of social justice that must be enlivened within the lifeworld of our everyday practices and social interactions. Gorz (1989) states in the quotation given at the opening of this chapter that, "*Technical culture is lack of culture in all things non-technical.*" The danger is that as the lifeworld becomes subsumed by *technique*, we will have lost the capacity to notice. At this point we become engaged within an unfortunate paradox: Technology expressed as *technique* surpasses its function of reflexivity and thus engenders the absolute power to control *because* technology reflects the abdication of our responsibility toward it. Thus, the question is, how may we regain a sense of responsibility about technology? The reader may guess from the title of this book that it begins with questioning technology. For, to question something is not to deny its inherent value or to simply criticize. Rather, it is a form of engagement that reaches for understanding through inquiry. To question technology is to invite a responsible relationship with it. Thus, as educators, are we not obliged to engage in the practice of questioning technology if we care to teach such a responsibility to our students? Perhaps this reflective and questioning approach to technology adoption will serve as a means to balance aesthetic rationality with technological rationality and thus invite a more humane instructional environment so that even while educators acknowledge that the places we call schools reflect the larger social and cultural transformations that characterize a troubled postmodern technological society, they are also sacred places. What is most important is that we actively engage in the process of constructing our social visions and realize the power in their possibility to reanimate the dialectic of educational reform policy and the lost sensibility of social justice.

Notes

[1] This ephemeral expression of power is perhaps best exemplified by the deregulation of capital and financing. The globalization of markets, finance, and labor has been constituted through electronic systems of communication (and transportation of the new currency of information), and as such has reconfigured not only the economy but also the sociopolitical sphere. The amorphous "presence" of corporate institutions raise issues as to the traditional notions of their responsibility to the state and its citizens. For example, a 1990 *Business Week* cover story touted how such technologies engendered "stateless" megacorporations that were "leaping boundaries" to intimidate labor unions, elude domestic policies such as "regulatory hurdles" and trade restrictions, as well as seek the cheapest labor sources worldwide.

[2] Technological deterministic views, where technology itself molds society in varying degrees, has the danger that one can turn to the autonomous mechanism of technology and absolve all human enterprise of responsibility. Segal (1996) reminds us that American society and culture shapes American's technology "precisely as American's values and expectations change and evolve" (p. 35). If we reject postmodernist "sense of pleasurably self-abnegating acquiescence in the inevitable to melancholy resignation or fatalism" (Marx, 1994, p. 24), what other perspectives are plausible? Segal (1996) observes that certain social critics seek a "revived pastorialism," which envisions the centrality of society-nature connection, rejects maximization of resources to equitable distribution and sustainability, and rejects "crass economic criteria" (such as GNP) as the basis for determining public policy. Thus, such critics offer an "appropriate technology" for industrialized countries and a native-based vision for the entire world (p. 42). In the field of education, C. A. Bowers (1988, 1995, 2000) urges educators to adopt an ecologically centered framework toward reforming education.

[3] Although Segal's comments are generally true, there does exist specific applications of electronic technology such as computer supported collaborative learning (CSCL) which, based on a network configuration, emphasizes collaboration, not individualized learning, and also embodies social constructivist learning theory which requires the active participation of both teacher and students (Scardamalia & Bereiter, 1993; Scardamalia et al., 1994). However, successful adoption of CSCL requires great planning, support, and structural changes within a school (Christal et al., 1997) and thus CSCL has not been widely adopted. Indeed, this factor raises serious questions about the primacy of the technology to initiate collaborative instructional experiences because it is possible to create social constructivist learning environments without technology acting as the "trojan horse" of such reform. And, as explained in Chapter Two, the mediating process of social interaction inherent in such computer-based systems is highly problematic.

BIBLIOGRAPHY

American Academy of Pediatrics. (1999). Media education. *Pediatrics, 104,* 341–343.

Apple, M. (1986). *Teachers and texts: A political economy of class and gender relations in education.* New York: Routledge & Kegan Paul.

—— (1993). *Official knowledge: Democratic education in a conservative age.* New York: Routledge.

—— (1995). *Education and power (2nd ed.).*New York: Routledge.

—— (1996). *Cultural politics and education.* Columbia University: Teachers College Press.

Armstrong, A. & Casement, C. (2000). *The child and the machine: How computers put our children's education at risk.* Beltsville, MD: Robins Lane Press.

Aronowitz, S. & Giroux, H. (1985). *Education under siege: The conservative, liberal and radical debate of schooling.* South Hadley, MA: Bergin & Garvey.

—— (1991). *Postmodern education: Politics, culture and social criticism.* Minneapolis, MN: University of Minnesota Press.

Arons, S. (1997). *Short route to chaos: Conscience, community and the re-constitution of American schooling.* Amherst, MA: University of Massachusetts Press.

Ball, S. (2001). Performativities and fabrications in the education economy: Towards the performative society. In D. Gleeson & C. Husbands (Eds.), *The performity school: Managing, teaching and learning in a performance culture* (pp. 210–226), London: Routledge Falmer.

Barth, R. (1990). *Improving schools from within.* San Francisco, CA: Jossey-Bass.

Baudrillard, J. (1983). *Simulations.* New York: Semiotext(e).

Becker, H. J. (2000). Who's wired and who's not: Children's access to and use of computer technology. In R. E. Behrman (Ed)., *The future of children: Children and computer technology, 10*(2) (pp. 44–75), Los Altos, CA: David and Lucile Packard Foundation.

Bell, D. (1976). *The cultural contradictions of capitalism.* New York: Basic Books.

Bellah, R., Madsen, R., Sullivan, W., Swidler, A., & Tipton, S. (1986). *Habits of the heart: Individualism and commitment in American life.* New York: Harper & Row.

Bennett, W. (1984). *To reclaim a legacy: A report on the humanities in higher education.* Washington, DC: National Endowment for the Humanities.

Bennis, W. & Nanus, B. (1985). *Leaders: The strategies for taking charge.* New York: Harper & Row.

Berliner, D. (1993). Mythology and the American system of education. *Phi Delta Kappan, 47*(8), 632–640.

Berliner, D. & Biddle, B. (1995). *The manufactured crisis: Myths, fraud and the attack on American public schools.* New York: Addison-Wesley.

Bloom, A. (1987). *The closing of the American mind: How higher education has failed democracy and impoverished the souls of today's students.* New York: Simon & Schuster.

Borgmann, A. (1984). *Technology and the character of contemporary life.* Chicago, IL: University of Chicago Press.

Bowers, C. A. (1988). *The cultural dimensions of educational computing: Understanding the non-neutrality of technology.* New York: Teachers College Press.

—— (1995). *Educating for an ecologically sustainable culture: Rethinking moral education, creativity, intelligence and other modern orthodoxies.* Albany, NY: State of New York University Press.

—— (2000). *Let them eat data: How computers affect education, cultural diversity, and the prospects of ecological sustainability.* Athens, GA: University of Georgia Press.

Brasington, R. (1990). Nintendinitis. *New England Journal of Medicine, 322*, pp. 1473–1474.

Bredo, E. (1989). Supportive contexts for learning. *Harvard Educational Review, 59*, 206–212.

Bronfenbrenner, U. (1979). *The ecology of human development*. Cambridge, MA: Harvard University Press.

———— (1989). Ecological systems theory. In R. Vasta (Ed.), *Annals of child development--Six theories of child development: Revised formulations and content issues* (pp. 1–103). Greenwich, CT: JAI Press.

Bruner, J. (1990). *Acts of meaning*. Cambridge, MA: Harvard University Press.

Burniske, R. W. & Monke, L. (2001). *Digital walls: Learning to teach in a post-modem world*. Albany, NY: SUNY Press.

Campbell, P. (1984). The computer revolution: Guess who's left out? *Interracial Books for Children, 15(3)*, 3–6.

Carey, J. (1989). *Communication as culture*. New York: Routledge.

———— (1990). The language of technology: Talk, text and template as metaphors for communication. In M. Medhurst, A. Gonzalez, & T. R. Peterson (Eds.), *Communication and the culture of technology* (pp. 19–39). Pullman, WA: Washington State University Press.

Castells, M. (1993). The informational economy and the new international division of labor. In M. Carnoy, M. Castells, S. Cohen, & F. M. Cardoso, *The new global economy in the information age: Reflections on our changing world*. University Park, PA: Pennsylvania State University Press, 15–43.

Chaney, H. (2000). The US "digital divide" is not even a virtual reality. *Bridge News*, March 12, 2000.

Chann, C. (1989). Computer use in the elementary classroom—An assessment of CAI software. *Computers and Education, 12(2)*, 109–115.

Christal, M., Ferneding, K., Kennedy-Puthoff, A., & Resta, P. (1997). *Schools as knowledge-building communities*. Denton, TX: Texas Center for Education Technology.

Chubb, J. E. & Moe, T. E. (1990*). Politics, markets and America's schools*. Washington, DC.: The Brookings Institute.

Clandinin, D. & Connelly, F. (1995). *Teachers' professional knowledge landscapes*. New York: Teachers College Press.

Clinton, W. (1994, January 26). Excerpts from President Clinton's State of the Union Message. *New York Times*, A9.

Connelly, F. M. & Clandinin, D. J. (1988). *Teachers as curriculum planners: Narratives of experience*. New York: Teachers College Press.

Cortes, E. Jr. (1995). Reweaving the fabric: The iron rule and the IAF strategy for power and politics. In Henry Cisneros (Ed.), *Interwoven Destinies* (pp. 294–319).

Cremin, L. (1988*). Popular education. The Carnegie Foundation for the Advancement of Teaching, An imperiled generation: Saving urban schools*. Princeton, NJ: Carnegie Foundation for the Advancement of Teaching.

Cuban, L. (1986). *Teachers and machines: The classroom use of technology since 1920*. New York: Teachers College Press.

———— (1996, October 9). Technology reformers and classroom teachers. *Education Week*, pp. 37, 39.

———— (1997). High-tech schools and low tech teaching. *Education Week, 16(34)*, pp. 38, 41.

———— (2001). *Oversold and underused: Computers in the classroom*. Cambridge, MA: Harvard University Press.

Davis, M. (1986). *Prisoners of the American dream*. London: Verso.

de Alba, A, Gonzalez-Baudiano, E., Lankshear, C. , & Peters, M. (2000*). Curriculum in the postmodern condition.*New York: Peter Lang.

Dewey, J. (1916). *Democracy and education*. New York: MacMillan Company.

——— *(1954)*. *The public and its problems*. Athens, OH: The Swallow Press.

DuBord., G. (1994). *The society of the spectacle*. New York: Zone Books.

Duffey, T. & Jonassen, D. H. (Eds.). (199*2)*. *Constructivism and the technology of instruction: A conversation*. Hillsdale, NJ:Lawrence Earlbaum.

Eldeman, M. (197*1)*. *Politics as symbolic action: Mass arousal and quiesance*. New York: Academic Press.

——— (1985). *The symbolic use of politics*. Urbana, IL: University of Illinois Press.

Elliott, D. S. (199*4)*. *Youth violence: An overview*. Congressional Program: Children and Violence, 9(2), 15–20.

Elliott, D., Hamburg, B. & Williams, K. (Eds.) (1998). *Violence in American schools*. Cambridge, England: Cambridge University Press.

Ellul, J. (1964). *The technological society*. New York: Vantage. (Original work published in 1954.)

Executive Office of the President of the United States, President's Committee of Advisors on Science and Technology. *Report to the President on the use of technology to strengthen K-12 education in the United States*. Washington, DC: U.S. Government Printing Office, March 1997.

Ezrahi, Y. (1994). Technology and the illusion of the escape from politics. In Yaron Ezrahi, Evertt Mendelsohn, & Howard P. Segal (Eds.), *Technology, pessimism, and postmodernism* (pp. 29–38). Amherst, MA: University of Massachusetts Press.

Fine, M. (1993). [Ap]arent involvement: Reflections on parents, power and urban public schools. *Teachers College Record*, 94.

Finkelstein, B. (1984). Education and the retreat from democracy in the United States— 1979–1984*Teachers College Record, 86*, 273–282.

Fox, S. (1991). The production and distribution of knowledge through open and distant learning. In Denis Hlynka & John Belland (Eds.), *Paradigms regained* (pp. 217–240). Englewood Cliffs, NJ: Educational Technology Publications.

Freire, P. (1970). *Pedagogy of the oppressed*. New York: Continuum.

Fullan, M. (1993). Why teachers must become change agents. *Educational Leadership, 50*(6), 12–18.

Geertz, C. (1973). *The interpretation of cultures*. New York: Basic Books.

Gergen, K. (1991). *The saturated self: Dilemmas of identity in contemporary life*. New York: Basic Books.

Gingrich, N. *(1995)*. *To renew America*. New York: HarperCollins.

Giroux, H. ((1997). *Channel surfing: Race talk and the destruction of today's youth*. New York: St. Martin's Press.

——— (2000). *Stealing innocence: Corporate culture's war on children*. New York: Palgrave.

Gleeson, D. & Gunter, H. (2001). The performing school and the modernization of teachers. In D. Gleeson & C. Husbands (Eds.), *The performing school: Managing, teaching and learning in a performance culture*. New York: RoutledgeFalmer, 139–158.

Glista, G. G., Frank, H. G., & Tracy, W. F. (1983). Video games and seizures. *Arch Neurology, 40*, 588.

Goleman, D. (1995a). *Emotional Intelligence: Why it can matter more than IQ*. New York: Bantam Books.

Goleman, D. (1995b, October 3). Early violence leaves its mark on the brain. *New York Times*, p. C10.

Goodman, J. (1995). Change without difference: School restructuring in historical perspective. *Harvard Educational Review, 65*(1), 1–29.

Goodson, I. F. (1995). The story so far: Personal knowledge and the political. In J. A. Hatch & R. Wisniewski (Eds.), *Life History and Narrative* (pp. 89–98). Washington, DC: The Falmar Press.

Gordon, D. (1996). *Fat and mean: The corporate squeeze of working Americans and the myth of managerial "downsizing."* New York: Free Press.

Gorz, A. (1989*). Critique of economic reason.* New York: Verso.

Graf, W. D., Chatrian, G., & Glass, S. T. (1994). Video game-related seizures: A report on 10 patients and a review of the literature. *Pediatrics, 93,* 551–56.

Graybill, D., Kirsh, J. R., & Esselman, E. D. (1985). Effects of playing violent versus non-violent video games on the aggressive ideation of aggressive and non-aggressive children. *Child Study Journal, 15,* 199–205.

Greene, M. (1978). *Landscapes of learning.* Columbia University: Teachers College Press.

——— (1988). *The dialectic of freedom.* Columbia University: Teachers College Press.

——— (1995). *Releasing the imagination.* Columbia University: Teachers College Press.

——— (1996). Perspectives and imperatives: Reflection and passion in teaching. In Fritz Mengert, Kathleen Casey, Delores Liston, David Purpel, & Svi Shapiro (Eds.) *The Education Institution (2nd ed.)* (pp. 419–429). Needham Heights, MA: Simon & Schuster. (Reprinted from *The Journal of Curriculum and Supervision,* Fall 1986, Volume 2, Issue No. 1.)

Habermas, J. (1989). Technology and science as "ideology." In Steven Seidman (Ed.), *Jurgen Habermas on society and politics: A reader.* Boston, MA: Beacon Press.

Harding, S. (1986). *The science question in feminism.* Ithaca, NY: Cornell University Press.

——— (1991). *Whose science? Whose knowledge?: Thinking from women's lives.* Ithaca, NY: Cornell University Press.

Hargraves, A. (1994). *Changing teachers, changing times.* London, England: Cassell.

——— (1995). Renewal in the age of paradox. *Educational Leadership, 52*(7), 14–20.

——— (1997, March). *The emotional politics of teaching and teaching development: With implications for educational leadership.* Paper presented at the American Educational Research Association, Chicago, IL.

Harris, P. (1996). Technology interview: Deborah W. Meier. *Technos, 5*(2), 6–13.

Hartley, D. (1999). Marketing and the "re-enchantment" of school management. *British Journal of Sociology of Education, 20*(3), pp. 309–23.

Harvey, D. (1990). *The condition of postmodernity.* Cambridge, MA: Blackwell.

Healy, J. (1990). *Endangered minds: Why children don't think and what we can do about it.* New York: Touchstone.

——— (1998). *Failure to connect: How computers affect our children's minds—for better and worse.* New York: Simon & Schuster.

Hearnstein, R. & Murray, C. (1994). *The bell curve: Intelligence and class structure in American life.* New York: Free Press.

Heinich, R. (1984). The proper study of instructional technology. *Educational Communications and Technology Journal, 32*(2), 67–87.

Hirsh, E. D. Jr. (1987). *Cultural literacy: What every American needs to know.* New York: Vintage Books.

Hood, C. (1990). De-Sir Humphrey frying the Westminster model of bureaucracy: A new style of governance? *Governance, 3*(2), 205–214.

Hutchins, R. M. (1969). *The learning society.* New York: Mentor Books.

Ihde, D. (1979). *Techniques and science.* Boston, MA: Reidel Publishing Co.

Illich, I. (1973). *Tools for conviviality.* Berkeley, CA: Heyday.

Innis, H. (1951). *The bias of communication.* Toronto: University of Toronto Press.

——— (1952). *Changing concepts of time.* Toronto: University of Toronto Press.

Irwin, A. R. & Gross, A. M. (1995). Cognitive tempo, violent video games and aggressive behavior in young boys. *Journal of Family Violence, 10,* 337–50.

Jacobson, L. (1997, September 3). Long-term achievement study shows gains, losses. *Education Week, 3,* p. 12.

Johnson, R. (1991). A new road to serfdom? In Education Group II (Eds.), *Education Limited.* London: Unwin Hyman.

Jupiter Communications (1999). *Kids and teens to spend $1.3 billion online in 2002: Parents' concerns rising as postmodern kids enter the age of digital commerce.* Press Release, New York: Jupiter Communications, June 7, 1999.

Kahne, J. (1996). *Reframing educational policy: Democracy, community and the individual.* New York: Teachers College Press.

Kenway, J. (1998). Pulp Fictions? Education, Markets, and the Information Superhighway. In D. Carlson & M. W. Apple (Eds.), *Power/Knowledge/Pedagogy: The meaning of democratic education in unsettling times.* Boulder, CO: Westview Press.

Kerr, S. (1996). Visions of sugarplums: The future of technology, education and the schools. In Stephen T. Kerr (Ed.), *Technology and the future of schooling.* (pp. 1–25). Chicago, IL: University of Chicago Press.

Kirsh, S. J. (1998). Seeing the world through Mortal Kombat-colored glasses: Violent video games and the development of a short-term hostile attribution bias. *Childhood: A global Journal of Child Research, 5,* 177–184.

Kleibard, H. (1992). *Forging the American curriculum.* New York: Routledge.

Kolderie, T. (1990). *Beyond choice to new public schools: Withdrawing the exclusive franchise on public education.* Policy Report, No. 8. Washington, DC: Progressive Policy Institute.

Kozal, J. (1991). *Savage inequalities: Children in America's schools.* New York: Crown Publishers.

Kozma, R. & Croninger, R. (1992). Technology and the fate of at-risk students. *Education and Urban Society, 24*(4), 440–453.

Kraut, R., Patterson, M., & Lundmark, V. (1998). Internet paradox: A social technology that reduces social involvement and psychological well-being? *American Psychologist, 53,* 1017–1031.

Laclau, E. & Mouffe, C. (1985). *Hegemony and socialist strategy: Towards a radical democratic politics.* London:Verso.

Labaree, D. F. (1987). Politics, markets and the compromised curriculum. *Harvard Educational Review, 57,* 483–494.

Lankshear, C. (1997, March). *Language and the new capitalism.* Paper presented at the American Educational Research Association, Chicago, IL.

Lasch, C. (1979). *The culture of narcissism: American life in an age of diminishing expectations.* New York: W. W. Norton & Company.

Loop, L. (Ed.) (1986). *The new information technology and the education of Hispanics: The promise and the dilemma.* (Policy Pamphlet Series No. 1). Claremont, CA: The Thomas Rivera Center, a National Institute for Policy Studies.

Lyotard, J. (1984). *The postmodern condition.* Minneapolis, MN: University of Minnesota Press.

Macdonald, J. B. (1995). *Theory as a prayerful act.* New York: Peter Lang.

Mander, J. (1978). *Four arguments for the elimination of television.* New York: William Morrow & Company.

Martinez, M. & Mead, N. (1988). *Computer competence: The first national assessment* (Tech. Rep. No. 17–CC–01). Princeton, N.J.: National Assessment of Educational Progress and Educational Testing Service.

Marx, L. (1994). The idea of "technology" and postmodern pessimism. In Y. Ezrahi, E. Mendelsohn, & H. Segal (Eds.), *Technology, pessimism and postmodernism* (pp. 11–28). Amherst, MA: University of Massachusetts Press.

McLaren, P. (1995). *Critical pedagogy and predatory culture.* New York: Routledge.

Montgomery, K. C. (2000). Children's media culture in the new millennium: Mapping the digital landscape. In R. E. Behrman (Ed.), *The future of children: Children and computer technology, 10*(2). Los Altos, CA: The David & Lucile Packard Foundation, 145–167.

Morley, L. & Rassool, N. (1999). *School effectiveness: Fracturing the discourse*. New York: Falmer Press.

Morrison, D. & Goldberg, B. (1996). New actors, new connections: The role of local information infrastructures in school reform. In Timothy Koshman (Ed.), *CSCL: Theory and practice of an emerging paradigm* (pp. 125–145). Mahwah, NJ: Lawrence Earlbaum.

Mumford, L. (1934). *Technics and civilization*. New York: Harcourt, Brace.

——— (1962). The case against modern architecture. In Donald L. Miller (Ed.), *The Lewis Mumford reader*. New York: Pantheon Books.

Murname, R. J. & Levy, F. (1996, September 11). Why money matters sometimes. *Education Week, 16*(2), pp. 36, 48.

Nasbitt, J. (1982*). MegaTrends: Ten new directions transforming our lives*. New York: Warner Books.

National Association of Secondary School Principals (1996). *An executive summary of breaking ranks: Changing an American institution*. Reston, VA: National Association of Secondary School Principals.

National Center for Educational Statistics. (1997). *Advanced telecommunications in U. S. public elementary and secondary schools. Fall 1996*. Washington, DC: U.S. Department of Education, Office of Educational Research and Improvement.

——— (2000, February). *Stats in brief: Internet access in public schools and classrooms: 1994–99*. Washington, DC: U.S. Department of Education, Office of Educational Research and Improvement.

National Commission on Excellence in Education (1983). *A nation at risk: The imperatives for educational reform*. Washington, DC: U.S. Government Printing Office.

National Educational Commission on Time and Learning (1994). *Prisoners of time*. Washington, DC: U. S. Government Printing Office.

National Educational Goals Panel (1994). *Goals 2000: Educate America Act*. Washington, DC: U.S. Government Printing Office.(Public Law 103–227, 20 USC 5897).

National Task Force (1986). Transforming American education: Reducing the risk to the nation. In Lewis J. Perelman (Ed.), *Technology and the transformation of schools, Appendix E*. Alexandria, VA: National School Boards Technology Leadership Network Special Report.

Newman, D. (1992). Technology as support for school structure and school restructuring. *Phi Delta Kappan, 74*(4), 308–315.

Newmann, F. (1993). Beyond common sense in educational restructuring. *Educational Researcher, 22*(2), 4–13.

Noble, D. (1991). *The classroom arsenal: Military research, information technology and public education*. New York: The Falmer Press.

Noddings, N. (1992). *The challenge to care in schools: An alternative approach to education*. New York: Teachers College Press.

Nunan, T. (1983). Countering educational design. New York: Nicols Publishing.

Oppenheimer, T. (1997, July). The computer delusion. *The Atlantic Monthly*, pp. 45–62.

Osborne, D. & Gaebles, T. (1993*). Reinventing government: How the entrepreneurial spirit is transforming the public sector*. New York: Penguin Press.

Perelman, L. J. (1987). *Technology as the transformation of schools*. Alexandria, VA: National School Board Technology Leadership Network Special Report.

Pepi, D. & Scheurman, G. (1996). The emperor's new computer: A critical look at our appetite for computer technology. *Journal of Teacher Education, 47*(3), 229–236.

Peters, M. (1996). *Poststructuralism, politics and education*. Westport, CT: Bergin & Garvey.

Platoni, K. (1999). The Pentagon goes to the video arcade. *Progressive, 63*, 27.

Poster, M. (1990). *The mode of information*. Chicago: University of Illinois Press.

——— (1993). *Politics, theory and contemporary culture*. New York: Columbia University Press.

Postman, N. (1993). *Technopoly: The surrender of culture to technology.* New York: Vintage Books.

———— (1995). *The end of education: Redefining the value of school.* New York: Knopf.

President's Educational Summit with Governors (1991). *America 2000: An Educational Strategy.* Washington, DC: U. S. Government Printing Office.

Provenzo, E. F. Jr. (1991). *Video kids: Making sense of Nintendo.* Cambridge, MA: Harvard University Press.

Purpel, D. (1996). Education as a sacrament. In Fritz Mengert, Kathleen Casey, Delores Liston, David Purpel, & Svi Shapiro (Eds.), *The Education Institution (2nd ed.)* (pp. 207–218). Needham Heights, MA: Simon & Schuster. (Reprinted from Independent School, Spring, 1991.)

Putnam, R. (2000). *Bowling alone: The collapse and revival of American community.* New York: Simon & Schuster.

Reich, R. (1991). *The work of nations: Preparing ourselves for 21st century capitalism.* New York: Alfred Knopf.

Reid, W. (1979). Schools, teachers and curriculum change: The moral dimension of theory-building. *Educational Theory, 29*(4), 325–336.

Reigeluth, C. (1987). The search for meaningful reform: A third-wave educational system. *Journal of Instructional Development, 10*(4), 3–14.

Rozak, T. (1986). *The cult of information.* Berkeley, CA: University of California Press.

Russakoff, D. (1999, April 19). Marketers following youth trends to the bank. *Washington Post,* A15–16.

Sarason, S. (1995). *School change: The personal development of a point of view.* New York: Teachers College Press.

———— (1996). *Revisiting the culture of school and the problem of change.* New York: Teachers College Press.

Scardamalia, M. & Bereiter, C. (1993). Schools as knowledge-building communities. In S. Strauss (Ed..), *Human development: The Tel-Aviv annual workshop: Vol. 7. Development and learning environments.* Norwood, NJ: Ablex.

Scardamalia, M., Bereiter, C. & Laman, M. (1994). CSILE project: Trying to bring the classroom into world 3. In Kate Mcgilly (Ed.), *Classroom lessons: Integrating cognitive theory and classroom practice.* Cambridge: Bradford Books/MIT Press.

Scheffler, I. (1990). Computers at school? In V. A. Howard (Ed.), *Varieties of thinking: Essays from Harvard's philosophy of education research center.* New York: Routledge, 93–109.

Schlechty, P. (1990). *Schools for the 21st century: Leadership imperatives for educational reform.* San Francisco, CA: Jossey-Bass.

Schofield, J. W. (1995). *Computers and classroom culture.* New York: Cambridge University Press.

Schwab, J. J. (1962). The teaching of science as enquiry. In J. J. Schwab and P. F. Brandwein (Eds.), *The teaching of science.* Cambridge: Harvard University Press.

———— (1983). The practical 4: Something for curriculum professors to do. *Curriculum Inquiry, 12*(3), 239–265.

Schwarz, M. & Thompson, M. (1990). *Divided we stand: Redefining politics, technology and social choice.* Philadelphia, University of Pennsylvania Press.

Sclove, R. E. (1995). *Democracy and technology.* New York: The Guilford Press.

Segal, H. P. (1994). The cultural contradictions of high tech: Or the many ironies of contemporary technological optimism. In Yaron Ezhari, Evertt Mendelsohn, & Howard. P. Segal (Eds.), *Technology, pessimism and postmodernism* (175–216). Amherst, MA: University of Massachusetts Press.

———— (1996). The American ideology of technological progress: Historical perspectives. In Stephen Kerr (Ed.), *Technology and the future of schooling* (pp. 28–48). Chicago: University of Chicago Press.

Seng, P. (1990). *The fifth discipline: The art and practice of the learning organization*. New York: Doubleday.

Sergiovanni, T. (1994). *Building community in schools*. San Francisco: Jossey-Bass.

Shapiro, S. (1990). *Between capitalism and democracy*. New York: Bergin & Garvey.

———— (1996). Memo to the president: Clinton and education: Policies without meaning. In Fritz Mengert, Kathleen Casey, Delores Liston, David Purpel, & Svi Shapiro (Eds.), *The Education Institution (2nd ed.)* (pp. 219–231). Needham Heights, MA: Simon & Schuster. (Reprinted from *Tikkun Magazine*, Spring, 1994.)

Shenk, D. (1997). *Data smog: Surviving the information glut*. San Francisco: Harper Edge.

Smith, F. (1995a). *Between hope and havoc: Essays into human learning and education*. Portsmouth, NH: Heinemann.

Smith, M. S. (1995b). Educational reform in America's public schools: The Clinton agenda. In Diane Ravitch (Ed.), *Debating the future of American education: Do we need national standards and assessments?* Washington, DC: The Brookings Institute.

Snauwaert, D. (1993). *Democracy, education and governance: A developmental conception*. Albany, NY: State University of New York Press.

Snyder, T. (1997, July). Paper given at the *National Educational Computing Conference*, Seattle, WA.

Spring, J. (1997). *Political agendas for education: From the Christian Coalition to the Green Party*. Mahwah, NJ: Lawrence Erlbaum.

Steinberg, L. (1996). *Beyond the classroom: Why school reform has failed and what parents need to do*. New York: Simon & Schuster.

Steinberg, S. & Kincheloe, J. (Eds.), (1997). *Kinder-culture: The corporate construction of childhood*. Boulder, CO: Westview Press.

Stohr-Hunt, P. M. (1997). An analysis of frequency of hands-on experience and science achievement, *Journal of Research in Science Teaching, 33*(1), 101–109.

Stoll, C. (1995). *Silicone snake oil: Second thoughts on the information highway*. New York: Doubleday.

———— (1999). *High-tech heretic: Why computers don't belong in the classroom and other reflections by a computer contrarian*. New York: Doubleday.

Street, J. (1992). *Politics and technology*. New York: Guilford Press.

Streibel, M. J. (1986/1994). A critical analysis of the use of computers in education. In Denis Hlynka and John C. Belland (Eds.), *Paradigms regained: The uses of illuminative, Semiotic and Post-modern criticism as modes of inquiry in educational technology*, (pp. 283–334). Englewood Cliffs, NJ: Educational Technology Publications. (Reprinted from *Educational Communications and Technology, 34*(3), 1986).

Subrahmanyam, K., Kraut, R. Greenfield, P. & Gross, E. (2000). The impact of home computer use on children's activities and development. In Richard E. Behrman (Ed.), *The Future of Children: Children and Computer Technology, 10*(2). Los Altos, CA: The David and Lucile Packard Foundation, 123–144.

Sutton, R. (1991). Equity and computers in the schools: A decade of research. *Review of Educational Research, 61*(4), 475–503.

Talbot, S. L. (1995). *The future does not compute: Transcending the machines in our midst*. Sebastopol, CA: O'Reilly & Associates.

Task Force on Education for Economic Growth. (1983). *Action for excellence: A comprehensive plan to improve our nation's schools*. Denver, CO: Education Commission of the States.

Toffler, A. (1980). *The third wave*. New York: Bantam Books.

Tom, A. (1984). *Teaching as a moral craft*. New York: Longman.

Trotter, A. (1997). Taking technology's measure. *Education Week: Technology Counts, 17*(11), pp. 6–11.

———— (1998). Question of effectiveness. *Education Week: Technology Counts'98*, 18, pp. 6–9.

Turkle, S. (1984). *The second self: Computers and the human spirit.* New York: Simon & Schuster.

——— (1997). Seeing through computers: Education in a culture of simulation. *The American Prospect, 31,* 76–82.

Turow, J. (1999). *The Internet and the family: The view from parents, the view from the press.* Philadelphia: Annenberg Public Policy Center, University of Pennsylvania, pp. 14, 25.

Tyack, D. (1974). *The one best system.* Cambridge, MA: Harvard University Press.

Tyack, D. & Cuban, L. (1995). *Tinkering towards utopia: A century of school reform.* Cambridge, MA: Harvard University Press.

Tyack, D. & Tobin, W. (1993). The "grammar" of schooling: Why has it been so hard to change? *American Educational Research Journal, 3*(3), 453–479.

Uchitelle, L. (1994, September 5). A degree's shrinking returns. *New York Times,* pp. 33–34.

U.S. Congress, Office of Technology Assessment (1995). *Teachers and Technology: Making the connection, OTA-EHR-616.* Washington, DC: Government Printing Office.

U.S. Department of Education (1984). *The nation responds: Recent efforts to improve education.* Washington, DC: U. S. Government Printing Office.

——— (1994). *Digest of education statistics 1994.* Washington D. C.: Office of Educational Research and Improvement.

——— (1991). *America 2000: An Education Strategy.* Washington, DC: Department of Education

U.S. Department of Health and Human Services 1996). *Physical activity and health: A report of health of the surgeon general.* Atlanta, GA: U.S. Department of Health and Human Services, Centers for Disease Control and Prevention, National Center for Chronic Disease Prevention and Health Promotion.

Welker, R. (1991). Expertise and the teacher as expert: Rethinking a questionable metaphor. *American Educational Research Journal, 28*(1), 19–35.

Weston, N. & Ingram, J. H. (1997). Whole language and technology: Opposites, or opposites in harmony? *Educational Horizons, 75*(2), 83–89.

White, K. (1997). A matter of policy. *Education Week, 17*(11), 40–42.

Whitty, G. (1994). *Consumer rights versus citizen rights in contemporary education policy.* Unpublished paper, University of London Institute of Education.

Winner, L. (1980). Do artifacts have politics? *Daedalus, 109,* 121–136.

——— (1986). *The whale and the reactor.* Chicago, IL: University of Chicago Press.

——— (1996). Who will be in cyberspace? *The Information Society, 12,* 63–72.

Woodward, E. H. IV & Gridina N. (2000). *Media in the home 2000: The fifth annual survey of parents and children.* Philadelphia: Annenberg Public Policy Center, University of Pennsylvania, p. 11.

Young, R. (1990). *A critical theory of education: Habermas and our children's future.* New York: Teachers College Press.

Zehr, M. (1997, November 10). Partnering with the public. *Education Week, 17*(11), 36–39.

INDEX

Note: Page numbers followed by a "t" indicate a table

Studies in the Postmodern Theory of Education

General Editors
Joe L. Kincheloe & Shirley R. Steinberg

Counterpoints publishes the most compelling and imaginative books being written in education today. Grounded on the theoretical advances in criticalism, feminism, and postmodernism in the last two decades of the twentieth century, Counterpoints engages the meaning of these innovations in various forms of educational expression. Committed to the proposition that theoretical literature should be accessible to a variety of audiences, the series insists that its authors avoid esoteric and jargonistic languages that transform educational scholarship into an elite discourse for the initiated. Scholarly work matters only to the degree it affects consciousness and practice at multiple sites. Counterpoints' editorial policy is based on these principles and the ability of scholars to break new ground, to open new conversations, to go where educators have never gone before.

For additional information about this series or for the submission of manuscripts, please contact:

> Joe L. Kincheloe & Shirley R. Steinberg
> c/o Peter Lang Publishing, Inc.
> 275 Seventh Avenue, 28th floor
> New York, New York 10001

To order other books in this series, please contact our Customer Service Department:

> (800) 770-LANG (within the U.S.)
> (212) 647-7706 (outside the U.S.)
> (212) 647-7707 FAX

Or browse online by series:

> www.peterlangusa.com